HOCKEY NOW!

The fourth edition of *Hockey Now!*
is dedicated to the fans who remained
loyal to the great game of hockey
during the lockout.

Enjoy the new NHL!

Fourth Edition

HOCKEY NOW!

MIKE LEONETTI

FIREFLY BOOKS

A FIREFLY BOOK

Published by Firefly Books Ltd. 2006

First printing

Publisher Cataloging-in-Publication Data (U.S.)
Leonetti, Mike, 1958-
    Hockey now! / Mike Leonetti.
4th ed.
[176] p. : col. photos. ; cm.
Summary: Profiles of over 90 National Hockey League players.
ISBN-13: 978-1-55407-037-4 (pbk.)
ISBN-10: 1-55407-037-6 (pbk.)
1. National Hockey League — Biography. 2. Hockey players — Biography. I. Title.
796.962/092 dc22   GV848.5 A1L45 2006

Library and Archives Canada Cataloguing in Publication
    Leonetti, Mike, 1958-
Hockey now! / Mike Leonetti. — 4th ed.
ISBN-13: 978-1-55407-037-4
ISBN-10: 1-55407-037-6
1. Hockey players—Biography. 2. National Hockey League—Biography.
3. Hockey players—Pictorial works. 4. National Hockey League—Pictorial
works. I. Title.
GV848.5.A1L455 2006 796.962'0922 C2006-901669-0

Published in the United States by
Firefly Books (U.S.) Inc.
P.O. Box 1338, Ellicott Station
Buffalo, New York 14205

Published in Canada by
Firefly Books Ltd.
66 Leek Crescent
Richmond Hill, Ontario L4B 1H1

Cover and interior design by Kimberley Young

Printed in Canada

The publisher gratefully acknowledges the financial support for our publishing program by the Government of Canada through the Book Publishing Industry Development Program.

TABLE OF CONTENTS!

INTRODUCTION

When you step back and think about it, what choice did the National Hockey League have? The game had become a cross between roller derby, wrestling and the rodeo on ice. Unskilled players were almost as valued as talented superstars, and for some the existence of the puck was merely a rumor. Goaltenders and defensive play dominated so strongly that the "action" consisted of watching the team with the lead stay back and kill off the clock any way possible – even if that included breaking all the rules. Smaller players had become virtually extinct, and large-sized performers were valued merely for their beef and brawn. Off the ice the game had descended into a comical and sometimes tragic tug of war between two sides (the owners in one corner, the players in the other), each determined to get their own way without any regard for the great game of hockey.

When the long and bitter labor dispute finally came to an end with one season (2004–05) wiped out, the NHL knew it had to come out with a revitalized look if its new collective agreement, which stressed a "partnership" between the parties, was going to make any sense. The NHL also remembered it had another "partner" – the fans – and finally did something for them.

By implementing new rules (two-line passes, smaller goalie equipment, enlarged offensive zones, use of the shootout to settle tie games, for instance) and enforcing the old rules (especially on the use of the stick) with a rigid standard, the game returned to its roots and became an exciting spectacle once again. Goal-scoring went from 5.14 goals per game to 6.05 in 2005–06, and the league produced five 50-goal scores compared to none in 2003–04. Shutouts dropped from 192 to 119, while 100-point players went from none in '03–'04 to seven in '05–'06. A 2–0 lead was no longer safe. Neither was a 3–0 advantage and, in a few cases, even a four-goal lead did not guarantee victory. The game has become more about skill, speed and skating – all qualities that made hockey one of the greatest spectator sports. Goals are now being scored in various ways, not just from scrambles and scrums around the net. A shooter suddenly has something to aim for as he comes down the wing, rushes are producing pretty passing plays that result in goals, and a long pass might spring someone in the open past all the defenders.

At first, players (defensemen in particular) had to re-program themselves, and it took some time before most caught on to the fact that referees were no longer going to look the other way. Once the players came to understand that it was a different world, the physical play that has always been part of hockey came back, with clean bodychecking again a valued trait (and unnecessary fighting greatly reduced as well).

By the time the 2006 playoffs began, the only question seemed to be whether the NHL would maintain the same standards when everything was on the line. The answer was a resounding yes, and the playoffs were the best in years. Many of the teams that were prepared for what has become popularly known as the "new NHL" did well not only in the regular season, but also in the post-season. Buffalo, Anaheim, Edmonton and Stanley Cup champion Carolina were good examples of this. The teams that missed out on the '06 playoffs had better make adjustments, or they will have no chance to win the championship.

While the fans have not forgotten that the game they love was taken away for an entire season, they did return in strong numbers to most of the arenas and helped to raise league revenues, and the salary cap will rise to $44 million for the 2006–07 season. As commissioner Gary Bettman indicated, this is a work in progress. The major overhaul has been implemented, and now the game in all aspects needs to tweaked, not ripped apart – a major step forward for this sport.

The missed season saw the end of many great careers (Brett Hull, Scott Stevens, Ron Francis, Al MacInnis, Mark Messier and eventually Mario Lemieux, Luc Robitaille and Steve Yzerman), but the '05–'06 campaign witnessed the rise of many new players (Sidney Crosby, Alexander Ovechkin, Dion Phanuef, to name the three brightest lights) who will be stars for years to come. We have profiled many of the new stars of the NHL while updating stories of veterans. We hope you enjoy the fourth edition of *Hockey Now!*

MASKED MARVELS!

Agile goaltenders with quick hands and feet, ready to challenge all shooters.

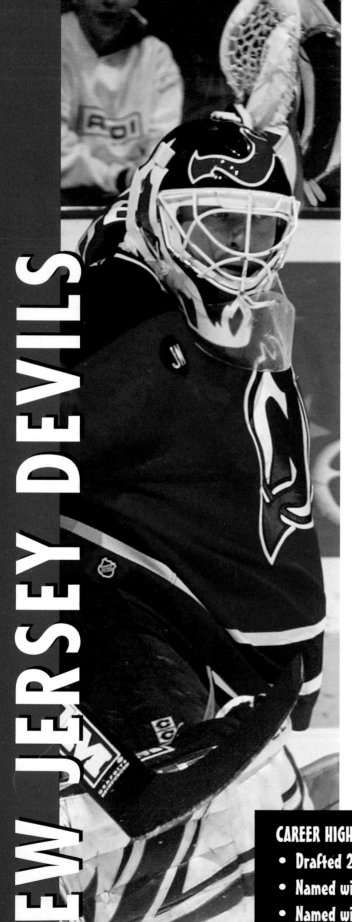

Martin BRODEUR

NEW JERSEY DEVILS

Martin Brodeur was just 14 years old when his home-town Montreal Canadiens won the Stanley Cup in 1986. The teenager skipped school to attend the victory parade held in the streets of the old town. One day he hoped to hoist the cup in a parade himself. His father, Denis, had been a goalie for the bronze medal Canadian team at the 1956 Olympics; young Martin eventually ended up in the net as well.

After a great junior career with St.-Hyacinthe in the Quebec junior league, Brodeur was selected in the first round of the 1990 NHL entry draft by the New Jersey Devils (20th overall). By the time the 1993–94 season began, the Devils had a solid team but lacked a quality front-line goalie. They decided to give Brodeur, who had spent a year at Utica in the American Hockey League, a chance at an NHL job. He played in 47 games that year, sporting a very impressive 27-11-8 record, and took away the Calder Trophy as the league's best rookie. He cemented a rock-solid reputation by beating Buffalo in the first round of the 1994 playoffs, which featured a Game 7 overtime victory over Sabre goalie Dominik Hasek. The New York Rangers eventually derailed the dream, but the best was yet to come for the Devils.

In the shortened 1994–95 season, Brodeur won 19 of his 40 games, but he saved his best for the playoffs when he won 16 of 20 starts and the Devils took the Stanley Cup. Brodeur was spectacular at times and finished with a playoff goals-against average of 1.67,

CAREER HIGHLIGHTS
- Drafted 20th overall by New Jersey in 1990.
- Named winner of the Calder Trophy in 1994.
- Named winner of the Vezina Trophy twice (2003, 2004).
- Has won 446 games with 80 shutouts in 740 NHL career games.

tops in the post-season. At the very tender age of 23, Brodeur had won a cup. The parade for the Devils was held in the arena parking lot in East Rutherford, New Jersey; not exactly like the parade in Montreal years earlier, but it would have to do.

Since the 1995 cup victory, Brodeur has proven to be a steady and consistent goalie. He has been a workhorse for the Devils, averaging 70 games in the years that have followed. Brodeur makes the most of his size (6'1", 205 pounds) and mostly plays a classic stand-up style, but he has been going down more and more like the other goalies do. He has a great glove hand and high confidence in his abilities. Rarely does he get much support in terms of goals (although New Jersey did lead the NHL in goals scored in 2000–01), but the Devils have been defensively oriented for the last number of years, which helps out Brodeur greatly.

A technically sound goalie, Brodeur is also very tough mentally and bounces back from the few goals he gives up. After a few shocking first-round losses following the 1995 Stanley Cup win, Brodeur finally took the Devils all the way back with a fine performance in the 2000 post-season. The Devils' second championship secured Brodeur's place among the elite in the NHL. They made the finals again in 2001, and the next year Brodeur topped his father by backstopping Canada to the 2002 Olympic gold.

With Pat Burns behind the bench, New Jersey tied with Philadelphia for fewest goals allowed in 2002–03; Brodeur led the league with nine shutouts, and had his lowest goals-against average (2.02) in five years. He also became the first goalie in NHL history to record his fourth 40-win season (41). For that, Brodeur won his first Vezina and was named to the NHL's first All-Star team. In the playoffs, Brodeur won game 7 against Ottawa in the eastern finals and

shut out Anaheim 3–0 in game 7 of the Stanley Cup final to win his third cup in nine years.

Brodeur has had to face many new challenges in the past couple of seasons. The decline and ultimate retirement of Scott Stevens was a blow to the defense, as was the loss of free agent blueliner Scott Niedermayer. As well, goaltending equipment shrunk somewhat even though Brodeur never really used the huge pads and gloves. Still, he won a league best 43 games in 2005–06 and got the Devils back into the playoffs when it looked they were going to miss the post-season. The New Jersey club will have to add more offense if they hope to take advantage of having a future Hall of Fame netminder guarding the net.

ICE CHIPS

Martin Brodeur has won 40 or more games five times in his career and has played 70 or more games in a season nine times (including the last eight consecutively from 1995–96 to 2005–06).

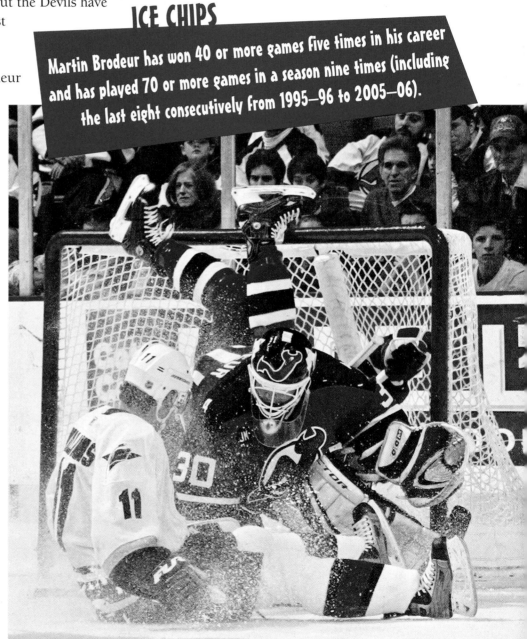

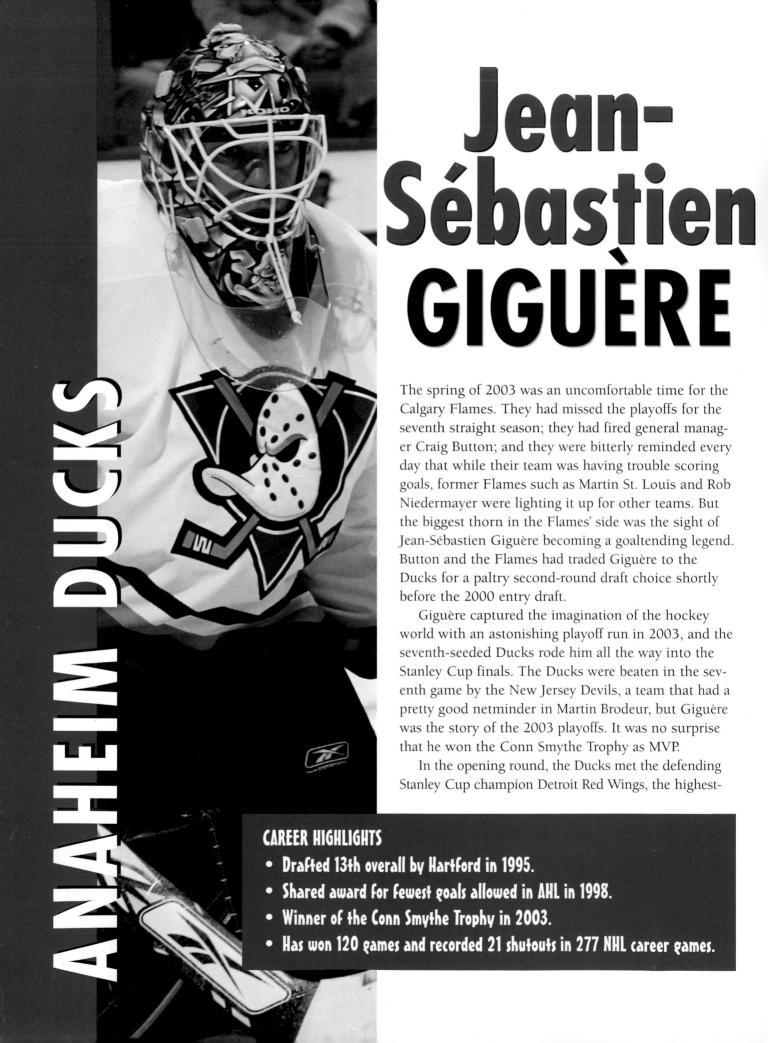

Jean-Sébastien GIGUÈRE

ANAHEIM DUCKS

The spring of 2003 was an uncomfortable time for the Calgary Flames. They had missed the playoffs for the seventh straight season; they had fired general manager Craig Button; and they were bitterly reminded every day that while their team was having trouble scoring goals, former Flames such as Martin St. Louis and Rob Niedermayer were lighting it up for other teams. But the biggest thorn in the Flames' side was the sight of Jean-Sébastien Giguère becoming a goaltending legend. Button and the Flames had traded Giguère to the Ducks for a paltry second-round draft choice shortly before the 2000 entry draft.

Giguère captured the imagination of the hockey world with an astonishing playoff run in 2003, and the seventh-seeded Ducks rode him all the way into the Stanley Cup finals. The Ducks were beaten in the seventh game by the New Jersey Devils, a team that had a pretty good netminder in Martin Brodeur, but Giguère was the story of the 2003 playoffs. It was no surprise that he won the Conn Smythe Trophy as MVP.

In the opening round, the Ducks met the defending Stanley Cup champion Detroit Red Wings, the highest-

CAREER HIGHLIGHTS
- Drafted 13th overall by Hartford in 1995.
- Shared award for fewest goals allowed in AHL in 1998.
- Winner of the Conn Smythe Trophy in 2003.
- Has won 120 games and recorded 21 shutouts in 277 NHL career games.

scoring team in the NHL. Giguère immediately gave a hint of what was to come when he faced 63 shots in the first game, the most ever for a goalie making his playoff debut, and the Ducks won 2–1 in triple overtime. The Ducks went on to an improbable sweep of one of the most powerful teams in hockey history, as the big (6'1", 200 pounds) butterfly-style netminder stopped 165 of 171 shots. Giguère then led the Ducks to an upset of the Dallas Stars. But he saved his best for the Western Conference final against another upstart team, the Minnesota Wild. He shut out the Wild for the first three games, and when Andrew Brunette scored at 4:47 of the first period in Game 4, it snapped Giguère's shutout streak at 217 minutes and 44 seconds. The Ducks swept the Wild to qualify for their first Stanley Cup final, and Giguère ended the Western Conference playoffs with a .960 save percentage, the highest in the past 30 years.

The Hartford Whalers made Giguère the first goalie taken (13th overall) in the 1995 draft. During his final junior season in 1996–97, he played eight games for the Whalers, with a 3.65 goals-against average. But that summer, the Whalers moved to Carolina and moved Giguère to the Flames along with Andrew Cassels for comeback-bound Gary Roberts and goalie Trevor Kidd. Giguère spent the entire 1997–98 season sharing goaltending duties with Tyler Moss in Saint John as the Baby Flames allowed the fewest goals in the AHL. Flames general manager Al Coates viewed the big goalie as the heir apparent in Calgary, and Giguère played 15 games for the Flames in 1998–99. The next season, he looked set

to join the Flames for good, but Grant Fuhr was signed and "Jiggy" was bumped.

Coates had planned to keep Giguère in the expansion draft of 2000, but he was fired and replaced by Craig Button, who wanted to protect only one goalie, Fred Brathwaite. So Giguère was traded to Anaheim for a draft choice that was dealt away to Washington.

Once he joined the Ducks, Giguère's career took off. In 2000–01 he spent 34 games with Cincinnati of the AHL, but was called up to start a franchise-record 23 straight games for Anaheim. The next year he became the No. 1 goalie as the Ducks floundered, losing 21 games by a score of 3–2 or 2–1. With off-season improvements, the Ducks began winning those close games in 2002–03. But nobody expected them, or their goalie, to have the kind of playoff they did in the Stanley Cup finals.

Giguère has not been as good since his magical run in the '03 playoffs. He posted a poor 17-31-6 record and the Ducks missed the playoffs in 2003–04. He rebounded in 2005–06 to win 30 games despite the reduced equipment size (which was a very noticeable part of his appearance in years past) of goaltending gear. His good record helped the Ducks make the post-season, but he was replaced in the middle of the first round by backup Ilya Bryzgalov. Giguère's days in Anaheim may soon come to an end.

CALGARY FLAMES

Miikka KIPRUSOFF

Fans of the Calgary Flames thought they were getting the short-term solution to Roman Turek's injury problems. But coach and general manager Darryl Sutter was taking the longer view. Sutter completed a trade in November 2003, acquiring goalie Miikka Kiprusoff for a second-round draft choice. Sutter thought he was getting a number one netminder.

Almost immediately, Kiprusoff established himself as one of the best netminders in the league, getting the Flames into the playoffs for the first time in seven years and carrying them all the way to the seventh game of the Stanley Cup final. Two days after his trade to Calgary, Kiprusoff started his first game for the Flames, won it and never looked back. By early March, he was running one-two with Martin Brodeur as the best goaltender in the NHL, and he had turned the Flames into self-believers.

Kiprusoff had always displayed streaks of brilliance, but most hockey observers felt he still needed consistency. It turned out that what he really needed was a chance. The native of Turku, part of a new generation of spectacular Finnish goalies to emerge during the mid '90s, was drafted by San Jose, 116th overall, in 1995. After being named the best goalie in the Finnish Elite League and the most valuable player in the playoffs (both in 1999), the Sharks brought Kiprusoff to North America to replace Evgeny Nabokov on their Kentucky farm club. His goals-against average of 2.48 was fourth best in the AHL and helped Kentucky win its first division championship.

CAREER HIGHLIGHTS
- Drafted 116th overall by San Jose in 1995.
- Led the NHL with a 1.69 goals-against average in 2003–04.
- Named to the NHL's First All-Star team in 2006.
- Has won 80 games and recorded 17 shutouts in 159 NHL career games.

The next season with Kentucky, he not only ranked third in the AHL in goals-against average and save percentage, but also got into five NHL games, providing a glimpse of what was to come. He won two of three decisions and also won a playoff game against St. Louis as he and Nabokov became the first goaltending duo in six years to capture their first post-season victories in the same series.

The Sharks traded Steve Shields because they thought Kiprusoff was ready for the NHL. They gave him 20 appearances in 2001–02, while Nabokov handled the bulk of the work. In one stretch, Kiprusoff won three straight starts, including his first NHL shutout, and posted a blistering 0.78 goals-against average and a .974 save percentage. But the following season he played in only 22 games and had a poor 5–14 record; and by the start of 2003–04, he had fallen behind both Nabokov and fellow Finn Vesa Toskala on the depth chart. So Kiprusoff was shipped off in the deal that changed the future of the Calgary Flames.

Using positioning and body size to play large in net, Kiprusoff went on to lead the league with a stingy 1.69 goals-against average, an NHL record. He tied for the league lead with a .933 save percentage and finished runner-up to Martin Brodeur for the Vezina Trophy. He was a clutch playoff performer, making 26 saves in a seventh-game overtime victory over Vancouver in round 1, shutting out Detroit in games 5 and 6 of the next round, and exacting revenge on the Sharks by winning four of six games in the conference final. The incredible run did not stop until he was beaten 2–1 in the seventh game of the Stanley Cup final.

In September 2004, Kiprusoff backstopped the underdog Finns to the World Cup final, where they lost to Canada. He then played in Sweden during the lockout before picking up in 2005–06 where he had left off in the NHL. Although his scoring-challenged Flames were upset by San Jose in the opening round of the 2006 playoffs, Kiprusoff was their most valuable player all season, leading the NHL with a 2.07 goals-against average and 10 shutouts and finishing second in wins (42) to Brodeur's 43. He also played more minutes than any netminder in the league. For that stellar performance, he was named a finalist for two major NHL awards, the Hart Trophy as MVP and the Vezina Trophy (which he won) as leading goalie, proving that he was a lot more than a temporary replacement in the Flames' net.

ICE CHIPS

Miikka Kiprusoff's older brother Marko is a defenseman who is back playing in Finland after two different stints in North America. He played mostly in the minor leagues, but did get into 51 games over parts of two seasons (1995–96, 2001–02) with the Montreal Canadiens and New York Islanders.

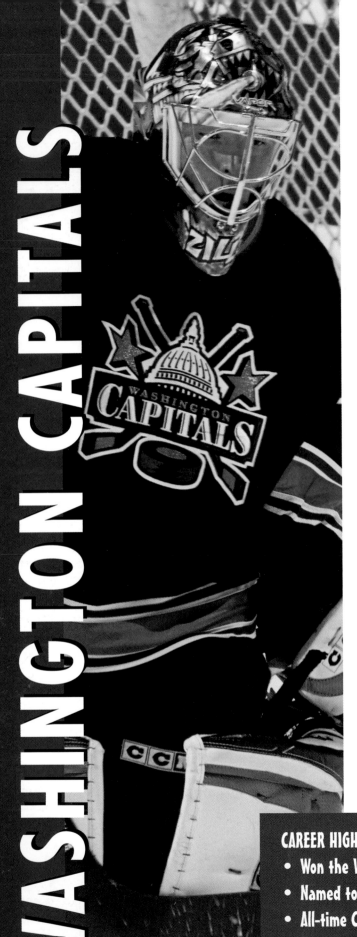

WASHINGTON CAPITALS

Olaf KOLZIG

The Washington Capitals figured having Bill Ranford in goal would start to pay some big dividends in the 1997–98 season. After all, Ranford had won the Stanley Cup with the Edmonton Oilers and had taken the highly coveted Conn Smythe Trophy in the process. The Capitals had swung a major deal to land the veteran netminder, so it was to be expected that Ranford would start in goal as the season opened in Toronto on October 1, 1997, at Maple Leaf Gardens. But then the unexpected happened – Ranford badly strained his groin area, and the backup goalie was forced into action. Most in the crowd at the Gardens knew little if anything about Olaf Kolzig, but by the end of the evening the brilliant performance of the young goalie allowed the Capitals to walk away with a 4–1 win. It would be the start of something big for both Kolzig and the Caps.

If the rest of the NHL was taken by surprise by Kolzig, the Capitals were quietly hoping the large net-minder would fulfill the promise he had displayed in junior and the minors. Washington selected Kolzig with their first choice (19th overall) in the 1989 draft. He played junior with the Tri-City Americans and then worked to establish himself in the minors, where he played in Baltimore, Rochester and Portland. In the 1994 playoffs, Kolzig took the Portland Pirates all the way to the American Hockey League championship, winning 12 of his 17 playoff starts. He then split the

CAREER HIGHLIGHTS
- Won the Vezina Trophy in 2000.
- Named to First All-Star team in 2000.
- All-time Capitals leader in goaltending wins, with 254.
- Named winner of the King Clancy Trophy in 2006.

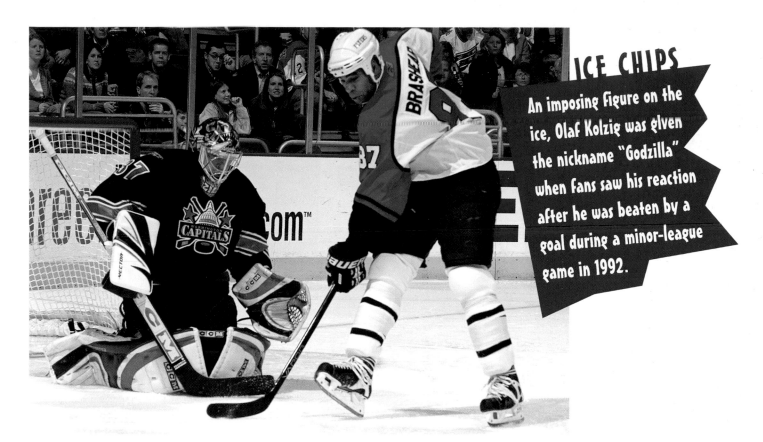

next two years between Portland and Washington before sticking with the Caps for the 1996–97 season, when he appeared in 29 games but posted a mediocre record of 8-15-4.

Ranford's injury proved to be Kolzig's big break at the NHL level. His 1997–98 record shows a 33-18-10 mark with a goals-against average of 2.58 and five shutouts. But he really shone in the playoffs, when he took the Capitals to the Stanley Cup finals with series wins over Boston, Ottawa and Buffalo before losing to the powerful Detroit Red Wings in four games. Kolzig was the main reason Washington made its first appearance in the finals, but the next season proved to be more difficult for the goaltender and the team. He posted a 26-31-3 record, and the Capitals missed the playoffs altogether. He rebounded in 1999–2000 to win 41 games and take the Vezina Trophy along with a place on the first All-Star team. The career of the native of Johannesburg, South Africa, was back on track.

Kolzig started out as a defenseman when he was nine years old and growing up in Edmonton, Alberta. When the regular goalie on his team was hurt, Kolzig played in net. And he's stayed there ever since. At 6'3" and 225 pounds, Kolzig is another one of the large men who play goal in the modern NHL. An agile goalie for a man of his size, Kolzig uses a butterfly

style that gives the shooter little of the net to see. He teases with the opening between his pads, but then closes quickly. The feisty Kolzig positions himself very well and has proven to be a durable performer for the Caps – a team that's not the same without him in net.

The playoff success of 1998 has proven difficult to recapture. The Capitals have either missed the playoffs (out of the post-season in '99, '02, '04 and '06) or been eliminated in the first round (in '00, '01 and '03). Kolzig has generally performed very well for Washington through all the ups and downs the franchise has undergone since '98, winning 37 games in '00–'01 and another 33 in '01–'02. The addition of Jaromir Jagr proved to be a total bust, and he was moved to the New York Rangers as soon as a deal could be arranged. It was expected that Kolzig was going to move on as well as the 2005–06 season progressed, but the Capitals left the decision to the netminder, who decided he wanted to stay and see the rebuilding process work around his goaltending and the spectacular play of Alexander Ovechkin. With a very raw defense around him, Kolzig still managed to win 20 games in '05–'06 and took great delight in seeing his team knock the Atlanta Thrashers from the playoff picture with a late-season victory. The veteran netminder is very much a leader for the Capitals.

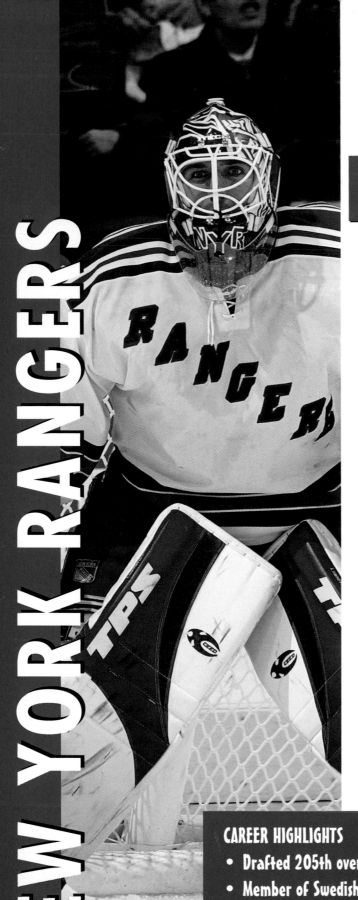

Henrik LUNDQVIST

Goaltender Henrik Lundqvist came to North America a decorated player in his native Sweden. He had been on the team (Frolunda) that won the Swedish Elite League championship and named the most valuable player in that circuit. He had also played in the World Hockey Championships for his country. The 23-year-old brought all this experience with him when he reported to the New York Rangers for the 2005–06 season. The Rangers were essentially starting over with many new players on their roster and were trying to shed their reputation as a high-payroll, low-result team. But could they count on a goalie drafted 205th overall in 2000 to lead them back into the playoffs after missing the post-season for seven straight years? The answer was a resounding yes.

The Rangers had actually signed perennial backup netminder Kevin Weekes in the hope that he might give the team a veteran presence in goal. While Weekes performed well in 32 games, he was still no better than a number-two goalie. Lundqvist on the other hand quickly adapted to his new environment and grabbed the number one netminding reins and never let go all season long. New York also brought in goaltending coach Benoit Allaire to help out the young man, but the mentor quickly found that all he had to do with Lundqvist was assist him with his angles and teach him how to play in the smaller North American rinks.

CAREER HIGHLIGHTS

- Drafted 205th overall by New York Rangers in 2000.
- Member of Swedish team that won the Olympic gold medal in 2006.
- Recorded his first NHL shutout 5–0 versus Atlanta on October 15, 2005.
- Has won 30 games and recorded two shutouts in 53 NHL career games.

ICE CHIPS

Henrik Lundqvist recorded 30 wins as a rookie netminder, breaking the Rangers' team mark for first-year netminders held by Johnny Bower and "Sugar" Jim Henry (both had 29 wins).

The 6'1", 192 pound goalie builds his game around positioning – getting square to the shooter consistently and controlling his rebounds effectively. His style of game is somewhere between standup and butterfly, and he moves easily from side to side to get proper positioning. Like all top goalies, Lundqvist is very competitive and hates to lose. He is so driven that he may be a little too intense (especially on game days) for his own good, but he might be able to overcome this with good coaching and more maturity.

Lundqvist was so well known in his native Sweden that he actually came to New York to seek a level of anonymity. However, by the third game of the 2005–06 season, the Madison Square Garden fans were chanting his name. That made the young netminder feel at home, and he fed off the energy of the crowd and his new teammates. Early in the year, Lundqvist had allowed two goals or fewer in 12 of his starts and was near the top of all the goaltending categories. Coach Tom Renney was at first reluctant to name Lundqvist as the number-one goalie, but the more he played the more it was obvious who should be the main starter. By the time the season was over, the Rangers had secured a playoff spot (44 wins and 100 points) and Lundqvist posted a record of 30-12-4 in 53 games played. He also had a sparkling .922 save percentage and a 2.44 goals against average.

As if his NHL performance wasn't enough, Lundqvist was selected to play for the Swedish national team for the 2006 Winter Olympic Games in Turin, Italy. The Swedes desperately wanted to atone for their terrible performance at the 2002 Games in Salt Lake City and decided Lundqvist was going to be their man in the nets. It proved to be a wise choice. Lundqvist won five games and took his team past the Czech Republic in the semifinal and then past ancient rival Finland 3–2 in the gold medal game. The victory only solidified Lundqvist's position in Sweden as the best goalie since the late Pelle Lindbergh, and the country had a great party after the Olympic Games were over.

However, the 2006 NHL playoffs did not go as well for a sick and battered New York team. The New Jersey Devils took advantage and knocked them off in four games. While that was a great disappointment to all Ranger fans, they at least have the knowledge that the goaltending duties are in good hands for a long time.

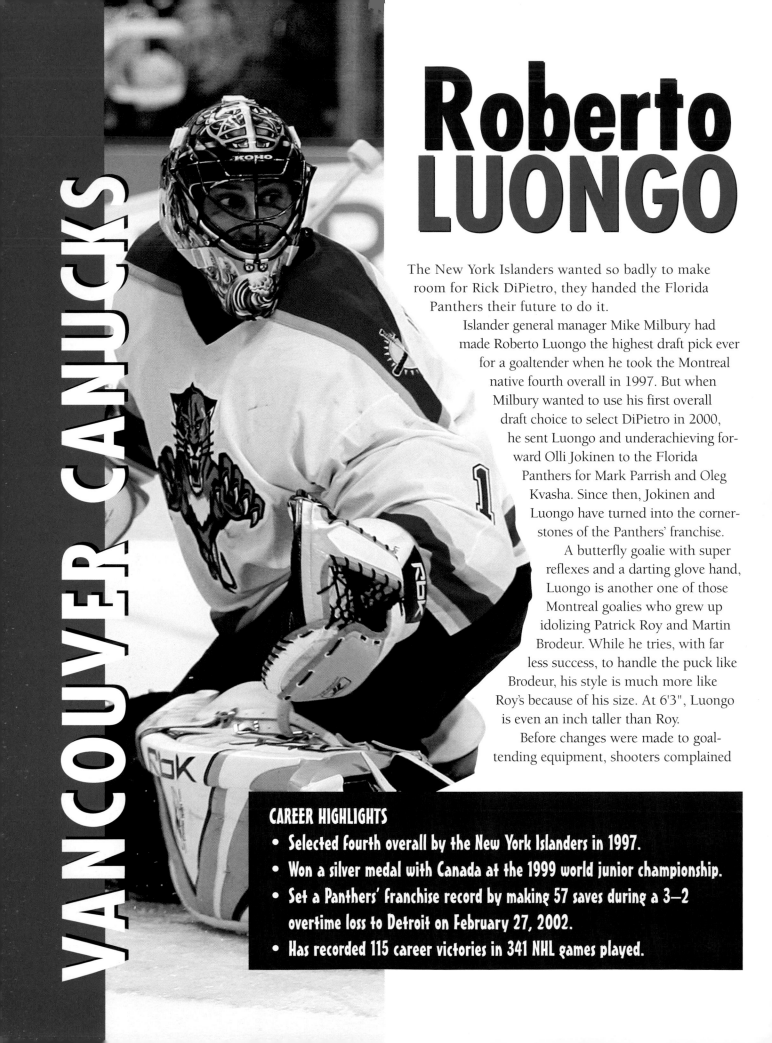

VANCOUVER CANUCKS

Roberto LUONGO

The New York Islanders wanted so badly to make room for Rick DiPietro, they handed the Florida Panthers their future to do it.

Islander general manager Mike Milbury had made Roberto Luongo the highest draft pick ever for a goaltender when he took the Montreal native fourth overall in 1997. But when Milbury wanted to use his first overall draft choice to select DiPietro in 2000, he sent Luongo and underachieving forward Olli Jokinen to the Florida Panthers for Mark Parrish and Oleg Kvasha. Since then, Jokinen and Luongo have turned into the corner-stones of the Panthers' franchise.

A butterfly goalie with super reflexes and a darting glove hand, Luongo is another one of those Montreal goalies who grew up idolizing Patrick Roy and Martin Brodeur. While he tries, with far less success, to handle the puck like Brodeur, his style is much more like Roy's because of his size. At 6'3", Luongo is even an inch taller than Roy.

Before changes were made to goal-tending equipment, shooters complained

CAREER HIGHLIGHTS
- Selected fourth overall by the New York Islanders in 1997.
- Won a silver medal with Canada at the 1999 world junior championship.
- Set a Panthers' franchise record by making 57 saves during a 3–2 overtime loss to Detroit on February 27, 2002.
- Has recorded 115 career victories in 341 NHL games played.

that knee flaps at the top of the goalie's pads helped plug the five-hole, but Luongo realized that the opposition would say anything to unnerve a goalie. And Luongo is not easy to get to. He's always been a confident, mature athlete – and he was targeted for the NHL from the time he joined the Val-d'Or Foreurs of the Quebec Major Junior Hockey League at the age of 16. At 18, he led the Foreurs to the Quebec championship and all the way to the 1998 Memorial Cup finals, despite having to face as many as 60 shots per game.

Although the Islanders were eager to get Luongo into the pro ranks, they decided to leave him in junior for one more season because they had Tommy Salo and Felix Potvin. His junior rights were traded to Acadie-Bathurst during the season, and Luongo led them to the Memorial Cup finals as well. Luongo had a brilliant training camp in 1999, but the Islanders still had Potvin, so they sent their young goalie to Lowell, where he could play 60 AHL games as a starter. When Wade Flaherty was injured, Luongo was called back to Long Island and played 24 games.

His first NHL game was a 2–1 victory at Boston, where he was forced to make 43 saves. Behind a terrible defense, he finished the season with a 3.35 goals-against average and .904 save percentage, stats that weren't helped by a couple of one-sided losses late in the year. He had a lucrative bonus clause in his contract, which was to kick in after 25 games, and the Islanders refused to play him in the 25th game. That hurt Luongo – and he wasn't terribly upset when the Islanders traded him to Florida.

The Panthers immediately tabbed Luongo as the goalie of the future, and the future arrived in a hurry. He started 2000–01 behind veteran Trevor Kidd, but by the All-Star break he had become the No. 1 goalie. His 2.44 goals-against average in 47 games was nearly a goal per game better than Kidd's, and his .920 save percentage was ranked seventh in the league. His five shutouts also broke a Panthers record.

In 2001–02, Luongo was firmly established as the

starter and a key to Florida's rebuilding plans. Mike Keenan, who treated goalies like yo-yos, became the coach early in the season, and it took a little adjustment for Luongo to get used to him. But he's so mentally calm that he handled Keenan's antics like he dealt with bad goals. He forgot them quickly.

In February 2002 Luongo was brilliant in facing 51 shots at the Young Stars game during All-Star week-end. He finished the season with a 2.77 goals-against average in 58 games, and probably would have played close to 70 games, but he tore a ligament in his right ankle in mid-March and missed the rest of the season.

The Panthers have not been able to make the playoffs despite the impressive performance of Luongo. Keenan has returned to Florida as the general manager and has anxiously sought to get his star netminder signed to a new deal. Keenan may have made a strategic error by taking Luongo to salary arbitration for the 2005–06 season, but that didn't dampen the Panthers' hopes for signing Luongo to a long-term deal. His contractual status did not stop Luongo from posting his first ever winning season (35-30-5) in '05–'06, but when he could not reach an agreement with Florida he was quickly dealt to Vancouver for a package of players that included Todd Bertuzzi and goalie Alex Auld. Luongo then signed a four-year deal with the Canucks.

ICE CHIPS

During the 2005–06 season Luongo appeared in 75 games, the most of any goaltender in the league, and faced 2,488 shots, the most of any NHL netminder. As yet, Luongo has not played in a single NHL playoff game.

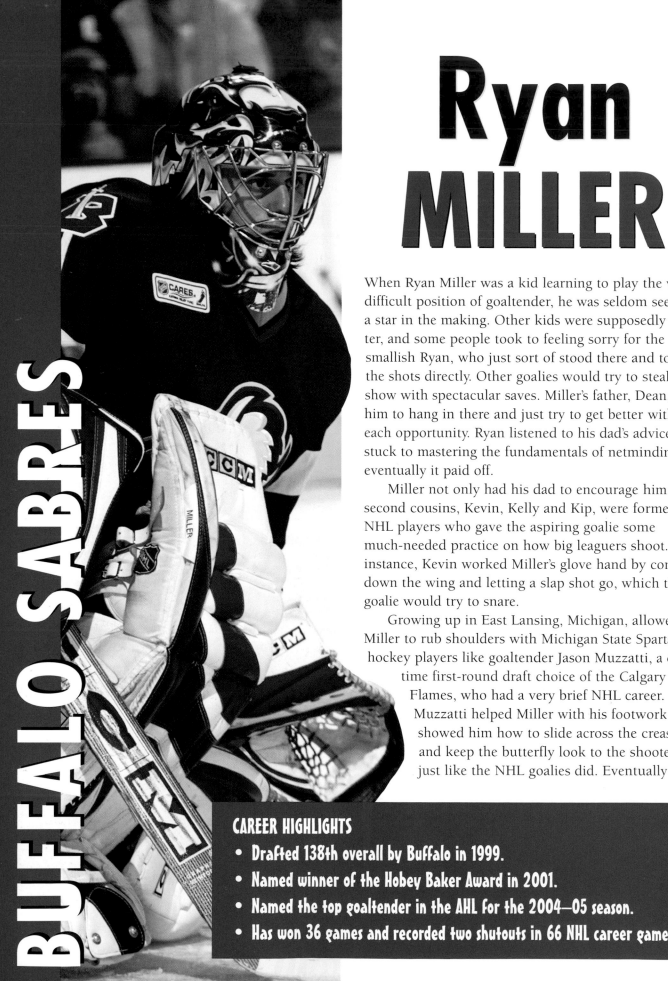

Ryan MILLER

BUFFALO SABRES

When Ryan Miller was a kid learning to play the very difficult position of goaltender, he was seldom seen as a star in the making. Other kids were supposedly better, and some people took to feeling sorry for the smallish Ryan, who just sort of stood there and took the shots directly. Other goalies would try to steal the show with spectacular saves. Miller's father, Dean, told him to hang in there and just try to get better with each opportunity. Ryan listened to his dad's advice and stuck to mastering the fundamentals of netminding; eventually it paid off.

Miller not only had his dad to encourage him. His second cousins, Kevin, Kelly and Kip, were former NHL players who gave the aspiring goalie some much-needed practice on how big leaguers shoot. For instance, Kevin worked Miller's glove hand by coming down the wing and letting a slap shot go, which the goalie would try to snare.

Growing up in East Lansing, Michigan, allowed Miller to rub shoulders with Michigan State Spartan hockey players like goaltender Jason Muzzatti, a one-time first-round draft choice of the Calgary Flames, who had a very brief NHL career. Muzzatti helped Miller with his footwork and showed him how to slide across the crease and keep the butterfly look to the shooter just like the NHL goalies did. Eventually

CAREER HIGHLIGHTS

- Drafted 138th overall by Buffalo in 1999.
- Named winner of the Hobey Baker Award in 2001.
- Named the top goaltender in the AHL for the 2004—05 season.
- Has won 36 games and recorded two shutouts in 66 NHL career games.

Miller played at Michigan State himself for a two-year period and was so good in the 2000–01 season (he won 31 games in 40 appearances) that he was named the winner of the Hobey Baker Award as the top U.S. collegiate player.

The Buffalo Sabres had already drafted the lanky (6'2", 170 pounds) Miller by that point but were not quite sure if Miller would make it to the big team anytime soon. The Sabres' scouts had gambled by taking Miller before he even got to college – based on what they saw of him in the North American Junior League, when he played for Sault Ste. Marie. They were not too worried about goalkeeping since they also had Martin Biron as their main backstopper, a good goalie in his own right. Miller got into 15 games for the Sabres in 2003–04 and was a rather ordinary 6-8-1 for a struggling team. He had bad outings first against the New York Islanders, giving up six goals, and then got whipped seven times by the Detroit Red Wings. Those kinds of numbers got him a ticket to the minors, but that was probably the best thing that happened to Miller. He got plenty of work with the Rochester Americans of the AHL over the next three years and became the top goalie prospect not playing in the

NHL. He won 41 games during the lockout season (leading the AHL) and was ready for the big league in the 2005–06 season.

The Sabres revamped their team for the 2005–06 season and the new rules. Part of the plan was to depend on Miller and many of his teammates who had played in Rochester the previous year. The confident netminder quickly showed that he was ready for the big league. Miller is effective because he uses his entire frame to cover as much of the net as possible. He has great flexibility and likes to sit back in his crease and read the play. His work ethic is very high and he is determined to forget any bad goals that beat him. The Sabres' leading scorer, Max Afinogenov, was 43rd overall in NHL scoring, which meant that Buffalo relied heavily on Miller to make the big save at the right time. Miller came through with a record of 30-14-1 (missing some of the year with a broken thumb) to help his team record a 110-point season. He led the Sabres to playoff victories over Philadelphia and Ottawa, and his save on Jason Spezza of the Senators was truly remarkable and saved the game for the Buffalo squad in the second game of the series – a 2–1 win for the Sabres.

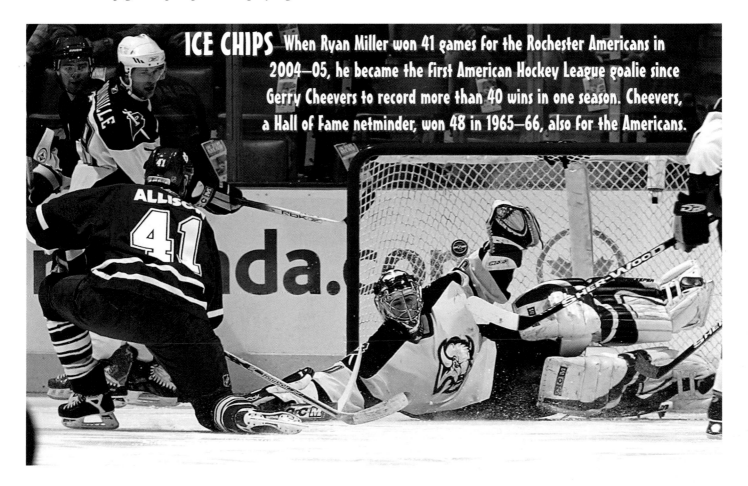

ICE CHIPS When Ryan Miller won 41 games for the Rochester Americans in 2004–05, he became the first American Hockey League goalie since Gerry Cheevers to record more than 40 wins in one season. Cheevers, a Hall of Fame netminder, won 48 in 1965–66, also for the Americans.

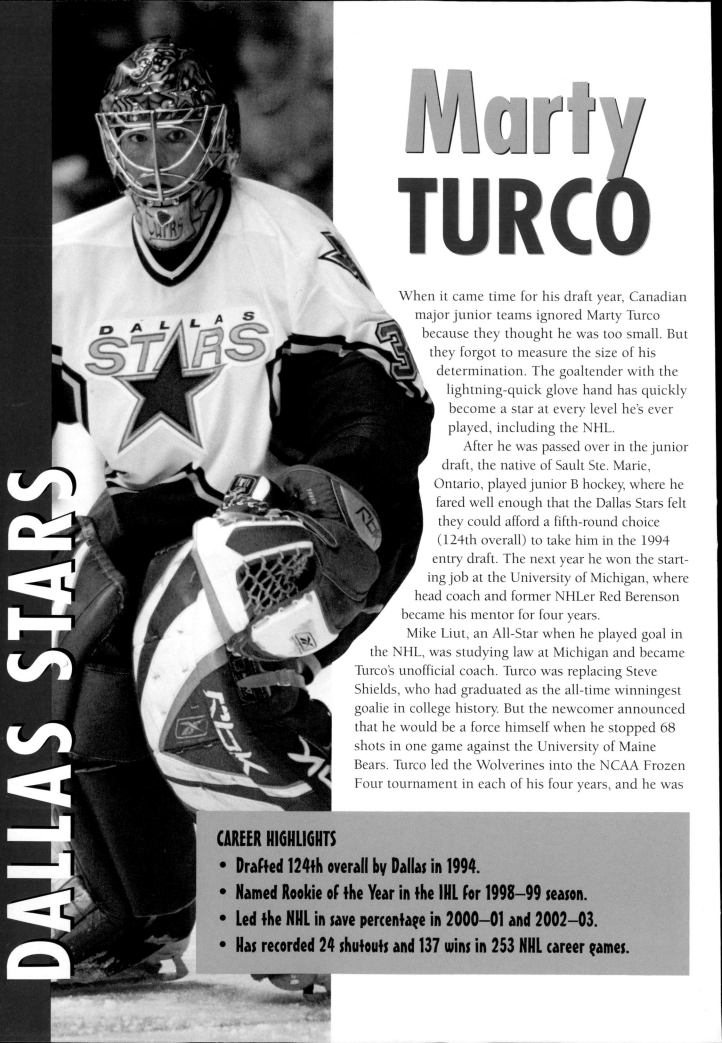

Marty TURCO

When it came time for his draft year, Canadian major junior teams ignored Marty Turco because they thought he was too small. But they forgot to measure the size of his determination. The goaltender with the lightning-quick glove hand has quickly become a star at every level he's ever played, including the NHL.

After he was passed over in the junior draft, the native of Sault Ste. Marie, Ontario, played junior B hockey, where he fared well enough that the Dallas Stars felt they could afford a fifth-round choice (124th overall) to take him in the 1994 entry draft. The next year he won the starting job at the University of Michigan, where head coach and former NHLer Red Berenson became his mentor for four years.

Mike Liut, an All-Star when he played goal in the NHL, was studying law at Michigan and became Turco's unofficial coach. Turco was replacing Steve Shields, who had graduated as the all-time winningest goalie in college history. But the newcomer announced that he would be a force himself when he stopped 68 shots in one game against the University of Maine Bears. Turco led the Wolverines into the NCAA Frozen Four tournament in each of his four years, and he was

CAREER HIGHLIGHTS
- Drafted 124th overall by Dallas in 1994.
- Named Rookie of the Year in the IHL for 1998–99 season.
- Led the NHL in save percentage in 2000–01 and 2002–03.
- Has recorded 24 shutouts and 137 wins in 253 NHL career games.

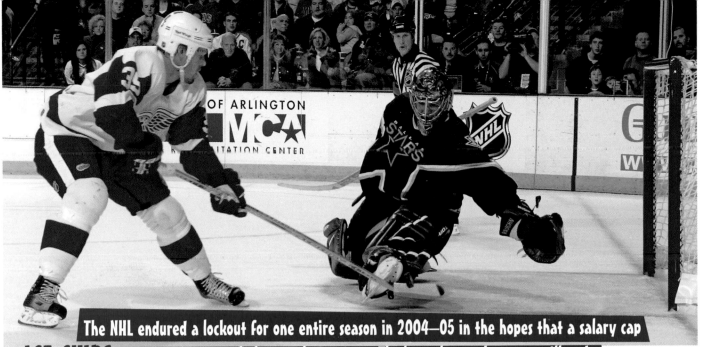

ICE CHIPS The NHL endured a lockout for one entire season in 2004–05 in the hopes that a salary cap system of pay would bring salaries down. The best players, however, still make a very good dollar as is evidenced by Marty Turco's new four-year deal for $22.8 million, an average of $5.7 million yearly over the length of the contract.

named tournament MVP in 1998. By the end of his Michigan career, Turco had surpassed Shields – with more wins (127) than any goaltender in the history of U.S. college hockey.

Turco didn't even have to leave the state to begin his pro career, as the Stars assigned him to the Michigan K-Wings of the now-defunct International Hockey League. He registered a 2.61 goals-against average and was chosen the IHL's Rookie of the Year. The next season, he lowered his average to 2.45 goals per game, was chosen top goalie in the All-Star Game and ran together a streak of four straight shutouts.

When the Stars promoted Turco to the NHL in 1999, it was to back up Ed Belfour, who'd led Dallas to a Stanley Cup in 1999 and the cup finals in 2000. Turco learned focus and discipline by watching Belfour, who was breaking in his third backup in three years. Turco quickly showed that he could handle NHL shooters, as he played only 26 games but led the entire NHL with a stunning .925 save percentage and 1.90 goals-against average.

The Stars knew for sure that they'd found Belfour's future replacement. That future arrived sooner than expected, when Dallas sputtered early in the 2001–02 season, and Belfour had some off-ice problems. Eventually, coach Ken Hitchcock was fired, the Stars missed the playoffs and Belfour had lost his No. 1 job.

Turco's agility, quick glove and improved positioning carried him to a 15-6-2 record in his 31 games, the fourth-best save percentage (.921) in the NHL and third-best goals-against average (2.09). At the end of the season, Belfour signed with Toronto as a free agent, and Turco had the Dallas netminding duties to himself.

The easygoing Turco has a completely different personality in the dressing room compared to the prickly Belfour. He improved his work ethic when he became the number-one goaltender because he knew his teammates expected more from him in that role. His first full season as the starter was 2002–03 and he proved he could do the job with a 31-10-10 record in 55 games and set a modern-day NHL mark by recording a minuscule 1.72 goals-against average. Turco showed that was no fluke with a 37-win season in 2003–04 and then set a franchise record with 41 wins in 2005–06. Only Martin Brodeur (Devils) and Miikka Kiprusoff (Flames) won more games during the regular season. Turco likes to play often and his 68 appearances in '05–'06 is certainly reflective of that fact, but his .898 save percentage has to be a concern. He is considered a team leader and is not afraid to speak out when necessary.

Turco's playoff performance has been less than stellar and the Colorado Avalanche added to his miseries when they ousted the Stars in just five games during the '06 post-season. A new contract virtually assures that Turco will be the Stars' main netminder for the foreseeable future, but they will expect much more from him in the playoffs. He is just now maturing as he hits the age of 30, so the Dallas club may very well come to realize that Turco's new deal was worth every penny.

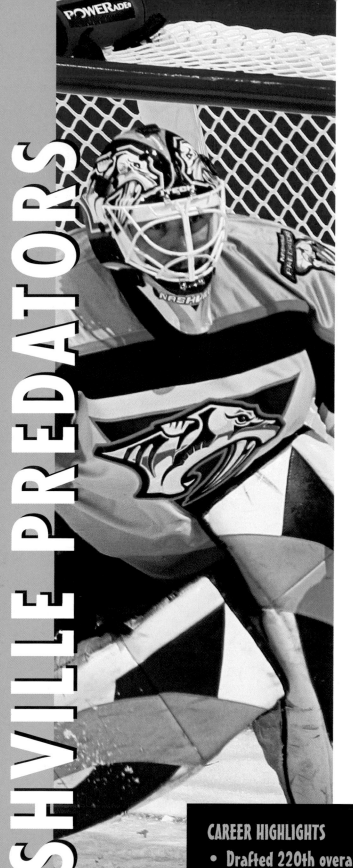

Tomas VOKOUN

The Montreal Canadiens have always had a good eye for goaltenders. A look through their long and illustrious history shows that team management was keenly aware of just how important netminding is to the success of a hockey team. Georges Vezina, George Hainsworth, Bill Durnan, Jacques Plante, Ken Dryden and Patrick Roy were all goalies developed by the organization, and they all led the Canadiens to Stanley Cup victories. In 1994 the Canadiens selected Jose Theodore who, on one occasion, was named the most valuable player in the NHL. He also helped Montreal pull off a couple of play-off upsets before he was dealt away (he now plays for the Colorado Avalanche). There was another netminder selected by Montreal in 1994 who received far less mention than Theodore and he got to play in only one game for the red, white and blue. Actually, Tomas Vokoun played just 20 minutes for the Canadiens (allowing four goals) before he found himself claimed by the Nashville Predators in the 1998 expansion draft.

Going to an expansion club is considered a big break for a goaltender who wants to get his career going. The downside is that he is often backstopping a weak team. But Vokoun (who got some further seasoning by playing in the American Hockey League) has the right attitude, and the other players like playing for him. He got off to a good start with the newly minted Predators by winning 12 games (in 37 appearances) as a rookie in the NHL. He won only nine games the following year and lost 20,

CAREER HIGHLIGHTS

- Drafted 220th overall by Montreal in 1994.
- Selected by the Nashville Predators in the 1998 expansion draft.
- Led the Czech Republic to the World Hockey Championship in 2005.
- Has won 139 contests and recorded 16 shutouts in 340 NHL career games.

but was back up to double digits in 2000–01 with 13 wins. He won only five contests in 2001–02 and his future appeared to be shaky in Nashville, where Mike Dunham was the regular goalie. The Predators kept adding good players through the draft and eventually the team got better through player development and some good trading. Injuries finally gave Vokoun the opportunity he needed to become the number-one goalie.

The 2002–03 season saw Vokoun play in 69 games, posting a very respectable 25-31-11 record. The following season was a major breakthrough for the entire organization, when the team secured its first playoff spot in its history and scared the Detroit Red Wings in the first round of the playoffs before losing in six games. Vokoun also had his first winning year, with a 34-29-10 record. By this point Vokoun was no longer looking over his shoulder for someone to take over his job, and he came back from the lockout year (he played in Europe in 2004–05) to have his best season to date in 2005–06. Vokoun was a workhorse, playing in 61 games and winning 36 contests while losing 18 with four ties. He had a .919 save percentage and added four shutouts to his total. More importantly, the Predators made it back to the playoffs for the second straight year and recorded franchise highs in wins (49) and points (106).

Vokoun is the type of goalie who uses his size (six feet, 195 pounds) to advantage by playing a mostly standup style. He has a good glove hand and is not especially exciting in terms of stopping the puck, but that's because he is so good at being in the right position most of the time. Vokoun is very strong and in good condition (he can handle the heavy workload this way), and his coaches and teammates know he can be relied upon with little fuss. He rebounds well from bad games or goals and does not take out any misfortune on his teammates.

The 2006 playoffs were a terrible disappointment for both Vokoun and the Predators. A serious ailment (blood clots) forced Vokoun out of the post-season, and backup Chris Mason was not equal to the task of stopping the hot San Jose Sharks in the first round of the playoffs. At the age of 29, Vokoun is now just heading into his prime years as a goalie. If the Predators continue to build their team, there is no telling how far they will go with him in net. Vokoun might just prove the Montreal Canadiens right again!

ICE CHIPS

Tomas Vokoun recorded his first NHL shutout and the first in Nashville team history by defeating Phoenix 3–0 on January 15, 1999.

27

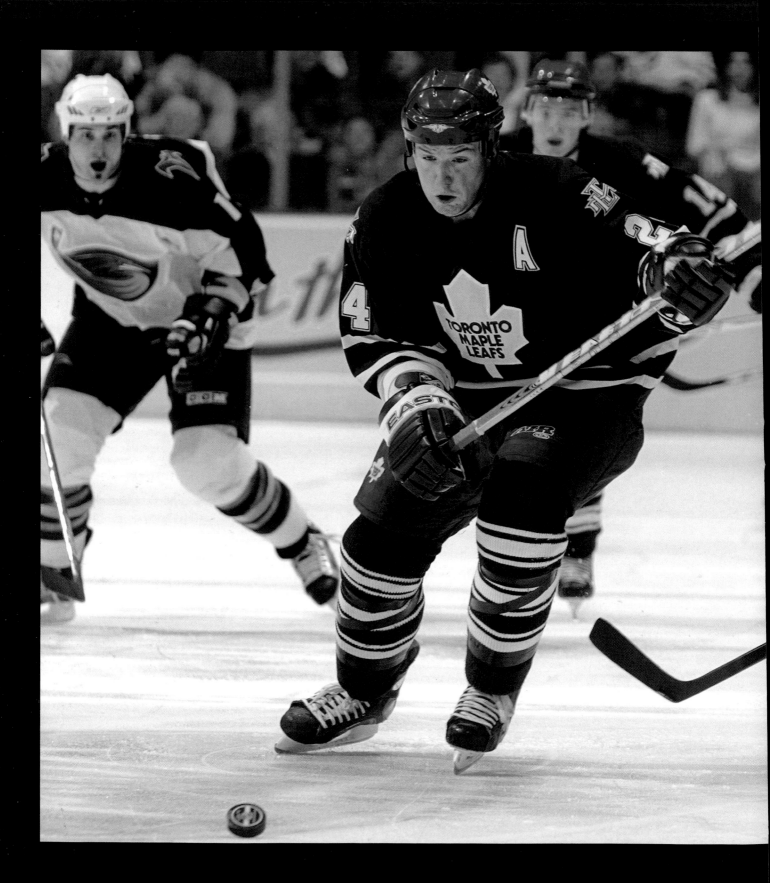

Strong, mobile defensemen who use their size and hard shots.

REARGUARDS!

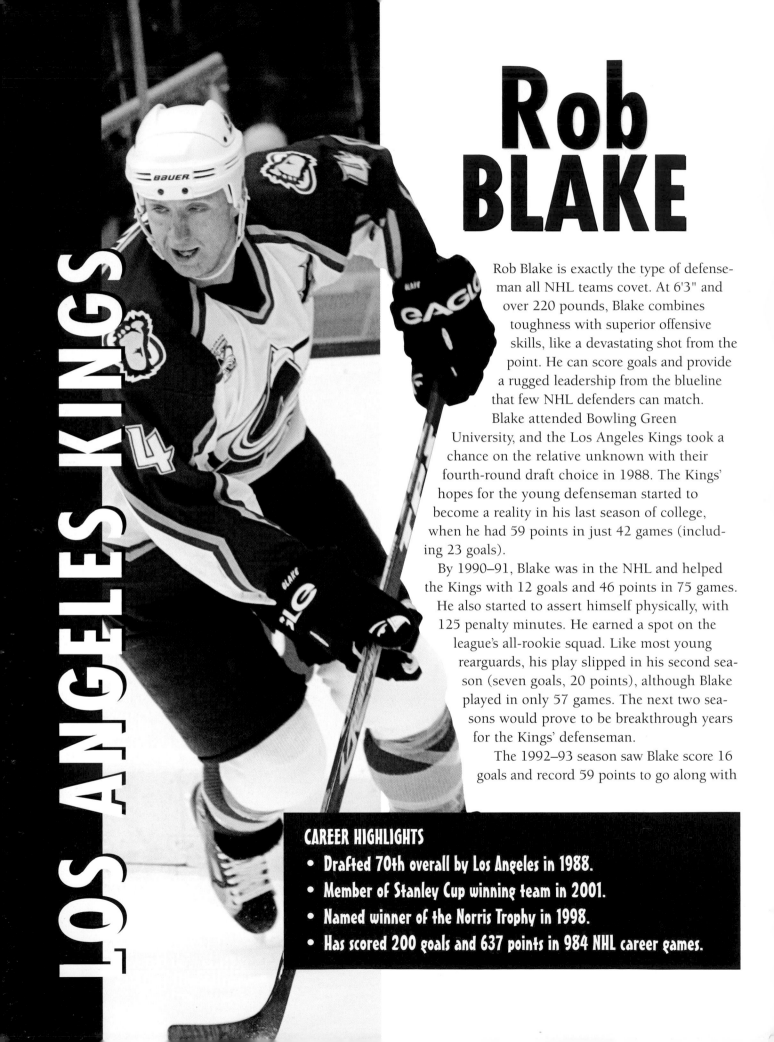

Rob BLAKE

LOS ANGELES KINGS

Rob Blake is exactly the type of defenseman all NHL teams covet. At 6'3" and over 220 pounds, Blake combines toughness with superior offensive skills, like a devastating shot from the point. He can score goals and provide a rugged leadership from the blueline that few NHL defenders can match.

Blake attended Bowling Green University, and the Los Angeles Kings took a chance on the relative unknown with their fourth-round draft choice in 1988. The Kings' hopes for the young defenseman started to become a reality in his last season of college, when he had 59 points in just 42 games (including 23 goals).

By 1990–91, Blake was in the NHL and helped the Kings with 12 goals and 46 points in 75 games. He also started to assert himself physically, with 125 penalty minutes. He earned a spot on the league's all-rookie squad. Like most young rearguards, his play slipped in his second season (seven goals, 20 points), although Blake played in only 57 games. The next two seasons would prove to be breakthrough years for the Kings' defenseman.

The 1992–93 season saw Blake score 16 goals and record 59 points to go along with

CAREER HIGHLIGHTS

- Drafted 70th overall by Los Angeles in 1988.
- Member of Stanley Cup winning team in 2001.
- Named winner of the Norris Trophy in 1998.
- Has scored 200 goals and 637 points in 984 NHL career games.

152 penalty minutes – and the Kings finally got a taste of what winning was all about when they made it to the Stanley Cup finals. Blake was a key component of the Kings' success, with 10 points in 23 post-season games as the Los Angeles club fell just three wins short of a championship. In 1993–94, the big blueliner scored 20 times and raised his point total to 68, even though the Kings failed to qualify for the play-offs. Using his rocket-like shot from the point, Blake found that he could be highly effective on the point during powerplays. He keeps the shot low, which is ideal for deflections and for getting the puck on net. Just as important is his ability to carry the puck and to crush opponents with bodychecks (he can throw an old-fashioned hip check as well as anybody). His two-way game was ready to take off when injuries took their toll for two years.

Healthy again for 1997–98, Blake recaptured his game and scored a career-high 23 goals, leading all NHL defensemen, and added a total of 50 points. He was easily the Kings' most important player now that Wayne Gretzky was gone, and he stepped up to fill the leadership void by taking on the team captaincy. His excellent play was rewarded with his first Norris Trophy win and a spot on the Canadian Olympic team. He was named best defenseman at the Nagano games.

Free agency was just around the corner (in the summer of 2001) for Blake, so the Kings were compelled to make a deal with Colorado near the trade deadline. Adam Deadmarsh and Aaron Miller went to Los Angeles, and Blake wound up with a Stanley Cup ring based on a terrific playoff that saw him score six goals and total 19 points. With the Avalanche, Blake joined Adam Foote and Ray Bourque to form a trio of defensemen the like of which has not been seen since the 1970s, when Montreal boasted three Hall of Famers on their blueline – Larry Robinson, Guy Lapointe and Serge Savard. Blake was a key member of the 2002 Canadian Olympic team that won the gold medal.

For the last two NHL seasons, Blake has settled around the 45- to 50-point range. He got off to a bad start in 2005–06 but bounced back to score 14 goals and 51 points and demonstrated that he could still be physical when he wanted to be. The Avalanche pulled off one playoff upset in '06 (over Dallas), but the glory days may be a thing of the past in Colorado (especially with the loss of Peter Forsberg and Adam Foote). Blake looked tired as the 2006 playoffs carried on, and the Avalanche are in need of rebuilding. However, that process will not include Blake, who signed a two-year deal with his original team, the Los Angeles Kings, when he became a free agent.

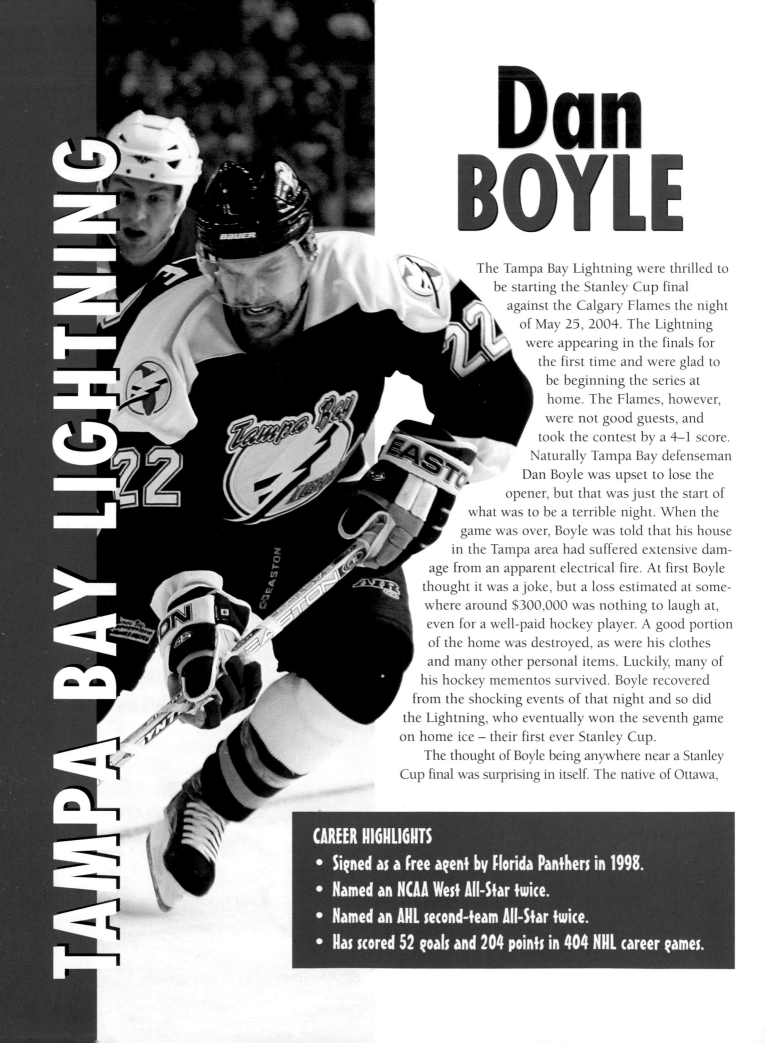

TAMPA BAY LIGHTNING

Dan BOYLE

The Tampa Bay Lightning were thrilled to be starting the Stanley Cup final against the Calgary Flames the night of May 25, 2004. The Lightning were appearing in the finals for the first time and were glad to be beginning the series at home. The Flames, however, were not good guests, and took the contest by a 4–1 score. Naturally Tampa Bay defenseman Dan Boyle was upset to lose the opener, but that was just the start of what was to be a terrible night. When the game was over, Boyle was told that his house in the Tampa area had suffered extensive damage from an apparent electrical fire. At first Boyle thought it was a joke, but a loss estimated at somewhere around $300,000 was nothing to laugh at, even for a well-paid hockey player. A good portion of the home was destroyed, as were his clothes and many other personal items. Luckily, many of his hockey mementos survived. Boyle recovered from the shocking events of that night and so did the Lightning, who eventually won the seventh game on home ice – their first ever Stanley Cup.

The thought of Boyle being anywhere near a Stanley Cup final was surprising in itself. The native of Ottawa,

CAREER HIGHLIGHTS
- Signed as a free agent by Florida Panthers in 1998.
- Named an NCAA West All-Star twice.
- Named an AHL second-team All-Star twice.
- Has scored 52 goals and 204 points in 404 NHL career games.

Ontario, had never played major junior hockey (he suited up for a tier II club in nearby Gloucester) before Miami (Ohio) University came along and offered him a scholarship. He put up good numbers while playing four years for the college team, the Redskins, and his final two seasons saw him record 54 and 40 points, respectively (14 goals in his final campaign with the college in 1997–98). Not many people noticed the 5'11", 190-pound defenseman and no NHL club drafted him. However, the Florida Panthers signed him as a free agent and he played 22 games for the NHL team in 1998–99, recording eight points. He spent the rest of the year with Kentucky of the American Hockey League, where he had a very respectable 42 points in 53 games. By the 2000–01 season, Boyle was more or less a regular with the Panthers and got into 69 contests, notching 22 points. About a quarter of the way through the next season, the Panthers suddenly traded him to the Lightning for a measly fifth-round draft choice. It was a move the Panthers would regret.

Boyle's game is more about finesse than anything else. Not a large defender by any means, Boyle has found a way to keep his offensive numbers reasonably high (generally, they keep improving each year) without sacrificing his defensive play. At first Boyle was seen as a rather questionable defender, but he worked very hard on his play in his own end because he knew that would ensure him NHL employment. Competent at both ends of the ice, Boyle's name now often comes up when the best defenders in the NHL are discussed (he was seriously considered for the Canadian Olympic team). He is not the dominating type of defenseman every team craves, but he will quarterback a powerplay with a good low shot that can be tipped in by forwards in front of the net. Boyle is not a speedster but is smart enough to know when to jump in and when to stay back. The Lightning are confident enough in his abili-

ties to use him against the opposition's best lines.

During the 2002–03 season, Boyle recorded 53 points (13 goals, 40 assists), and in the Lightning's cup year he had a 39-point regular season followed by 10 points in 23 playoff contests. The Tampa Bay club struggled mightily during the 2005–06 season, but Boyle matched his career best with 53 points based on 15 goals (a career high) and 38 assists. The Lightning were knocked out in the first round of the 2006 playoffs by Ottawa in just five games, but during one contest Boyle beat Senators goalie Ray Emery with one of the best goals of the post-season, spinning with the puck and firing in a shot on the glove side. Boyle should continue to develop and be an assist leader from his position for years to come.

ICE CHIPS

Players on the Stanley Cup winning team are each allowed to spend a couple of days with the coveted trophy, and Dan Boyle decided to take it to his hometown. Among other activities, Boyle took the Cup to his parents' home in Orleans, Ontario, and the next day to the downtown Ottawa co-op residence where he had done much of his growing up, so that lifelong friends could see the famed silver trophy.

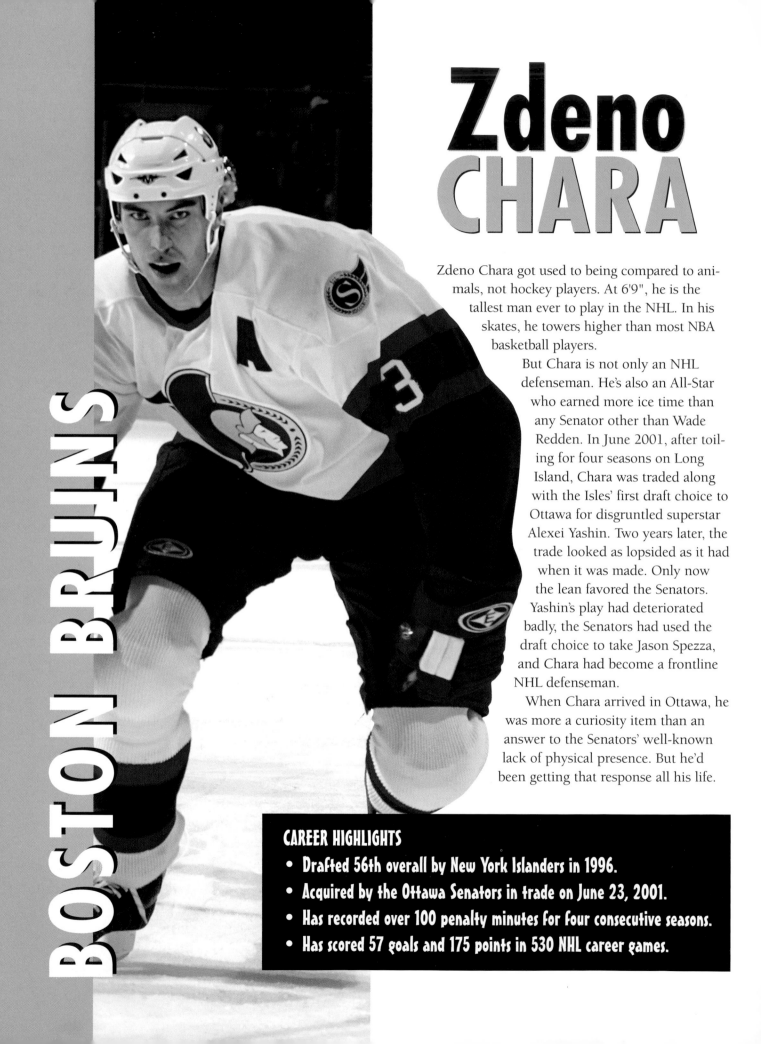

Zdeno CHARA

BOSTON BRUINS

Zdeno Chara got used to being compared to animals, not hockey players. At 6'9", he is the tallest man ever to play in the NHL. In his skates, he towers higher than most NBA basketball players.

But Chara is not only an NHL defenseman. He's also an All-Star who earned more ice time than any Senator other than Wade Redden. In June 2001, after toiling for four seasons on Long Island, Chara was traded along with the Isles' first draft choice to Ottawa for disgruntled superstar Alexei Yashin. Two years later, the trade looked as lopsided as it had when it was made. Only now the lean favored the Senators. Yashin's play had deteriorated badly, the Senators had used the draft choice to take Jason Spezza, and Chara had become a frontline NHL defenseman.

When Chara arrived in Ottawa, he was more a curiosity item than an answer to the Senators' well-known lack of physical presence. But he'd been getting that response all his life.

CAREER HIGHLIGHTS
- Drafted 56th overall by New York Islanders in 1996.
- Acquired by the Ottawa Senators in trade on June 23, 2001.
- Has recorded over 100 penalty minutes for four consecutive seasons.
- Has scored 57 goals and 175 points in 530 NHL career games.

When he started playing hockey in the Czech Republic town of Trencin, everyone told him he was too big for the game. Nothing on the ice for the next few years changed their minds. Chara's muscles and coordination could not keep up to his surging height. He was awkward and easy to get around. When he was 16, and playing junior B, he decided to quit at the end of the season. But he changed his mind and became determined to prove his critics wrong. It took him six or seven years, but he finally did it.

The Islanders selected Chara 56th overall in the 1996 draft. He came to Canada for his final year of junior hockey in Prince George, British Columbia, then spent 1997–98 and 1998–99 alternating between the Islanders and the American Hockey League. He found regular NHL employment the next two years, taking a lot of penalties but scoring only four goals and winding up at minus 27 each season.

The Islanders considered him highly expendable, especially when they could land the high-priced Yashin in return. But all Chara needed was to stop growing, fill out a bit and find a comfortable environment. He got all of that in Ottawa. By the end of the 2001–02 season he had become one of the Senators' most important players and one of the better defensemen in the NHL. He could move the league's biggest players from the front of the net with ease, and he was feisty enough to take 156 minutes in penalties.

His strength and lengthy reach make him difficult for forwards to beat to the outside. And he is developing a soft touch on the attack. His 10 goals in 2001–02 were four more than he totaled in his entire four years in New York, and his plus-minus marks zoomed to plus 30. He brought a certain edge to an Ottawa team that had always survived on speed and finesse. In fact, when the Senators lost games 6 and 7 to the undermanned Toronto Maple Leafs in the second round of the 2002 playoffs, it was widely attributed to Chara's absence (because of a knee injury). His physical presence had been an important factor in a first-round victory over the Flyers, and in the Senators' leading the Leaf series before he was hurt.

In 2002–03, Chara continued to improve. He set career marks in assists (30) and points (39). Coach Jacques Martin often used him as a forward on the powerplay, where he would park in front of the net like an apartment building. Chara was selected for the 2003 All-Star Game, along with fellow Trencin native

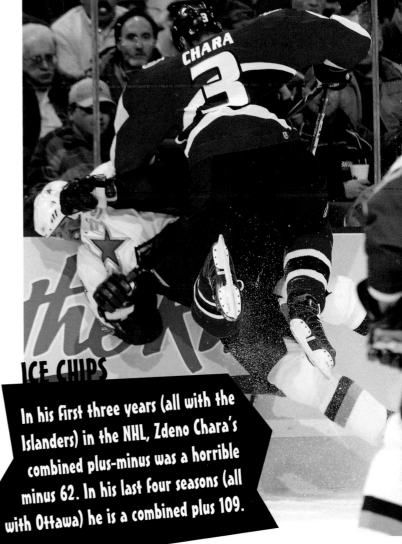

ICE CHIPS

In his first three years (all with the Islanders) in the NHL, Zdeno Chara's combined plus-minus was a horrible minus 62. In his last four seasons (all with Ottawa) he is a combined plus 109.

and Ottawa teammate Marian Hossa. And he led the Senators, who had suffered four straight springs of playoff disappointments, into the Eastern Conference final, although they lost to New Jersey in seven games.

Finally Zdeno Chara's reputation and his game had grown as tall as he was.

Chara had his terrific year in 2003–04 with 41 points (including 16 goals) but once again the Maple Leafs knocked the Senators out of the playoffs. The Senators had a great season in 2005–06 and Chara played 27:11 minutes per game while scoring 16 goals once again and totaling a career-high 43 points. Chara hurt his hand in a fight late in the season but was back for the playoffs. However, his play was not up to his usual standards and his overall effort appeared to be lagging. Once again the Senators got knocked out of the playoffs with a loss in the second round. Chara then joined the Boston Bruins by signing a five-year deal as a free agent.

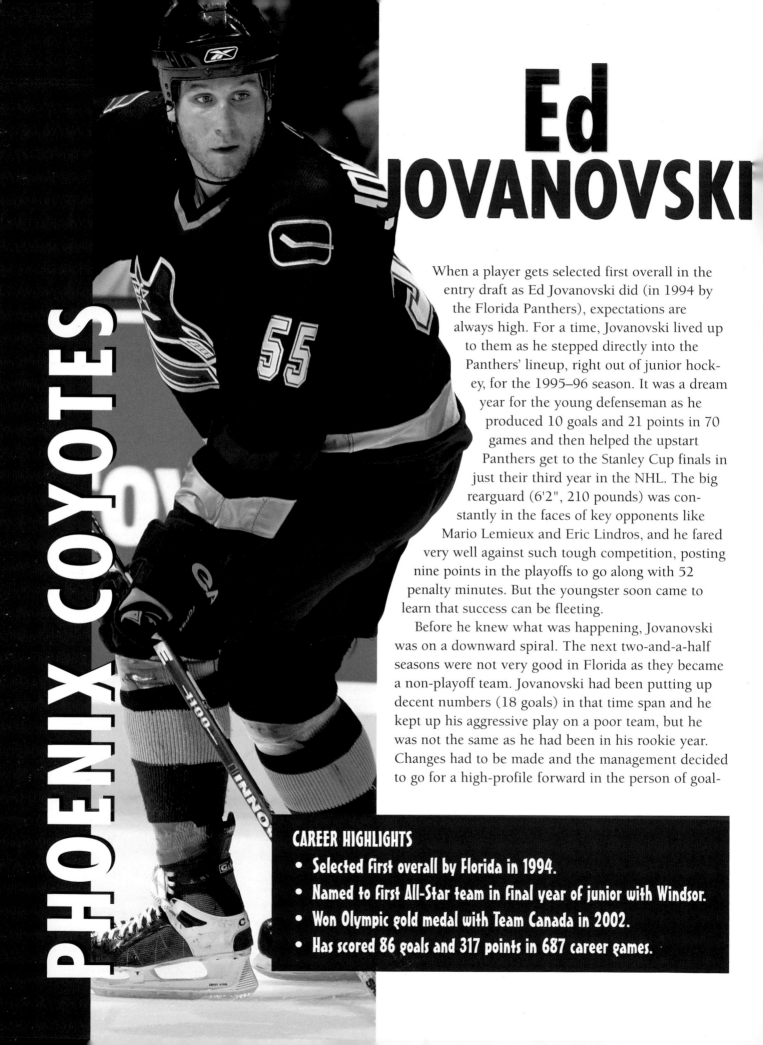

Ed JOVANOVSKI

PHOENIX COYOTES

When a player gets selected first overall in the entry draft as Ed Jovanovski did (in 1994 by the Florida Panthers), expectations are always high. For a time, Jovanovski lived up to them as he stepped directly into the Panthers' lineup, right out of junior hockey, for the 1995–96 season. It was a dream year for the young defenseman as he produced 10 goals and 21 points in 70 games and then helped the upstart Panthers get to the Stanley Cup finals in just their third year in the NHL. The big rearguard (6'2", 210 pounds) was constantly in the faces of key opponents like Mario Lemieux and Eric Lindros, and he fared very well against such tough competition, posting nine points in the playoffs to go along with 52 penalty minutes. But the youngster soon came to learn that success can be fleeting.

Before he knew what was happening, Jovanovski was on a downward spiral. The next two-and-a-half seasons were not very good in Florida as they became a non-playoff team. Jovanovski had been putting up decent numbers (18 goals) in that time span and he kept up his aggressive play on a poor team, but he was not the same as he had been in his rookie year. Changes had to be made and the management decided to go for a high-profile forward in the person of goal-

CAREER HIGHLIGHTS
- Selected first overall by Florida in 1994.
- Named to First All-Star team in final year of junior with Windsor.
- Won Olympic gold medal with Team Canada in 2002.
- Has scored 86 goals and 317 points in 687 career games.

ICE CHIPS

Ed Jovanovski played junior hockey in his hometown of Windsor, Ontario, where he starred for the Spitfires for two seasons. Always at his best when he plays a physical game, Jovanovski has recorded 1,085 penalty minutes in ten NHL seasons.

scoring Pavel Bure from Vancouver. Vancouver wisely asked for Jovanovski to be added to the package (which also included Kevin Weekes, Mike Brown, Dave Gagner and a first-round draft choice in the 2000 entry draft). Considering that Jovanovski was floundering along with the fortunes of the Panthers, the blockbuster trade could not have come at a better time for him.

Vancouver's general manager at the time, Brian Burke, saw the potential in the young blueliner. Blessed with offensively minded instincts and tough to play against, Jovanovski needed to use his size to become truly effective. Using all his assets would make Jovanovski a force to be reckoned with in the NHL. When Marc Crawford took over as coach of the Canucks, Jovanovski's career was rejuvenated. In 2000–01 the Canucks made it back to the playoffs and Jovanovski had a very good year with 12 goals and 47 points in 79 games. He followed that up with a career-best 17 goals and 48 points the next season. For four straight seasons he led all the Canuck defensemen in scoring and, in 2002–03, he finished among the NHL's top 10 blueliners in scoring when he had 46 points.

Jovanovski's fine play has been recognized with three appearances in the NHL's All-Star Game and his selection for Team Canada in 2002. He played well at the Salt Lake City Olympics and had five points during the Canucks playoff series against Detroit (which Vancouver eventually lost). An injury cost him 15 games in the 2002–03 season and hurt his chances to win the Norris Trophy, but he had clearly established himself as the leader of the Canucks blue-line as Vancouver won 45 games and recorded 104 points (a club record). He played in only 56 games in '03–'04 and recorded just 23 points, but his open-ice hits kept the opposition honest at all times.

The 2005–06 season was shortened to 44 games (he had to have abdominal surgery but still managed 33 points) and the Canucks missed Jovanovski's passionate play and leadership dearly (as did Team Canada at the Olympics). He returned late in the season, but it was too late for Vancouver to make the playoffs. He then signed with the Phoenix Coyotes as a free agent.

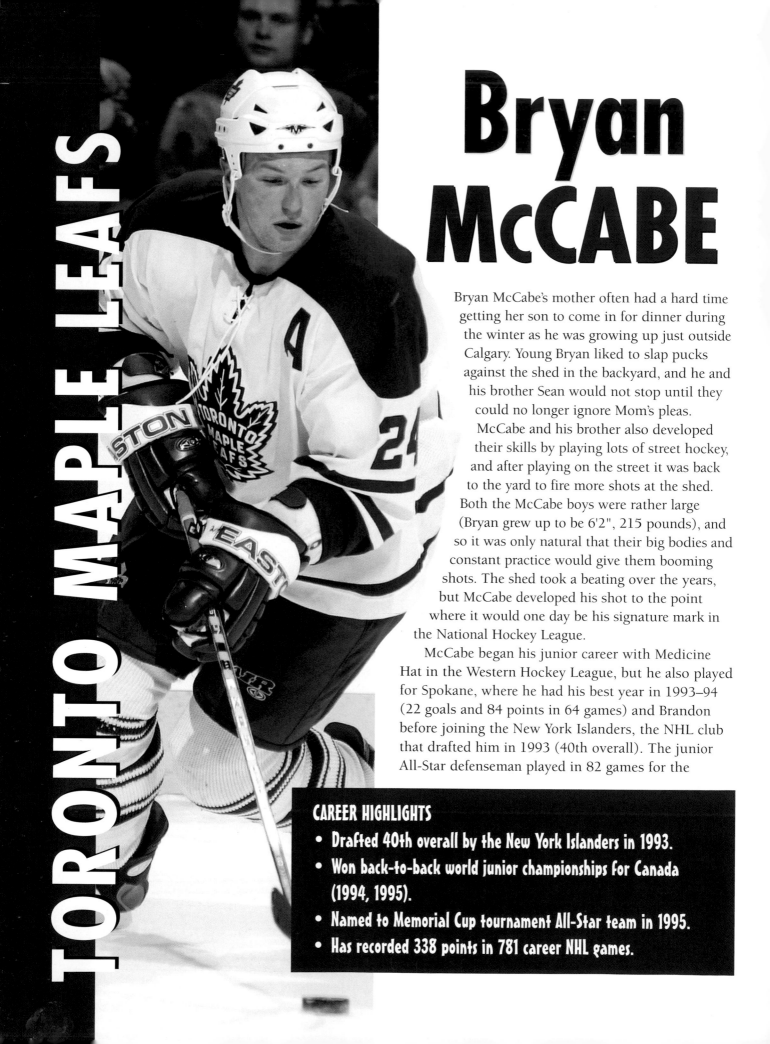

TORONTO MAPLE LEAFS

Bryan McCABE

Bryan McCabe's mother often had a hard time getting her son to come in for dinner during the winter as he was growing up just outside Calgary. Young Bryan liked to slap pucks against the shed in the backyard, and he and his brother Sean would not stop until they could no longer ignore Mom's pleas.

McCabe and his brother also developed their skills by playing lots of street hockey, and after playing on the street it was back to the yard to fire more shots at the shed. Both the McCabe boys were rather large (Bryan grew up to be 6'2", 215 pounds), and so it was only natural that their big bodies and constant practice would give them booming shots. The shed took a beating over the years, but McCabe developed his shot to the point where it would one day be his signature mark in the National Hockey League.

McCabe began his junior career with Medicine Hat in the Western Hockey League, but he also played for Spokane, where he had his best year in 1993–94 (22 goals and 84 points in 64 games) and Brandon before joining the New York Islanders, the NHL club that drafted him in 1993 (40th overall). The junior All-Star defenseman played in 82 games for the

CAREER HIGHLIGHTS
- Drafted 40th overall by the New York Islanders in 1993.
- Won back-to-back world junior championships for Canada (1994, 1995).
- Named to Memorial Cup tournament All-Star team in 1995.
- Has recorded 338 points in 781 career NHL games.

ICE CHIPS

Islanders in 1995–96 and had a respectable 23 points, although he was a terrible minus 24 for a bad team.

The next season saw McCabe get his defensive record to a much more respectable minus two while upping his point total to 28. So impressed were the Islanders with their young rearguard that they named the 22-year-old McCabe team captain, but then inexplicably traded him to Vancouver (along with Todd Bertuzzi and a third-round draft choice) in a deal involving Trevor Linden. The Canucks quickly flipped McCabe to the Chicago Blackhawks, and the Leafs were able to pry away the burly defender in an October 2000 trade that saw Toronto send the oft-injured Alexander Karpovtsev to Chicago in exchange. It was another famous Mike Smith deal featuring a European coming to his club in exchange for a youngster he saw little use for on his team. Not long after that, Smith was removed as Chicago's general manager (the same thing had happened to him in Toronto in 1999).

McCabe finally began to thrive on the Leafs blueline. He quickly established himself as a fast-skating defenseman who could shoot the puck from the point with great authority. While not overly physical, McCabe is certainly not afraid to throw his body around, and his hip checks (his big backside is a very useful tool in delivering a hit) have kept many forwards from getting around him. Soon he became the Leafs' best defenseman and gained a second-team All-Star berth in 2003–04, the first Leaf blueliner so honored since Borje Salming in 1979–80.

Recognition for his good play has not come easily to McCabe in spite of a 17-goal season in 2001–02 and a 16-goal year in 2003–04. In 2005–06 he got off to a blazing start, but the selectors for Canada's Olympic team were reluctant to consider him for that squad (he was eventually asked to play when injuries struck). Early in 2005–06 McCabe was firing bullets that were going in with great regularity, especially on the powerplay. Fed with great passes from teammate Tomas Kaberle, the Leaf defenseman looked like a sure bet to break the team mark for most goals in a season by a rearguard, but McCabe ended up three short of the total with 19 tallies (13 of which came with the extra man). His play declined somewhat after the Olympics, and McCabe could not find the net very often, but he did end up with a career-high 68 points. Talk of a Norris Trophy died away, and McCabe's poor playmaking decisions (his breakout pass attempts are often picked off) were once again a topic of conversation for his critics. Oftentimes McCabe will try to do things in a hurry, and it gets him into trouble. A calmer, more clearly thinking McCabe could easily regain his All-Star status.

Dion PHANEUF

CALGARY FLAMES

When hockey legends and luminaries take the time to comment on an NHL rookie, you know that he must be pretty special. Such is the case for Calgary Flames defenseman Dion Phaneuf, who took the league by storm during the 2005–06 regular season. Wayne Gretzky saw a lot of Phaneuf as coach of the Phoenix Coyotes and was effusive in his praise of the youngster. Phrases like "a tremendous hockey player" and "going to be a force for a long time" were just two of the accolades tossed Phaneuf's way by "The Great One." Even *Hockey Night in Canada* broadcaster Don Cherry got in on the act, saying Phaneuf was the best rookie defenseman in the NHL since Bobby Orr! The high praise did not seem to faze the youngster, who took it all in stride and turned in one of the best freshman seasons in NHL history.

The Calgary Flames were thrilled to take the 6'3", 213 pound defenseman as their first pick in the 2003 entry draft. Coach and general manager Darryl Sutter was well aware of Phaneuf, since the youngster

CAREER HIGHLIGHTS
- Drafted ninth overall by Calgary in 2003.
- Member of Canada's world junior championship team for two gold medals (2004, 2005).
- Named Defenseman of the Year in the WHL in 2004 and 2005.
- Has scored 20 goals and 49 points in 82 NHL career games.

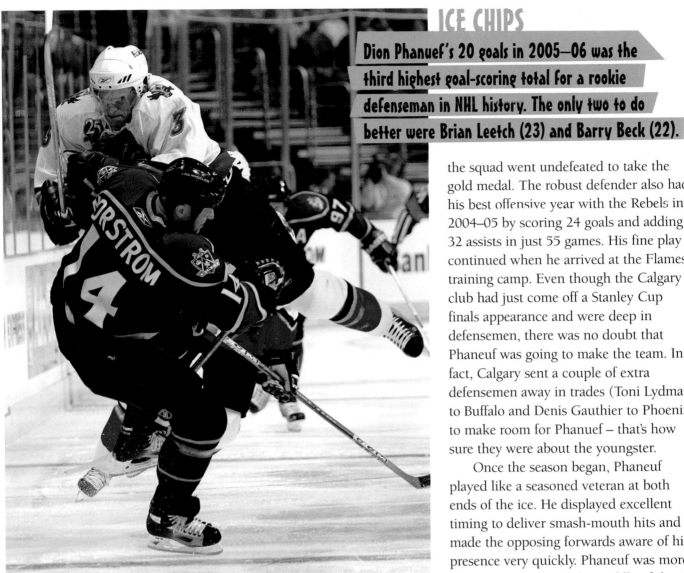

Dion Phanuef's 20 goals in 2005–06 was the third highest goal-scoring total for a rookie defenseman in NHL history. The only two to do better were Brian Leetch (23) and Barry Beck (22).

the squad went undefeated to take the gold medal. The robust defender also had his best offensive year with the Rebels in 2004–05 by scoring 24 goals and adding 32 assists in just 55 games. His fine play continued when he arrived at the Flames' training camp. Even though the Calgary club had just come off a Stanley Cup finals appearance and were deep in defensemen, there was no doubt that Phaneuf was going to make the team. In fact, Calgary sent a couple of extra defensemen away in trades (Toni Lydman to Buffalo and Denis Gauthier to Phoenix) to make room for Phaneuf – that's how sure they were about the youngster.

Once the season began, Phaneuf played like a seasoned veteran at both ends of the ice. He displayed excellent timing to deliver smash-mouth hits and made the opposing forwards aware of his presence very quickly. Phaneuf was more than willing to hit in the middle of the ice and did not hesitate to clear the front of the net when he had to (he also dropped the gloves when necessary). The Flames wanted him to be careful about picking his spots to deliver his hits because he might get overzealous and be out of position, but his great hockey sense did not let that happen very often. He was also a force on the attack, scoring 20 times (the most for any Calgary rookie defenseman since Gary Suter, who had 18 in 1985–86) by unloading a big bomb of a shot from the point. Phaneuf is also an excellent passer (29 assists) and likes getting into the middle of the action. What impressed most was his poise for such a young player and his ability to play in all situations.

The Flames were out of the playoffs early in the '06 post-season, and for the first time Phaneuf showed that all rookies do have weaknesses. In spite of that, hockey observers believe he will be a star in the NHL for many years to come.

had played for his brother Brent, who coached the Red Deer Rebels.

A native of Edmonton, Alberta, the large defenseman professed to liking the way hard-rock defenseman Scott Stevens (who retired prior to the start of the 2005–06 season) played the game and molded his approach around the style of the three-time Stanley Cup champion blueliner. His penalty-minute total in Red Deer was usually well over the 100-minute mark, and the Flames were certainly hoping he would bring that personality to the team. Phaneuf has a sort of quiet confidence about him and, while he will not brag, he knows he belongs among the best players in the world.

When the NHL players were locked out during the 2004–05 season, it meant that top prospects like Phaneuf could play in junior one more season. It also gave Phanuef an opportunity to play for the Canadian team at the world junior championships where he excelled, as

Chris PRONGER

ANAHEIM DUCKS

As general manager of the Hartford Whalers, Brian Burke felt that defenseman Chris Pronger could be just what his floundering club needed. Burke also knew that if he was to have any chance at taking Pronger, he would have to move up from his sixth position in the 1993 draft. He waited nervously while Ottawa selected first. They accommodated Burke nicely by taking Alex Daigle. Burke now had his opening and quickly struck a deal with San Jose that included a flip of first-round draft choices, and Burke, now picking second, grabbed Pronger's rights. Unfortunately, Burke would not be around to see the fruits of his selection (he would join the NHL's front office before returning to the general manager position in Vancouver, and then Anaheim).

Pronger played junior with the Peterborough Petes, and in his last two seasons there recorded 62 and 77 points. He was by far the best defenseman in Canadian junior hockey. What attracted all the scouts was Pronger's size (6'6", 207 pounds) and his incredible reach. Throw in some toughness and leader-

CAREER HIGHLIGHTS
- Drafted second overall by Hartford in 1993.
- Named captain of the St. Louis Blues in 1997.
- Named winner of the Hart and Norris trophies in 2000.
- Has scored 106 goals and 456 points in 802 NHL career games.

ship potential, and Pronger looked like a can't-miss prospect. But his youth and immaturity quickly showed up in Hartford and he developed a reputation off the ice that displeased Hartford management. Pronger's conditioning was also nowhere near where it needed to be. Soon the trade rumors began. He played just two years in Hartford and scored a total of 10 goals and 44 points.

By this time Mike Keenan was coaching and managing the St. Louis Blues. When he heard that Pronger might be available, he moved hastily to complete a deal. Keenan paid a high price for Pronger (it cost the Blues the rights to Brendan Shanahan), but the coach felt it was worth it. However, when he got a look at the shape Pronger was in, Keenan was furious and told Pronger in no uncertain terms that this was not acceptable. It was a turning point for the young blueliner – and he got the message that he would have to be serious about his career. His first season as a Blue, 1995–96, was rough, with only seven goals and 25 points (and a minus 18), but he started to bloom in the playoffs. Pronger has never looked back.

Keenan was eventually replaced as coach of the Blues by Joel Quenneville, a former NHL defenseman. This change helped Pronger enormously; he now had a mentor to teach him how to play on the blueline properly. In 1996–97, he scored 11 goals and 35 points and became a plus (15) player again. Now his name was being mentioned among the NHL's best defensemen as he developed a strong two-way game. He could contribute on the powerplay or dish out a terrific bodycheck. In 1999–2000, Pronger became the first defenseman since Bobby Orr to win the Hart and Norris trophies in the same year, when he had 14 goals and 62 points, helping the Blues to the best record in the NHL.

He had an injury-filled 2000–01 season, but still managed 47 points in 51 games. In the 2002 playoffs he had eight points in nine games but suffered a serious knee injury. That injury and three operations to his wrist kept him out of all but five games in 2002–03.

ICE CHIPS
Despite making it to the finals in 2006, Chris Pronger requested a trade out of Edmonton. On July 3, 2006, he was dealt to Anaheim in exchange for a package of players (including Joffrey Lupul and Ladislav Smid) and draft choices.

The Blues had learned to play without him, but were ecstatic to have their captain back the following year.

Pronger had a good season in St. Louis during 2003–04 with 54 points (including 40 assists) but, as usual, the Blues got nowhere in the playoffs. The rebuilding Blues could not see paying Pronger a big contract after the lockout and dealt him to Edmonton for younger defenseman Eric Brewer and two others. He had a difficult time adjusting to the new rule enforcement at first, but he came on strong at the end (finishing with 12 goals and 56 points) and the Oilers made the playoffs. He was their best player in the playoffs as Edmonton defeated Detroit, San Jose and Anaheim to make it to the finals.

Smooth-skating defensemen who can jump into the attack and control the power-play.

BLUELINE ATTACK!

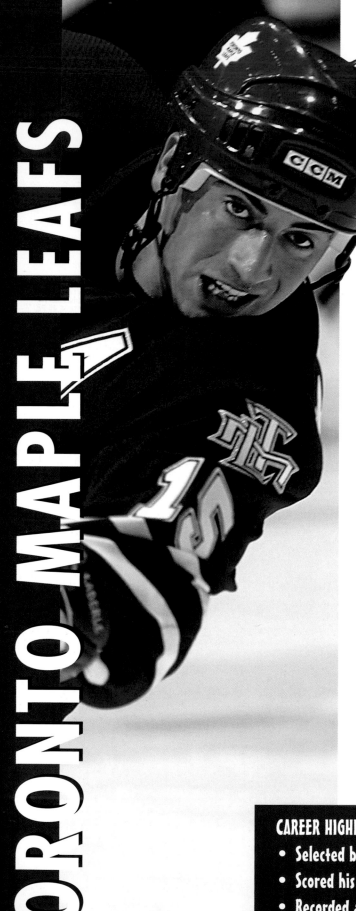

TORONTO MAPLE LEAFS

Tomas KABERLE

When the Toronto Maple Leafs hired coach Pat Quinn before the start of the 1998–99 season, he knew he had to make some significant changes if one of hockey's most storied franchises was going to get back on the winning track. It appeared the Leafs had little to offer the new coach in terms of young talent, especially on the blueline. But Tomas Kaberle changed all that with a surprising year that would launch his NHL career.

Not many expected the defenseman, who had been selected 204th overall in 1996, to make the Leafs' starting lineup. But Kaberle's poise with the puck made Quinn add him to his opening night roster. The youngster played 29:13 minutes (the most of any player) in the contest against Detroit, and the Leafs got off on the right foot with a 3–2 win over the Stanley Cup champions. It quickly became apparent that Quinn had found himself a gem.

Kaberle began playing hockey at the age of five and had a good chance to succeed in the sport, considering his father, Frantisek, was once an elite international player for the Czech Republic. His older brother, Frantisek Jr., was also playing the game. (He has played 386 NHL games for Los Angeles, Atlanta and Carolina.)

As Kaberle rose through the ranks of the system in the Czech Republic, his numbers were not exactly overwhelming, but he did manage about 20 points a season. Perhaps that's why he was available to the Leafs with their 13th selection of the 1996 entry draft.

CAREER HIGHLIGHTS
- Selected by Toronto in the 1996 entry draft, 204th overall.
- Scored his first NHL goal against Detroit (October 23, 1998).
- Recorded a career-high 67 points in 2005–06.
- Has recorded 291 points in 525 career games.

The baby-faced blueliner was ticketed for development in St. John's in the American Hockey League, but Kaberle never made it out to Canada's east coast. An impressive training camp earned Kaberle a start in Toronto and he has never looked back.

The Maple Leafs realized that the young defenseman still needed work and wisely held him out of some games when he began to struggle as a rookie. He played in 57 games in 1998–99 and contributed four goals (including an overtime winner against Montreal) and 22 points. He showed flashes of the qualities that got him on the team straight out of training camp, especially his deft puckhandling skills. Kaberle is a strong skater and a very good passer. He can read the play easily, with a strong knack for knowing when to jump into the attack.

Kaberle's shot is by no means devastating, but it is somewhat deceiving (especially when he gets good wood on his drives) and it tends to be accurate. Toronto fans keep encouraging him to shoot more. As with many skilled players in today's game, Kaberle tends to get into trouble when he over-handles the puck or when the game gets physical. He is listed at 6'2" and 200 pounds, but can have trouble handling the bigger NHL forwards in front of the Leafs' net.

During the 2000–01 season, the Maple Leafs had a chance to acquire superstar Eric Lindros from Philadelphia if they would include Kaberle in the deal. The Leafs coveted the former Flyers captain but balked at putting Kaberle into the package to complete the deal.

Hanging on to Kaberle has proven to be a wise move by the Leafs. During the 2005–06 season, Kaberle recorded a career-best 67 points (including a team-high 58 assists) and was a vital member of the Leafs' highly ranked powerplay. Kaberle set up fellow blueliner Bryan

McCabe with perfectly placed passes that McCabe could blast toward the opposition net. McCabe rightly credited Kaberle for much of his success in '05–'06 and Toronto management certainly agreed by locking Kaberle up to a long-term deal. The smooth-skating Kaberle is ideally suited to the new NHL, and there is no telling how more directed coaching will aid him in the future. If he improves his play in his own end (he still tends to give the puck away at the most inopportune time), the tireless Kaberle may become one of the truly elite defensemen in the league.

ICE CHIPS

Tomas Kaberle has recorded 30 or more assists four times in his career and was the only Maple Leaf player to dress for all 82 games in 2005–06.

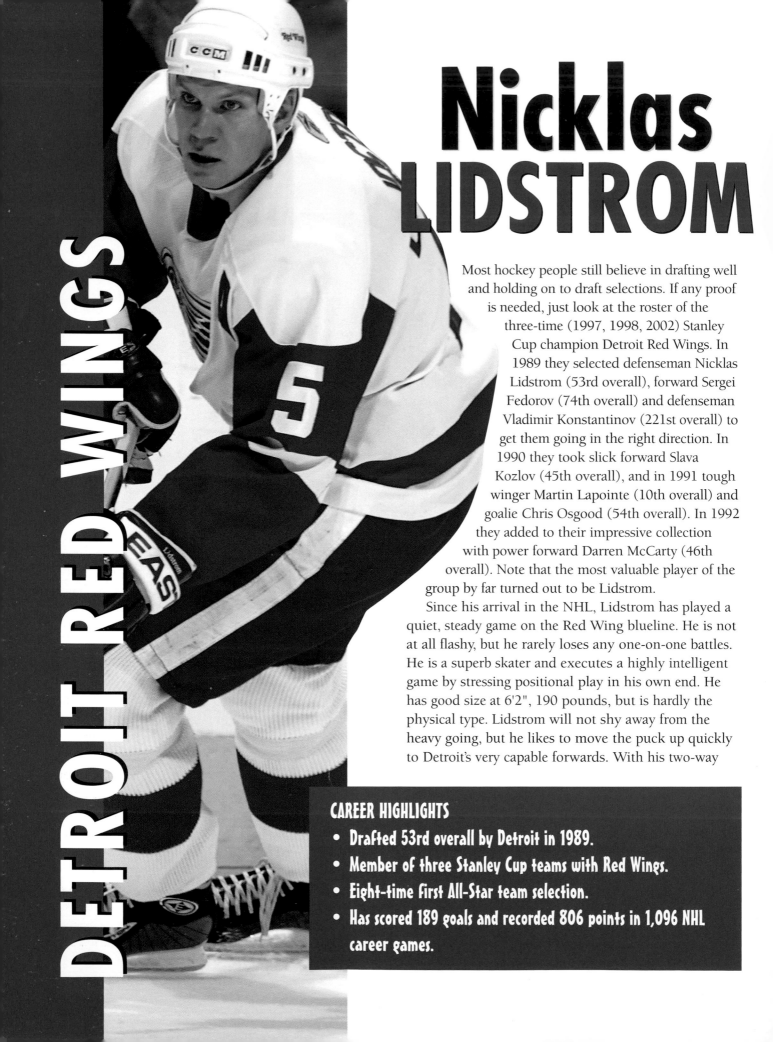

DETROIT RED WINGS

Nicklas LIDSTROM

Most hockey people still believe in drafting well and holding on to draft selections. If any proof is needed, just look at the roster of the three-time (1997, 1998, 2002) Stanley Cup champion Detroit Red Wings. In 1989 they selected defenseman Nicklas Lidstrom (53rd overall), forward Sergei Fedorov (74th overall) and defenseman Vladimir Konstantinov (221st overall) to get them going in the right direction. In 1990 they took slick forward Slava Kozlov (45th overall), and in 1991 tough winger Martin Lapointe (10th overall) and goalie Chris Osgood (54th overall). In 1992 they added to their impressive collection with power forward Darren McCarty (46th overall). Note that the most valuable player of the group by far turned out to be Lidstrom.

Since his arrival in the NHL, Lidstrom has played a quiet, steady game on the Red Wing blueline. He is not at all flashy, but he rarely loses any one-on-one battles. He is a superb skater and executes a highly intelligent game by stressing positional play in his own end. He has good size at 6'2", 190 pounds, but is hardly the physical type. Lidstrom will not shy away from the heavy going, but he likes to move the puck up quickly to Detroit's very capable forwards. With his two-way

CAREER HIGHLIGHTS

- Drafted 53rd overall by Detroit in 1989.
- Member of three Stanley Cup teams with Red Wings.
- Eight-time First All-Star team selection.
- Has scored 189 goals and recorded 806 points in 1,096 NHL career games.

skills (much like those of his idol, Hall of Famer Borje Salming), Lidstrom is in on virtually every important situation for the Red Wings. When fellow blueliner Konstantinov was injured in a car accident and his career tragically ended, Lidstrom's value to the Detroit club skyrocketed.

Lidstrom began his NHL career in 1991–92, when he scored 11 goals and 49 assists. His numbers slipped slightly the next season (only 41 points), but he quickly recovered in 1993–94 to post 56 points. In 1994–95 the rebuilt Red Wings got their first taste of success by making it to the finals, Lidstrom leading the way with 16 points in 18 playoff games. He followed up with a great regular season in 1995–96 of 17 goals and 50 assists, but the Wings lost in the playoffs to the Colorado Avalanche. The Detroit club was ready for the 1996–97 season, however. Lidstrom contributed 57 points in the season and then another eight points in the playoffs, as the Red Wings won the cup final in four straight games. In the sweep, Lidstrom and partner Larry Murphy effectively shut down Eric Lindros and his Flyer teammates to clinch the championship.

The classy defenseman was outstanding in 2000–01, when he finally won the Norris Trophy (15 goals, 56 assists) after three straight years as the runner-up. He won again in 2002 and in 2003, to become the first three-straight winner since Bobby Orr. When the Red Wings won the cup again in 2002, he won the Conn Smythe Trophy as playoff MVP. As the Detroit club has aged (especially on defense), the team relies more and more on Lidstrom; in 2002–03 he led the league in ice time per game (29:20 minutes), the highest of his career. He was also named a first-team All-Star, joining Orr and Doug Harvey as the only defensemen to be selected for six consecutive seasons.

Lidstrom had a rather dismal season in 2003-04, when he recorded just 38 points (his lowest full-season total since he joined the Red Wings). However, he came back strong in 2005–06 (after taking the lockout year

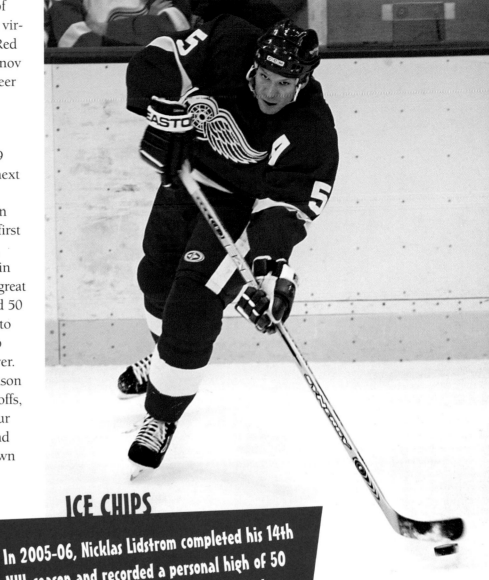

ICE CHIPS

In 2005-06, Nicklas Lidstrom completed his 14th NHL season and recorded a personal high of 50 penalty minutes. Over his career Lidstrom has only recorded 326 penalty minutes, proving that a defenseman can play a clean but effective style. Lidstrom is a four-time winner of the Norris Trophy (2001, 2002, 2003, 2006).

off from hockey) to score 16 goals and total a career-high 80 points. Urged to shoot more by new Detroit coach Mike Babcock, the consistent Lidstrom heeded the advice and worked his powerplay magic. He averaged 28:06 minutes of ice time each contest and proved to be durable by playing in 80 games. The Red Wings won the Presidents' Trophy for the league's best mark in the regular season, but were upset by the Edmonton Oilers in the first round of the '06 playoffs. Lidstrom and defensive partner Andreas Lilja had an especially difficult time in the post-season; however, he did help Sweden capture the gold medal at the Winter Olympics.

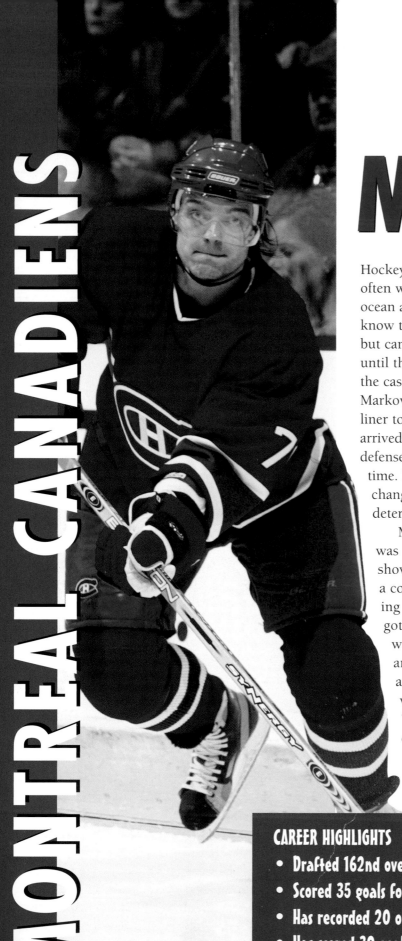

MONTREAL CANADIENS

Andrei MARKOV

Hockey players who are not born in North America often want to test themselves by coming across the ocean and playing in the best hockey league. They know they can dominate a game in Europe or Russia, but can never be sure if they are indeed elite players until they try the National Hockey League. Such was the case for Montreal Canadiens defenseman Andrei Markov. Born in Voskresensk, Russia, the sturdy blueliner took his time before going to Montreal. When he arrived, Markov suffered the growing pains that all defensemen do when they play in the NHL for the first time. He also had to adapt to a language and cultural change that he was not quite ready for, but he was determined to make it.

Markov started skating at the age of five and was playing hockey by the time he was eight. He showed promise playing hockey close to home, and a coach suggested that he might be suited to playing defense. It was good advice, and Markov first got noticed outside Russia when he played in the world junior tournament in 1998. His performance in that prestigious tournament caught the attention of the Canadiens, who selected him with their sixth choice in the '98 entry draft. The Habs were hoping to get him to Montreal quickly, but Markov decided to stay at home for two more years. He played for Moscow Dynamo, helping that club win one regular-

CAREER HIGHLIGHTS

- Drafted 162nd overall by Montreal in 1998.
- Scored 35 goals for Moscow Dynamo over three seasons.
- Has recorded 20 or more points five consecutive years.
- Has scored 30 goals and 112 points in 334 NHL career games.

season championship. In 1998–99 he scored 17 goals in 50 games, and in 1999–2000 he had 23 points in 29 games for Dynamo. He had established himself as the best Russian player not in the NHL, and while he did not wish to leave his family behind, Markov knew it was time to take the plane ride over the Atlantic.

The 2000–01 season saw Markov play in 63 games for Montreal (scoring six goals and adding 17 assists), but the Canadiens felt he could use some time in the minors and sent him to their farm club, the Quebec Citadelles of the American Hockey League, for 14 games. He did much the same thing the following season, when he had 24 points in 56 games for Montreal and 10 points in 12 games for the Citadelles. It was difficult for Markov to accept his time in the minors, and he very nearly went home. However, he did not want to give up his goal of playing in the NHL. He learned to play better defensively, and his minor league days were over by the 2002–03 season, when he firmly established himself as a regular on the Canadiens' blueline. In 79 games, Markov scored 13 goals and added 24 assists, and although his numbers dropped somewhat the following year (to 29 points), he was still considered a star in the making.

ICE CHIPS
When Andrei Markov played for Moscow Dynamo, he was named winner of the "Golden Helmet" as the most valuable player in the Russian League for the 1999–2000 season.

The six foot, 208-pound, broad-shouldered defenseman is quite comfortable moving the puck up the ice. He is very mobile and likes to join the attack into the offensive zone. Markov is a smooth skater and a good passer, but plays his best hockey when he has a bit of an edge in his game. He competes hard and also has a good shot from the point – which he can unleash anytime – especially on the powerplay (he had six goals with the extra man during the 2005–06 season). Although his drive from the blueline is not overwhelming, he can put something on it when he lets it go. He took only 88 shots on goal in '05–'06 and scored 10 times, indicating he should shoot more. (Fellow Montreal defenseman Sheldon Souray took 202 shots on goal.) Markov is now better able to handle the bigger forwards in the NHL (he was a plus 13 in '05–'06) and his penalty-minute total was a career-high 74, showing that he is getting more involved in the physical action. He has become the Canadiens' best and most reliable defenseman, and if he stays healthy (he played in 67 games last year, missing games because of a variety of ailments), he may be All-Star material in the near future.

Scott NIEDERMAYER

ANAHEIM DUCKS

The New Jersey Devils were down 2–1 in the second game of the 1995 Stanley Cup final to the Detroit Red Wings. The Red Wings were looking to even the series after a loss in the opener, and it appeared they were on their way to doing so. Then Devils defenseman Scott Niedermayer decided to show his superior skills and took off with the puck. He weaved his way down the ice, through the entire Detroit team, then took a shot on goalie Mike Vernon. It did not go in, but the speedy defender easily beat Detroit's Paul Coffey (ironically Niedermayer's childhood idol) to the disk. This time he made no mistake; the game was tied. Niedermayer's goal seemed to break the backs of the Red Wings and they never recovered. New Jersey put in two more and won the contest 4–2. Two games later, Niedermayer and the Devils won the Stanley Cup. That goal that Niedermayer scored against Detroit exemplified all that is good about his game. A speed merchant with a scoring touch, Niedermayer is at his absolute best when he is carrying the puck. His natural offensive instincts take over, and his vision on the ice allows him to make pinpoint passes that often lead to goals. Niedermayer can go on these offensive forays because his great speed lets him get back to cover up defensively so his partner is not left in the lurch. The slick defenseman developed his skating skills by taking power and figure skating

CAREER HIGHLIGHTS
- Drafted third overall by New Jersey in 1991.
- Member of gold medal-winning Canadian team at 2002 Olympics.
- Member of Stanley Cup winning team in 1995, 2000 and 2003.
- Has scored 125 goals and 539 points in 974 NHL career games.

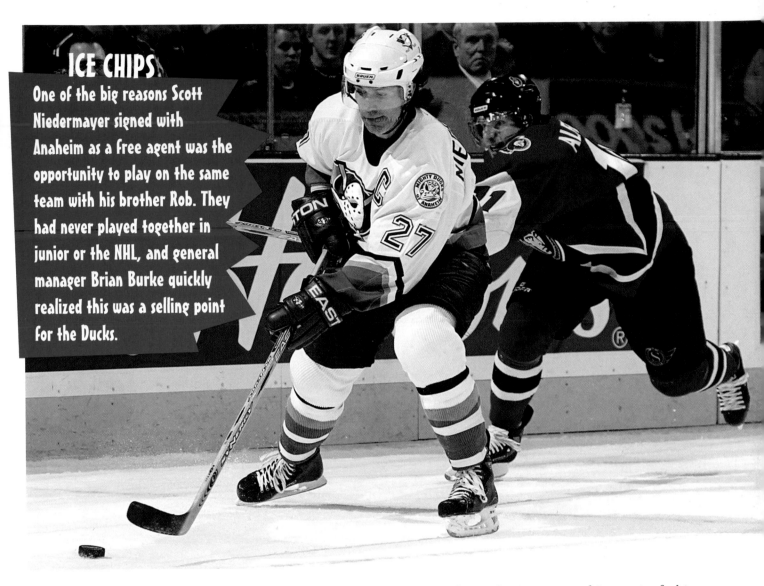

lessons. When he is in full flight his turns and cuts on the ice are a joy to behold.

Although he probably did not score as many goals as he might have in New Jersey, Niedermayer was an invaluable asset to the Devils. New Jersey was fortunate to be in a position where they could draft Niedermayer. Through a trade with the Maple Leafs in 1989, the Devils ended up with the third overall pick in the 1991 entry draft (all the Devils gave up was defenseman Tom Kurvers).

Niedermayer developed as a junior with the powerful Kamloops Blazers of the Western Junior Hockey League. His best year in Kamloops had Niedermayer score 26 times and add 56 assists in 1990–91. In 1992 he had 23 points in 17 games and he won the Memorial Cup tournament's Most Valuable Player award.

Playing for the Devils proved to be stifling at times but they did win many games with a defense-first approach. Niedermayer has built his game around quarterbacking the powerplay and setting up his teammates for goals. At times and in a quiet fashion, Niedermayer complained about the defensive system the Devils employed, but he recognized that it did win championships. In 2000, the Devils reclaimed the Stanley Cup, with Niedermayer scoring five times in the post-season. In the 2001 playoffs, he was struck with a vicious elbow that took him out of the lineup for a while. He recovered well and scored 11 times in both 2001–02 and in 2002–03 under new coach Pat Burns. Niedermayer was a plus 23 in 2002–03, his best-ever rating, and he played a key role as the Devils won the 2003 Stanley Cup.

The Devils were gone very quickly in the playoffs of 2004, and for the first time Niedermayer was an unrestricted free agent. New Jersey was desperate to have him return, but he signed with Anaheim and had his best offensive year with 63 points (including 50 assists). He was a first-team All-Star in '06 and looks forward to playing with Chris Pronger.

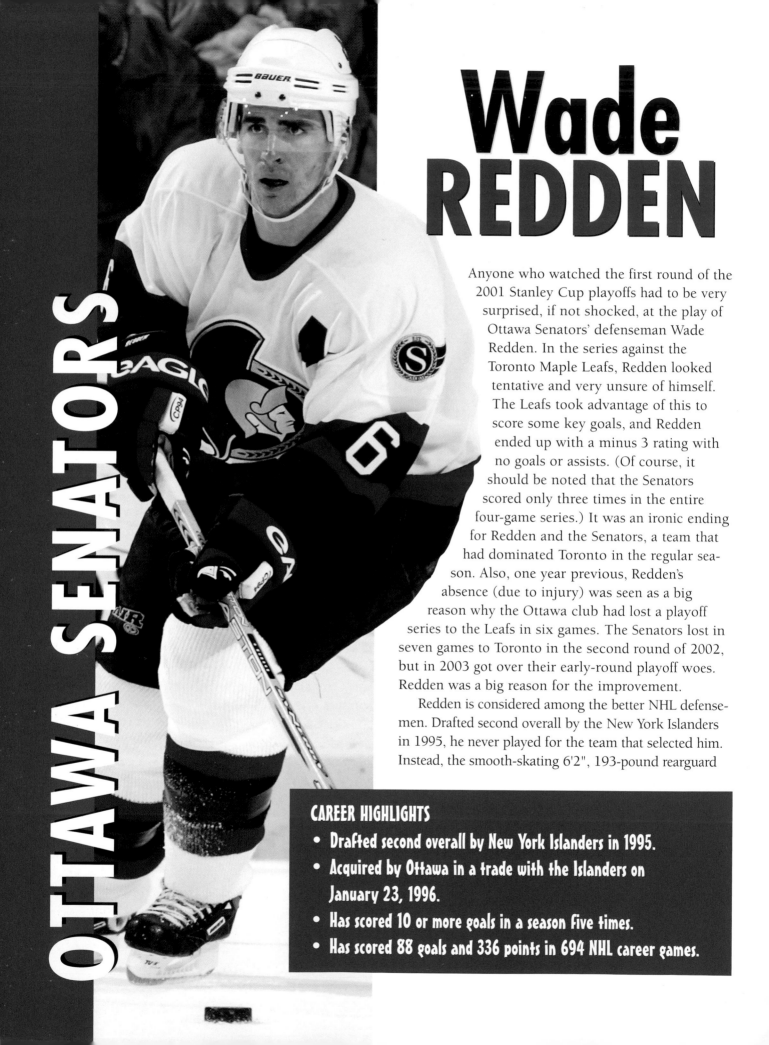

Wade REDDEN

Anyone who watched the first round of the 2001 Stanley Cup playoffs had to be very surprised, if not shocked, at the play of Ottawa Senators' defenseman Wade Redden. In the series against the Toronto Maple Leafs, Redden looked tentative and very unsure of himself. The Leafs took advantage of this to score some key goals, and Redden ended up with a minus 3 rating with no goals or assists. (Of course, it should be noted that the Senators scored only three times in the entire four-game series.) It was an ironic ending for Redden and the Senators, a team that had dominated Toronto in the regular season. Also, one year previous, Redden's absence (due to injury) was seen as a big reason why the Ottawa club had lost a playoff series to the Leafs in six games. The Senators lost in seven games to Toronto in the second round of 2002, but in 2003 got over their early-round playoff woes. Redden was a big reason for the improvement.

Redden is considered among the better NHL defensemen. Drafted second overall by the New York Islanders in 1995, he never played for the team that selected him. Instead, the smooth-skating 6'2", 193-pound rearguard

CAREER HIGHLIGHTS
- Drafted second overall by New York Islanders in 1995.
- Acquired by Ottawa in a trade with the Islanders on January 23, 1996.
- Has scored 10 or more goals in a season five times.
- Has scored 88 goals and 336 points in 694 NHL career games.

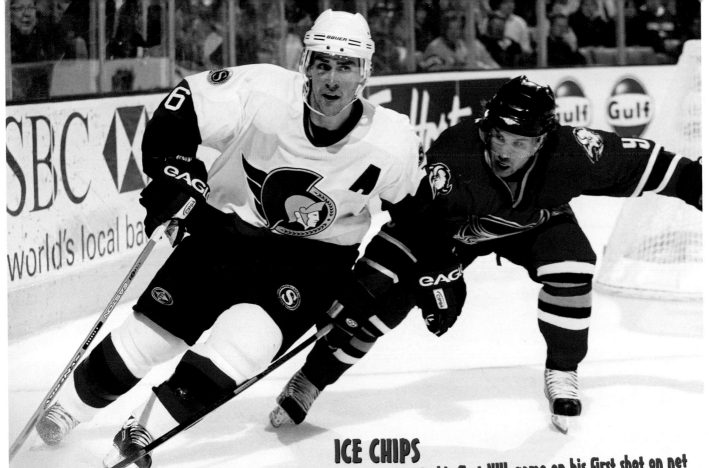

ICE CHIPS

Wade Redden scored in his first NHL game on his first shot on net when he beat Montreal goalie Jocelyn Thibault on October 5, 1996, breaking a 3–3 tie between the Senators and the Canadiens.

was traded to the Senators in return for fellow defenseman Bryan Berard. (Berard had been selected first overall by Ottawa in the same draft; ironically, Berard's career would be nearly ended in a game against the Senators by the careless stick of Ottawa's Marian Hossa, which caught Berard in the eye.) If the surprising deal had any effect on Redden, he certainly did not show it. He continued his fine performance with Brandon of the Western Hockey League and wrapped up a fine junior career in 1995–96. (He was named to the Memorial Cup All-Star team.) He made the jump to the NHL the next season, and has displayed the poise of a veteran despite his youth. Before his 26th birthday Redden had seven NHL seasons and six playoffs under his belt.

Redden's main strength is that he likes the puck. He will not hesitate to carry the disk and is able to move it quickly with a good pass. His work on the powerplay is highlighted by his good shot (although not devastating by any means) and his vision from the point. Redden's passing skills are especially vital to his game, and his assist total in seven NHL seasons now stands at 182 in 548 career games.

In 2000–01 Redden enjoyed one of his best years when he had 10 goals and 47 points. He slipped to 34 points the next season but had 10 goals again in 2002–03, and added 35 assists, the second highest total Redden has produced.

Redden had made himself an offensive force in the NHL when he might have been thought of primarily as a stay-at-home rearguard. He is not afraid to use his body and, while his 47-minute per year average in penalties for his first six years did not indicate an overly aggressive defenseman, he upped that total to 70 as the Sens got much tougher in 2002–03. With a well-rounded game to his credit, Redden plays a lot for the Senators (well over 20 minutes per game) and is used in all situations.

Redden's offensive output the last two years has been very consistent. In 2003–04 he set a career high with 17 goals and in 2005–06 he had a career-best 50 points (including 40 assists). It was a difficult year for Redden with the passing of his mother, but he came back to play very well in the opening round of the playoffs, helping to get the Senators past Tampa Bay. He was not nearly as good against Buffalo in the next round, but Redden should remain in Ottawa as a franchise cornerstone for years to come.

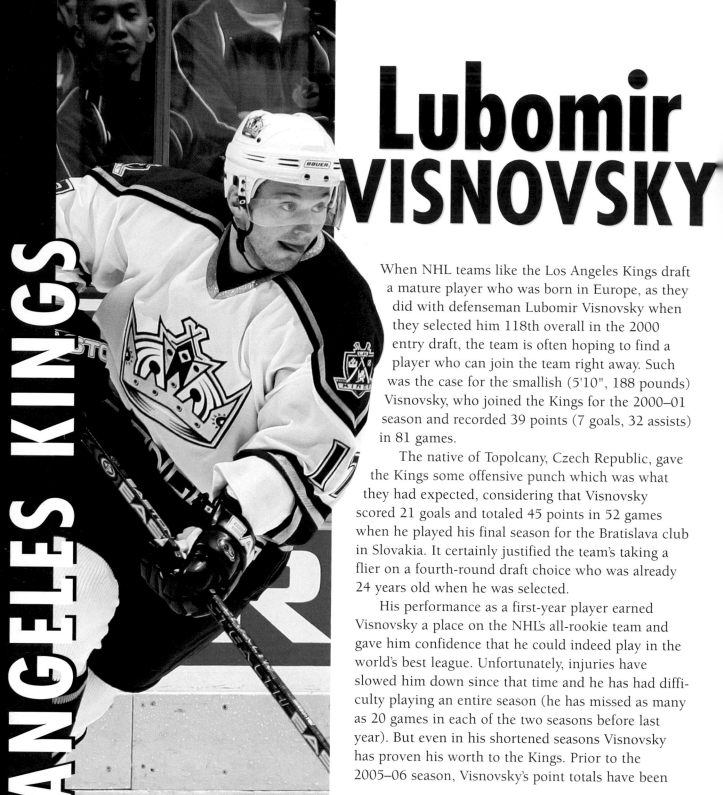

Lubomir VISNOVSKY

When NHL teams like the Los Angeles Kings draft a mature player who was born in Europe, as they did with defenseman Lubomir Visnovsky when they selected him 118th overall in the 2000 entry draft, the team is often hoping to find a player who can join the team right away. Such was the case for the smallish (5'10", 188 pounds) Visnovsky, who joined the Kings for the 2000–01 season and recorded 39 points (7 goals, 32 assists) in 81 games.

The native of Topolcany, Czech Republic, gave the Kings some offensive punch which was what they had expected, considering that Visnovsky scored 21 goals and totaled 45 points in 52 games when he played his final season for the Bratislava club in Slovakia. It certainly justified the team's taking a flier on a fourth-round draft choice who was already 24 years old when he was selected.

His performance as a first-year player earned Visnovsky a place on the NHL's all-rookie team and gave him confidence that he could indeed play in the world's best league. Unfortunately, injuries have slowed him down since that time and he has had difficulty playing an entire season (he has missed as many as 20 games in each of the two seasons before last year). But even in his shortened seasons Visnovsky has proven his worth to the Kings. Prior to the 2005–06 season, Visnovsky's point totals have been

CAREER HIGHLIGHTS

- Drafted 118th overall by the Los Angeles Kings in 2000.
- Selected for the NHL's all-rookie team for the 2000–01 season.
- Named to Slovakia's Olympic team in 2002 and 2006.
- Has scored 44 goals and 180 points in 348 career games.

under 30 despite his obvious offensive capabilities.

Although he is not the best skater in the league, Visnovsky is an effective small defenseman because he handles the puck so well. He is better at dishing the puck off than shooting it, but his slapshot can be accurate and effective. Visnovsky has found that playing the point on the powerplay is his way of making a mark in the NHL. It is unlikely that Visnovsky will win many physical battles, but in the new-look game, his lack of size will not be as big a detriment as it might once have been.

Now 29 years old, Visnovsky, in his fifth full season with the Kings, led the team in points during the 2005–06 season, with 67. Teamed with fellow blueliner Joe Corvo, Visnovsky showed he could play almost a full season (81 games) and that he has the confidence to play a smart game. He scored 17 goals (10 of which came on the powerplay) and added 50 assists, all his numbers adding up to career highs. He even recorded his first career hat trick when he scored three against Dallas in November 2005. Perhaps he benefited more than some other players who played in Europe during the lockout season of 2004–05 (he had 38 points in 43 games for his old team in Slovakia) and it seemed he came back to North America determined to put up better numbers. With Corvo willing to play back when he jumped into the play, Visnovsky had the opportunity to freelance a little more and it worked out well. Visnovsky has also become much more comfortable off the ice. He can joke easily, and although speaking English can still be a bit of a problem, his personality has made him a favorite around the Kings' dressing room.

Despite Visnovsky's efforts during

the season, the Kings were unable to make the playoffs. Coach Andy Murray was fired just before the season ended and longtime general manager Dave Taylor also lost his job once the year was over. It will be interesting to see how Visnovsky adjusts to the new general manager (Dean Lombardi) and coach (Marc Crawford) once the season begins. One thing is certain: Lubomir Visnovsky is no longer one of the best-kept secrets in hockey.

ICE CHIPS

Lubomir Visnovsky finished fourth in scoring for defensemen in 2005–06 when he had 67 points (only Nicklas Lidstrom, Sergei Zubov and Bryan McCabe had more). He averaged 23:16 minutes in ice time and had a ranking of plus seven.

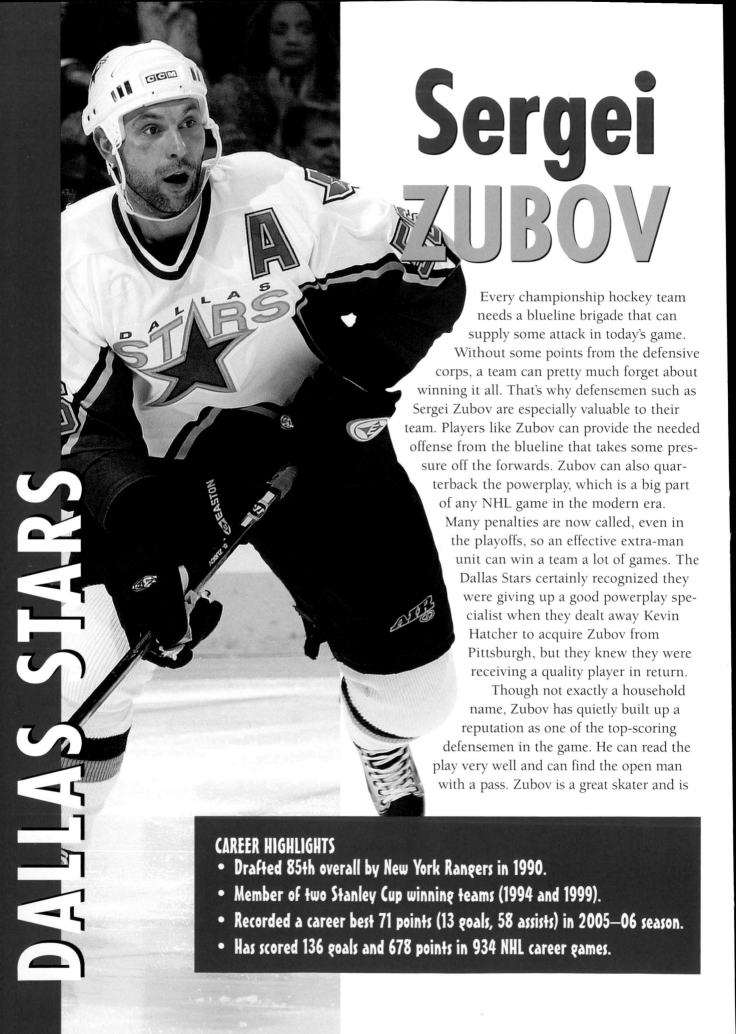

Sergei ZUBOV

Every championship hockey team needs a blueline brigade that can supply some attack in today's game. Without some points from the defensive corps, a team can pretty much forget about winning it all. That's why defensemen such as Sergei Zubov are especially valuable to their team. Players like Zubov can provide the needed offense from the blueline that takes some pressure off the forwards. Zubov can also quarterback the powerplay, which is a big part of any NHL game in the modern era. Many penalties are now called, even in the playoffs, so an effective extra-man unit can win a team a lot of games. The Dallas Stars certainly recognized they were giving up a good powerplay specialist when they dealt away Kevin Hatcher to acquire Zubov from Pittsburgh, but they knew they were receiving a quality player in return.

Though not exactly a household name, Zubov has quietly built up a reputation as one of the top-scoring defensemen in the game. He can read the play very well and can find the open man with a pass. Zubov is a great skater and is

CAREER HIGHLIGHTS
- Drafted 85th overall by New York Rangers in 1990.
- Member of two Stanley Cup winning teams (1994 and 1999).
- Recorded a career best 71 points (13 goals, 58 assists) in 2005–06 season.
- Has scored 136 goals and 678 points in 934 NHL career games.

exceptional at handling the puck, the qualities most teams want from their offensive blue-liners. He is not afraid to rush the puck out of his own end and he picks up a lot of loose disks by positioning himself properly. At 6'1" and 200 pounds, Zubov cannot be run over by opposing forwards, yet he is not an overly physical player. His penalty minutes are generally low (only 26 minutes in 2002–03, for example), but Zubov's game is to get the puck and move it up to the forwards as quickly as possible.

ICE CHIPS

Sergei Zubov has recorded 30 assists and at least 40 points for 10 consecutive seasons (1995–96 to 2005–06). He has now had seven seasons of 40 or more assists and has scored 10 or more goals 10 times in his career.

Selected 85th overall by the New York Rangers in 1990, Zubov played in the former Soviet Union before he joined the NHL in 1992–93. He was a member of the Unified team that won the Olympic gold medal in 1992, and then he joined Binghamton of the AHL before going up to the big club the same year. He played in 49 games for the Rangers in 1992–93 and had a very respectable 31 points. The following year was a big one for Zubov and the Rangers. He scored a club-high 89 points and then added 19 points in 22 playoff games as the New York club won the Stanley Cup for the first time since 1940. His play in the post-season earned Zubov some well-deserved critical acclaim. Zubov had 36 points in 38 games during the shortened 1994–95 season, but the team became disenchanted with him for some reason (there were rumors that he was not a favorite of team captain Mark Messier) and he was dealt to the Pittsburgh Penguins.

Zubov enjoyed a good season in Pittsburgh with 66 points in 64 games and recorded a career-high plus 28 rating. Once again, however, he found himself on the move, this time to Dallas. The Stars were starting to stress a defensive game, but they still liked what Zubov could bring to their team. Zubov seemed to find the right mix of offense and defense to suit the Dallas system and he led all NHL blueliners with 47 assists in 1997–98. He had 57 points in 73 games in 1997–98, then added 51 points in 81 contests during the 1998–99 season. During the 1999 playoffs, Zubov showed that his previous experience was invaluable, and he was one of the Stars' best players. Coach Ken Hitchcock gave him plenty of ice time and Zubov enjoyed a second Stanley Cup triumph.

He hasn't slowed his pace since then, recording seasons of 42, 51, 44, 55 and 42 points. He is usually among the top point producers for defensemen and in the 2005–06 season, he finished second among all blueliners with 71 points. Zubov clearly thrived as the quarterback of the powerplay with so many penalties being called and had the best year of his career. One thing that has not changed about the star defenseman is that he is still very shy about self-promotion and does not seek the spotlight at all. If he were a little more outgoing, Zubov's chances of winning the Norris Trophy would increase greatly, but Stars coach Dave Tippett appreciates what he does in his own end and on the attack. Many, including Zubov, felt that Dallas was a legitimate contender for the Stanley Cup in '06, but they fell flat in the playoffs and were out after the first round. The Stars will count on Zubov to keep up his fine play and get over their playoff woes as they did in 1999.

POWER FORWARDS!

Aggressive, goal-scoring forwards who can handle the heavy traffic in front of the net.

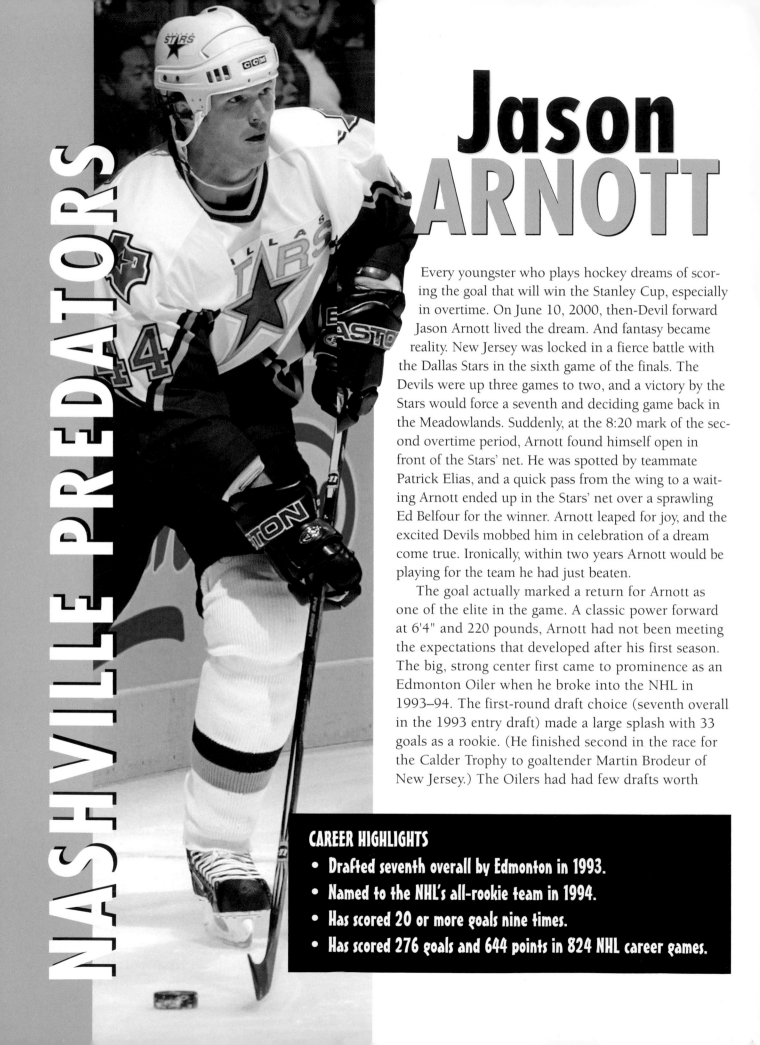

Jason ARNOTT

Every youngster who plays hockey dreams of scoring the goal that will win the Stanley Cup, especially in overtime. On June 10, 2000, then-Devil forward Jason Arnott lived the dream. And fantasy became reality. New Jersey was locked in a fierce battle with the Dallas Stars in the sixth game of the finals. The Devils were up three games to two, and a victory by the Stars would force a seventh and deciding game back in the Meadowlands. Suddenly, at the 8:20 mark of the second overtime period, Arnott found himself open in front of the Stars' net. He was spotted by teammate Patrick Elias, and a quick pass from the wing to a waiting Arnott ended up in the Stars' net over a sprawling Ed Belfour for the winner. Arnott leaped for joy, and the excited Devils mobbed him in celebration of a dream come true. Ironically, within two years Arnott would be playing for the team he had just beaten.

The goal actually marked a return for Arnott as one of the elite in the game. A classic power forward at 6'4" and 220 pounds, Arnott had not been meeting the expectations that developed after his first season. The big, strong center first came to prominence as an Edmonton Oiler when he broke into the NHL in 1993–94. The first-round draft choice (seventh overall in the 1993 entry draft) made a large splash with 33 goals as a rookie. (He finished second in the race for the Calder Trophy to goaltender Martin Brodeur of New Jersey.) The Oilers had had few drafts worth

CAREER HIGHLIGHTS
- Drafted seventh overall by Edmonton in 1993.
- Named to the NHL's all-rookie team in 1994.
- Has scored 20 or more goals nine times.
- Has scored 276 goals and 644 points in 824 NHL career games.

talking about since their glory days, but they finally hit on a winner with the selection of Arnott. It also looked like he would be a future leader and a likely replacement for Mark Messier. However, things just as quickly unraveled in Edmonton, and soon Arnott found himself incurring the wrath of Oiler fans and facing some off-ice problems.

Oilers general manager Glen Sather quickly solved the problems surrounding Arnott by dealing him to New Jersey for Bill Guerin (who was holding out in a contract dispute) in January 1998. With the Devils, Arnott rediscovered his game. Shifted back to center where he belongs, Arnott was teamed with Elias and Petr Sykora to form one of the top lines in the entire NHL. The Devils made the finals again in 2001, but Arnott missed a couple of key playoff games with injuries. He had held out at the start of the season, but signed on to play 54 games and record 55 points. At the trade deadline the next March, manager Lou Lamoriello traded Arnott and tough guy Randy McKay to Dallas in a monster deal for Joe Nieuwendyk and Jamie Langenbrunner. It was a good deal for both teams. Although McKay opted for free agency, Arnott's 47 points (23 goals) helped Dallas finish first in the Western Conference in 2002–03, after they had missed the playoffs in 2002. The Devils, meanwhile, paced by Langenbrunner and Nieuwendyk, won the Stanley Cup in 2003.

Arnott uses his body to great effectiveness. He combines that skill with a heavy shot that he can one-time as well as anyone in the NHL. A solid passer, Arnott is able to keep up with speedy wingers; and, most of all, he gives them the room they need to operate. Arnott has come to understand that he must keep his intensity up at all times to be effective.

After a mediocre season in 2003–04 saw Arnott score just 21 goals, he came back in the 2005–06 season to record a career-best 76 points and was second on his team with 32 goals. Arnott played with a leaner, more sculpted body and proved he could keep up in the new style of NHL play (some were concerned he would be a plodding type of player with the different rule enforcement). The Stars won 53 games in the '05–'06 season but did not appear to be ready for the playoffs and were quickly disposed of by Colorado. The abrupt end of the season gave the team more time to consider signing the 32-year-old Arnott. Some have suggested that his career season came as result of looking for a new deal, but that would ignore the fact that Arnott has been a consistent performer over his entire NHL career. Perhaps that is why the Nashville Predators signed him to a five-year contract.

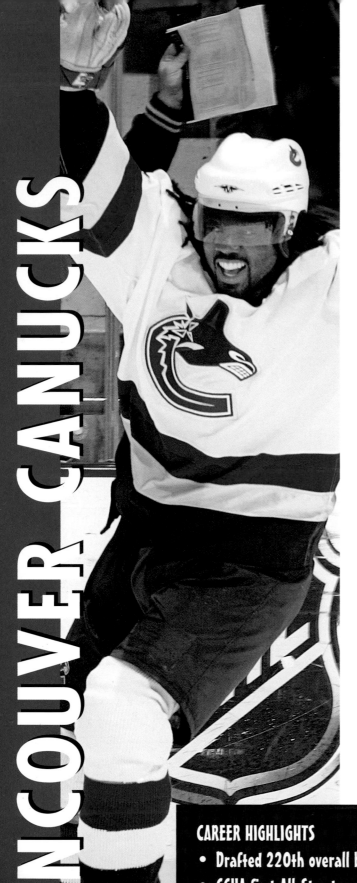

Anson CARTER

There's an old saying that Canadians care about the world hockey championships only when Canada wins them. In May 2003, Anson Carter made Canadians care about the world championships again.

On Sunday, May 11, the gold medal game between Canada and Sweden at the world championships in Helsinki went into overtime – the score tied at 2–2. Nine years earlier the same two nations had met in the final of the 1994 Olympics, and Sweden won the gold in a shootout. At the time, Anson Carter was a sophomore at Michigan State and had just helped Canada win gold at the world junior championships.

In the 14th minute of overtime in the gold medal game of the 2003 worlds, Carter carried the puck from the left side of the Swedish net, swept behind the net and cut in front from the right side, trying for a classic wraparound. He stuffed the puck past the sliding pads of Swedish netminder Mikael Tellqvist. But as his teammates mobbed him, the referee called for a replay, uncertain if the puck had actually entered the net. After seven minutes – during which off-ice officials studied replays, blowing up the image of the puck – the referee got the word and signaled that it was a goal, and a gold for Canada. The delayed Canadian celebration erupted again. It was Canada's first world gold since 1997, and Carter was on that team too, notching six points in 11 games.

Carter suddenly became a national hero. His team jer-

CAREER HIGHLIGHTS

- Drafted 220th overall by Quebec in 1992.
- CCHA First All-Star team for Michigan State (in 1994 and 1995).
- Won gold medal with Team Canada at 1997 and 2003 world championships.
- Has scored 191 goals and 393 points in 610 career NHL games.

sey and goal-scoring stick were placed in the Hockey Hall of Fame, as was the Canadian dollar coin – the loonie – that team trainers had placed in the padding beneath the crossbar of the Swedish net before the gold medal game.

Anson Carter, the son of parents who had immigrated to Toronto from Barbados, had come a long way from the player who did not play major junior hockey and had only one season of tier two junior A before accepting a scholarship to Michigan State. In his four years at Michigan State, Carter passed the 30-goal and 50-point barriers twice and, after his 54-point sophomore season, was chosen by the Quebec Nordiques as a lowly 220th pick in the 1994 draft. The next year he was a finalist for the Hobey Baker Award as the best college hockey player in the United States, and when he finished his college career in 1996, he had 106 goals – just one short of fifth place on the all-time MSU list. By then the Nordiques had moved to Colorado, and in April 1996 Carter's rights were traded to Washington for a draft choice, Ben Storey, who never played in the NHL.

Carter made the NHL the next season, splitting time between the Capitals, for whom he scored three goals in 19 games, and their AHL affiliate in Portland, where he scored 19 goals and 38 points in just 39 games. Just before the trading deadline, he was included in a major deal between the Capitals and Boston Bruins. Boston was about to miss the playoffs for the first time in 30 years and wanted to rebuild, while the Capitals were trying to reach the final playoff spot and needed experienced players. The Bruins really wanted goalie Jim Carey and budding superstar Jason Allison, and Carter was tossed in to balance the deal.

Carter has good hands and a good shot, and he knows what he's doing around the net. He has excellent timing when it comes to moving in and out of the area around the crease for scoring chances. But he is not a classic power forward and averages only about 30 penalty minutes per season. Although he doesn't beat many defenders to the outside, he has a very explosive first three steps.

After his trade to the Bruins, Carter had 13 points in the remaining 19 games. Then in 1997–98, his first full NHL season, he scored 16 times and had 43 points. He

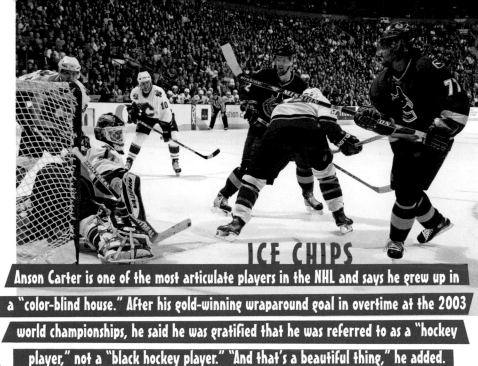

ICE CHIPS

Anson Carter is one of the most articulate players in the NHL and says he grew up in a "color-blind house." After his gold-winning wraparound goal in overtime at the 2003 world championships, he said he was gratified that he was referred to as a "hockey player," not a "black hockey player." "And that's a beautiful thing," he added.

held out in a contract dispute the next fall and played six games with the independent Utah Grizzlies of the IHL before coming to terms with the Bruins. He had 24 goals in 55 games. Although the Bruins missed the playoffs again in 1999–2000, Carter had 22 goals and 47 points in a season shortened by injury to 59 games. When he sat out in another contract dispute with the notoriously cheap Bruins, he was swapped in November 2000 to Edmonton for Bill Guerin. Carter scored only 16 goals for the Oilers that season while Guerin starred for the Bruins, but in 2001–02, the Oiler line of Carter, Ryan Smyth and Mike Comrie was leading the NHL in scoring before Smyth was injured in November. Carter went on to finish third in team scoring with 28 goals and 60 points, by far his best NHL season.

The Oilers were going to trade Carter at the end of the 2002–03 season because his salary was climbing out of their range. But they made the move earlier, when the Rangers offered Radek Dvorak at the trade deadline. The move angered Edmonton fans because Carter was the Oilers' leading scorer. With the Rangers, he matched his career high of 60 points for the season.

The Rangers dealt him to Washington in the deal for Jaromir Jagr, but he was flipped to the Los Angeles Kings during the 2003–04 season. All the moving around led to a bad year, but he rebounded with a career-best 33 goals when he signed with the Vancouver Canucks as a free agent for the 2005–06 season. He played well with the Sedin twins and enjoyed playing for former Canucks coach Marc Crawford. A free agent once again, Carter was not expected back in Vancouver.

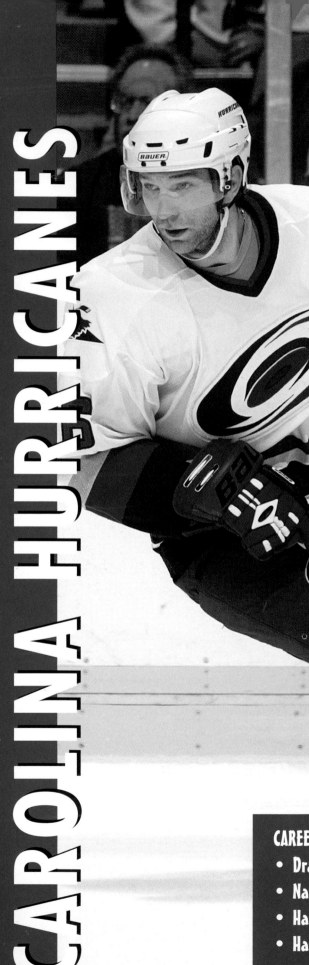

CAROLINA HURRICANES

Erik COLE

Carolina left-winger Erik Cole was enjoying a great 2005–06 season when disaster struck on March 4, 2006, during a game against the Pittsburgh Penguins. With Cole's back in full view, Pittsburgh defenseman Brooks Orpik knocked the 6'3", 200-pound Hurrican player into the boards from behind, causing Cole to suffer a compression fracture of the C5 vertebra in his neck. Doctors said he came within an inch of being paralyzed for life. It was the kind of hit that has no place in hockey, but those who dish out punishment deemed Orpik should serve a suspension that totaled four games. Cole, on the other hand, was out the rest of the season, had to endure a neck brace and months of rehabilitation, and played in just two playoff games. Maybe the NHL will wake up to the injustice one day.

Cole is no stranger to injuries, having suffered a broken leg during the 2002–03 season, so he is used to making full recoveries. He is determined to get back as soon as he can and resume a career that has so much promise.

A native of Oswego, New York, Cole played high school hockey locally (scoring 49 goals in 40 games in 1995–96) and then one year in the USHL with the Des Moines team (30 goals in 48 games). He then decided to attend college and had his best year for the Clarkson Knights, with 22 markers and 42 points in 36 games. The Hurricanes drafted the big winger 71st overall in 1998 after he had spent just one year at

CAREER HIGHLIGHTS
- Drafted 71st overall by Carolina in 1998.
- Named Rookie of the Year while attending Clarkson University.
- Has recorded 40 or more points in three of four NHL seasons.
- Has scored 78 goals and 168 points in 274 NHL career games.

Clarkson University. When his college days were over, Cole was assigned to Cincinnati of the American Hockey League for the 2001–02 season. He showed he could score as a professional, with 23 goals and 43 points in 69 games. Cole looked like he was ready for the NHL.

Cole played in 81 games for the Hurricanes in 2001–02 and recorded a very respectable 16 goals and 40 points. He also showed his game had a physical edge by leading all rookies in hits that year. Cole was also a strong playoff performer (six goals, three assists) when the surprising Hurricanes made it all the way to the Stanley Cup final in the 2002 post-season. The Carolina club was not nearly as good the following year, and then Cole suffered his leg injury, which cut his season to 53 games (14 goals, 13 assists). He was able to bounce back with a good year in 2003–04 when he scored 18 times and added 24 assists, but once again the Hurricanes missed the playoffs. Cole played in Germany during the lockout to try and stay sharp for the return of the NHL in 2005–06.

It's easy to see why Cole is a coveted player in spite of his bad run with injuries. He uses his size with great effectiveness when he is going strong and is very willing to get involved physically. He knows how to forecheck effectively and can dig a puck out to make something happen on the attack. He has a good goal-scoring touch, and there is no telling how many goals he might be able to get, but he should be a 30-goal scorer without too much difficulty. Cole is rapidly maturing as a power forward and his all-around game should improve with time.

Cole is part of an exciting Carolina lineup that features speed and skill and played the '05–'06 season on a line with Eric Staal and Cory Stillman. The fleet winger had 30 goals and 59 points in 60 games before his injury, and many thought the Hurricanes would suffer greatly without their number-one left-winger. Carolina has a deeper lineup than most would give them credit for and will be just that much better when Cole returns full time to the Stanley Cup champions. Once Cole recovers from his neck injury, the rest of the NHL will see one of the best power forwards back at work.

ICE CHIPS

With the new rule enforcement, referees were calling more penalty shots than ever in 2005–06. Erik Cole had two penalty shots (the first NHL player to do so) in one game against Buffalo on November 9, 2005, scoring on one attempt on goalie Martin Biron.

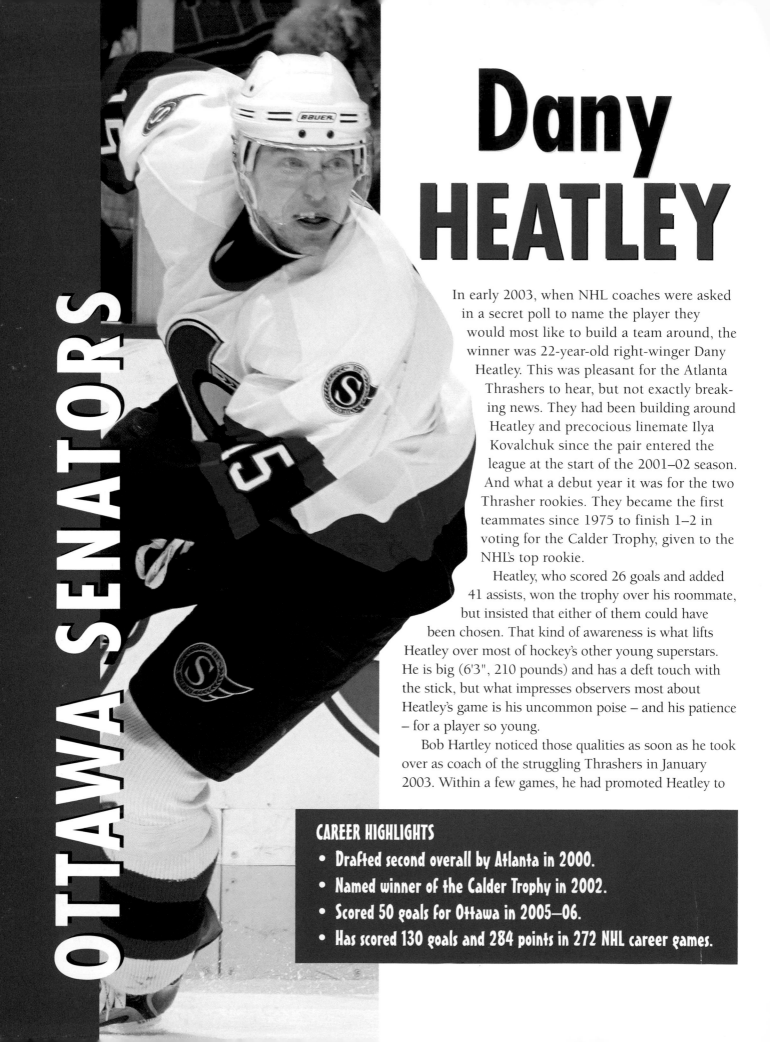

Dany HEATLEY

In early 2003, when NHL coaches were asked in a secret poll to name the player they would most like to build a team around, the winner was 22-year-old right-winger Dany Heatley. This was pleasant for the Atlanta Thrashers to hear, but not exactly breaking news. They had been building around Heatley and precocious linemate Ilya Kovalchuk since the pair entered the league at the start of the 2001–02 season. And what a debut year it was for the two Thrasher rookies. They became the first teammates since 1975 to finish 1–2 in voting for the Calder Trophy, given to the NHL's top rookie.

Heatley, who scored 26 goals and added 41 assists, won the trophy over his roommate, but insisted that either of them could have been chosen. That kind of awareness is what lifts Heatley over most of hockey's other young superstars. He is big (6'3", 210 pounds) and has a deft touch with the stick, but what impresses observers most about Heatley's game is his uncommon poise – and his patience – for a player so young.

Bob Hartley noticed those qualities as soon as he took over as coach of the struggling Thrashers in January 2003. Within a few games, he had promoted Heatley to

CAREER HIGHLIGHTS
- Drafted second overall by Atlanta in 2000.
- Named winner of the Calder Trophy in 2002.
- Scored 50 goals for Ottawa in 2005–06.
- Has scored 130 goals and 284 points in 272 NHL career games.

Dany Heatley got off to a great start when he joined the Ottawa Senators in 2005–06 by scoring 22 points in his first 22 games. He would set a franchise record for most goals (50) and points in a season (103) for the Senators.

one of his assistant captains. After his brilliant NHL debut, Heatley not only avoided the classic sophomore slump, but also advanced into the league's elite. In 2002–03, he finished ninth in NHL scoring, with 41 goals (sixth in the league) and 89 points. He scored 19 powerplay goals, good for third in the league, even though the talent-thin Thrashers were forced to use him on the point on the powerplay well into December.

Heatley's sudden impact in the NHL was a surprise, considering that he and Kovalchuk were soon confronted by the opposing team's best checkers, all game. He has been a remarkably consistent scorer since his first year of midget hockey in Calgary, when he rang up 91 points in just 25 games and was named MVP at the Air Canada Cup. Two years later he led the Alberta Junior Hockey League with 70 goals and 126 points for the Calgary Canucks. As a freshman with the University of Wisconsin, Heatley had 56 points in 38 games, prompting the Thrashers to select him second overall in the 2000 draft. He followed that up with a 57-point season at Wisconsin, and jumped directly from college hockey onto the Thrashers' top line.

Kovalchuk may be the flashier player, but it is Heatley who is more consistent and has a better all-round game. (Two years older than his roommate, he guided Kovalchuk through his initiation into North American culture.) Heatley led all NHL scorers with

13 goals in January 2003, and was selected for February's All-Star Game. There, he played on a line with Olli Jokinen and his childhood idol, Jaromir Jagr. But it was Heatley who put himself into the history books, becoming just the fifth player to score four goals in the mid-season classic. He also added an assist and later scored in the tie-breaking shootout. Needless to say, he was named the game's Most Valuable Player. And he was just 22 years old.

The Thrashers were not able to surround their two young stars with enough supporting talent to come close to making the playoffs. However, they did make a modest improvement in 2002–03, moving to 74 points from 54 points the previous season.

Heatley was the driver in a horrific car accident prior to the start of the 2003–04 season that killed teammate Dan Snyder and nearly ended his own career. Heatley recovered physically to return to the Thrasher lineup for 31 games (recording 29 points) but his days in Atlanta were numbered. He wisely asked for a trade prior to the start of the 2005–06 season and he was dealt to Ottawa for Marian Hossa. Heatley had a great year playing on a line with Jason Spezza and scored a career-best 50 goals and 103 points. He was not nearly as sharp in the playoffs, and Ottawa fans were disappointed with his production. It certainly led to the Senators' quick ouster by Buffalo in the second round.

COLUMBUS BLUE JACKETS

Rick NASH

Columbus general manager Doug MacLean has not had an easy time trying to build the expansion Blue Jackets into a contending team. They have yet to make the playoffs (expansion cousin the Minnesota Wild has at least made one playoff appearance) and have not been able to lure (or, perhaps, seek) a highly qualified and experienced coach to lead this young group of players, although MacLean has gone behind the bench for a period of time in hopes of shaking things up. However, one move made by MacLean that nobody can question was his maneuvering to select forward Rick Nash first overall at the 2002 entry draft. The Florida Panthers actually held the first pick (Columbus was slated to pick third) and knew they wanted to take defenseman Jay Bouwmeester, while Atlanta, picking second, was poised to take goaltender Kari Lehtonen. MacLean was able to secure the pick by promising the Panthers a swap of future first-round selections at Florida's discretion. It was the best move the Blue Jackets have made to date.

A native of Brampton, Ontario, Nash had actually thought about being a goaltender, since he played that position in lacrosse. His dad suggested he needed to make a choice when he was about 10 years old, and Nash decided to stay out of the hockey nets and play forward instead.

Nash first came to prominence when he scored 61 goals in the 1999–2000 season for the Toronto

CAREER HIGHLIGHTS
- **Drafted first overall by Columbus in 2002.**
- **Winner of Maurice Richard Trophy (tied) with 41 goals in 2002–03.**
- **Named to Team Canada for the world hockey championships in 2005.**
- **Has scored 89 goals and 150 points in 208 NHL career games.**

Marlboros in the Greater Toronto Hockey League. He then jumped to the London Knights of the Ontario Hockey League, where he was named to the all-rookie team by scoring 31 goals in 59 games. A 32-goal season in 2001–02 caught the eye of the scouts (although the goal total was not extraordinarily high), but the Blue Jackets had done their homework and knew what they wanted. Columbus saw no reason not to keep him with the big team after his first training camp, and Nash experienced the thrill of scoring a goal in his first NHL game, against Chicago on October 10, 2002. He would go on to score 17 times as a rookie and add 22 assists to earn a spot on the NHL's all-rookie team.

The next season saw the youngster score a league-leading 41 goals (tied with Jarome Iginla and Ilya Kovalchuk) and his performance got noticed all over the NHL. The 6'4", 206-pound left-winger started to emerge as a top power forward. He is very intense and has a great nose for the net. He is especially deadly around the crease and his quick release is difficult for goalies to handle. Nash is not afraid to battle for the puck and can use his large body (which is just now filling out at the tender age of 22) to get possession, and he can be a load for anyone to move once he

plants himself around the net. Even when it appears he is tied up, Nash is able to keep his stick free and easily get off his rocket shot.

Nash played in Switzerland during the lockout and knew that the 2005–06 season was supposed to be the year Columbus would make a big leap in the standings, but things got off to a terrible start as early as August when he badly sprained his ankle. He came back only to suffer a knee injury and played in a total of just 54 games. Still, he managed 54 points, including 31 goals. Nash felt he was looked upon to lead the team and to score goals. While he produced when he played, the rest of the team was not nearly as effective without him in the lineup. Only David Vyborny (65 points) and Nikolai Zherdev (27 goals) seemed to excel for coach Gerard Gallant, and even superstar Sergei Fedorov struggled after he was acquired in a deal. Columbus does have a good collection of young talent plus veterans like Fedorov and Adam Foote, so their playoff drought may soon come to an end. If it does, you can be sure it will be because Nash will score somewhere between 40 and 50 goals a season. That's why MacLean gave his budding superstar a five-year, $27 million deal!

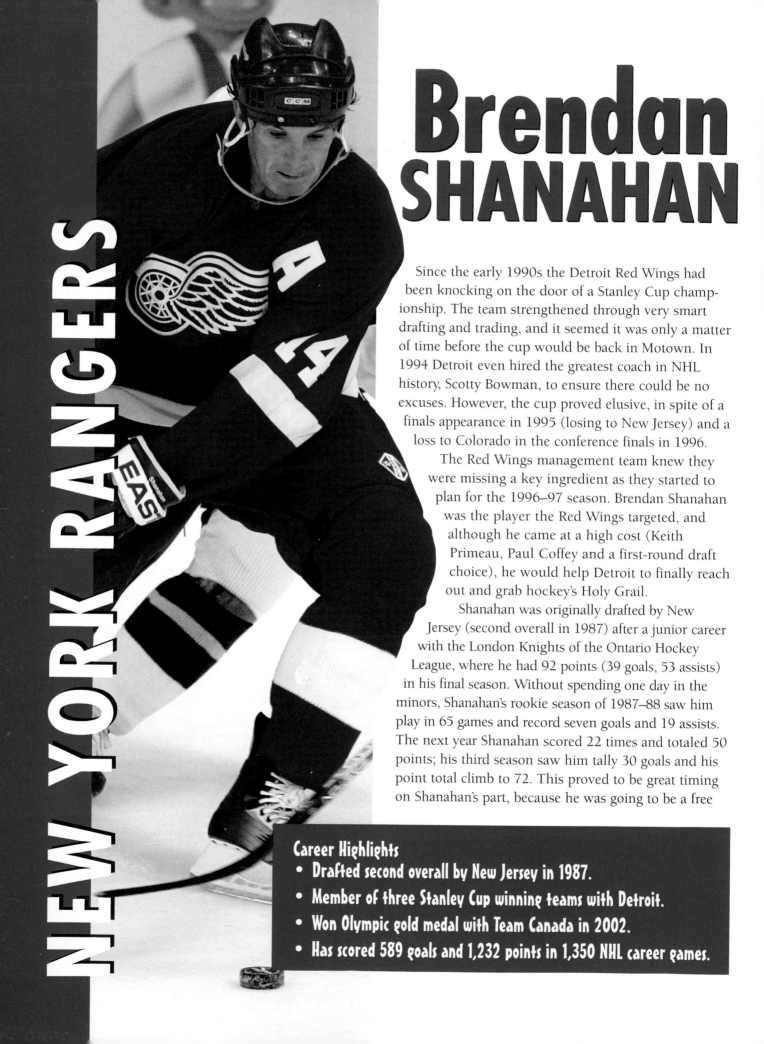

Brendan SHANAHAN

Since the early 1990s the Detroit Red Wings had been knocking on the door of a Stanley Cup championship. The team strengthened through very smart drafting and trading, and it seemed it was only a matter of time before the cup would be back in Motown. In 1994 Detroit even hired the greatest coach in NHL history, Scotty Bowman, to ensure there could be no excuses. However, the cup proved elusive, in spite of a finals appearance in 1995 (losing to New Jersey) and a loss to Colorado in the conference finals in 1996.

The Red Wings management team knew they were missing a key ingredient as they started to plan for the 1996–97 season. Brendan Shanahan was the player the Red Wings targeted, and although he came at a high cost (Keith Primeau, Paul Coffey and a first-round draft choice), he would help Detroit to finally reach out and grab hockey's Holy Grail.

Shanahan was originally drafted by New Jersey (second overall in 1987) after a junior career with the London Knights of the Ontario Hockey League, where he had 92 points (39 goals, 53 assists) in his final season. Without spending one day in the minors, Shanahan's rookie season of 1987–88 saw him play in 65 games and record seven goals and 19 assists. The next year Shanahan scored 22 times and totaled 50 points; his third season saw him tally 30 goals and his point total climb to 72. This proved to be great timing on Shanahan's part, because he was going to be a free

Career Highlights
- Drafted second overall by New Jersey in 1987.
- Member of three Stanley Cup winning teams with Detroit.
- Won Olympic gold medal with Team Canada in 2002.
- Has scored 589 goals and 1,232 points in 1,350 NHL career games.

the defending champion Colorado Avalanche in the 1997 playoffs, then went on to sweep the Philadelphia Flyers in four straight to capture their first cup since 1955. Shanahan scored nine goals in the post-season and, just as important, gave many of his smaller teammates the courage to play bigger. The Red Wings repeated their victory in 1998 with a sweep of the Washington Capitals, but missed out on their chance at three in a row with a loss to the Avalanche in 1999.

Shanahan has had remarkably consistent numbers since 1999–2000, with 78, 76, 75 and 68 points, plus an average of 100 penalty minutes. He was injured in the 2001 playoffs, a key factor, as the Red Wings went

ICE CHIPS

Brendan Shanahan took the initiative during the lockout year by organizing a summit to help improve the NHL game. He had a wide variety of people involved in hockey give input, and he then discussed these suggestions with commissioner Gary Bettman. Shanahan became a highly respected voice in leading the need to change the game.

agent that summer.

In a surprising move, the St. Louis Blues signed the big winger even though he was a restricted free agent, meaning the Blues would have to compensate the Devils. Signing Shanahan cost the Blues the services of star defenseman Scott Stevens, but they would not regret it. Shanahan quickly proved his worth by scoring 51 goals in 1992–93. He followed that up with 52 in 1993–94, a season that saw him record 102 points and gain a berth on the first All-Star team. Unafraid to go into the corners for the puck, Shanahan can beat an opponent with a bullet shot off the wing or by dropping his gloves to stick up for a teammate.

Despite all his achievements, in 1995 the very popular Shanahan was dealt to the Hartford Whalers in exchange for Chris Pronger. This trade shocked the affable Shanahan, but he responded with 44 goals and 78 points for the Whalers in 1995–96. He asked for a trade to a contender and soon was dealt to the Red Wings.

Back in a hockey environment, Shanahan scored 46 times for the Wings and totaled 87 points to go with 131 penalty minutes. The Red Wing opponents now had a large, aggressive, goal-scoring forward to defend against, something the Detroit club had lacked for some time. In a playoff rematch, the Red Wings knocked off

out in the first round. But he had 20 points in 23 playoff games as Detroit won the Stanley Cup in 2002, Bowman's final season.

The 2003–04 season was not a great one for the normally highly productive winger who scored only 25 goals and 53 points. He did not play hockey during the lockout and once hockey was back on the ice for the start of the 2005–06 season, many wondered how the aging Shanahan (he is now 37 years old) would fare in the new, speedier game. There was no need to worry – the burly winger scored 40 goals (including 14 power-play markers and six game-winning tallies) and totaled 81 points while playing in all 82 games. With Steve Yzerman's leadership role reduced somewhat because of injury, it was obvious that Shanahan was the leader of the Red Wings and he was as feisty as ever recording 105 penalty minutes. The playoffs were a big disappointment for the Red Wings as the Edmonton Oilers knocked them off in six games. The bad ending led to changes in Detroit, with Steve Yzerman retiring and Shanahan signing with the New York Rangers as a free agent.

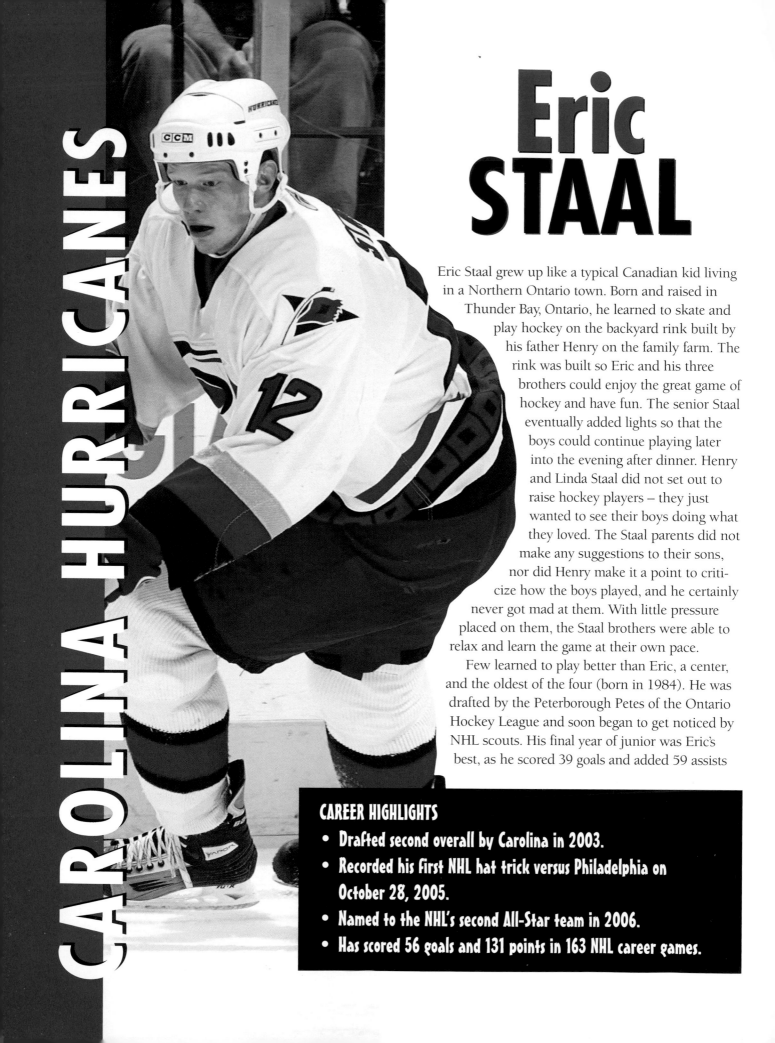

CAROLINA HURRICANES

Eric STAAL

Eric Staal grew up like a typical Canadian kid living in a Northern Ontario town. Born and raised in Thunder Bay, Ontario, he learned to skate and play hockey on the backyard rink built by his father Henry on the family farm. The rink was built so Eric and his three brothers could enjoy the great game of hockey and have fun. The senior Staal eventually added lights so that the boys could continue playing later into the evening after dinner. Henry and Linda Staal did not set out to raise hockey players – they just wanted to see their boys doing what they loved. The Staal parents did not make any suggestions to their sons, nor did Henry make it a point to criticize how the boys played, and he certainly never got mad at them. With little pressure placed on them, the Staal brothers were able to relax and learn the game at their own pace.

Few learned to play better than Eric, a center, and the oldest of the four (born in 1984). He was drafted by the Peterborough Petes of the Ontario Hockey League and soon began to get noticed by NHL scouts. His final year of junior was Eric's best, as he scored 39 goals and added 59 assists

CAREER HIGHLIGHTS
- Drafted second overall by Carolina in 2003.
- Recorded his first NHL hat trick versus Philadelphia on October 28, 2005.
- Named to the NHL's second All-Star team in 2006.
- Has scored 56 goals and 131 points in 163 NHL career games.

ICE CHIPS

Eric Staal's three brothers appear destined to follow in the path of their older sibling. Marc was drafted by the New York Rangers in 2005 and Jordan is expected to be a top choice in the 2006 entry draft after a junior career in Peterborough. Jared was selected by the Sudbury Wolves of the OHL and will play for them in 2006–07.

in 68 games. He was selected second overall by the Carolina Hurricanes at the 2003 entry draft and found himself playing on the big team the following season as an 18-year-old. Staal did not set the world on fire in his first year, recording 31 points in 81 games during the 2003–04 season. The next season was the year of the lockout, but Staal had the opportunity to play in the American Hockey League and had a banner season with 26 goals and 77 points in 77 games while playing for Lowell. As he began to feel more comfortable with the professional game, he realized that he could excel playing against men and not just juniors.

Nobody expected much from the Hurricanes or Staal for the 2005–06 season, but general manager Jim Rutherford felt he had made the right moves for the new NHL. Not only did the Hurricanes make the playoffs, they won the Stanley Cup. Much of Carolina's improvement is directly related to the rise of Staal as one of the best players in the league. From the beginning of the season, Staal showed an incredible drive to the net that usually started by undressing a defenseman or two. Using his long legs (he stands 6'3" and weighs 200 pounds) to great advantage, Staal embarrassed more than one defender by simply blowing past him and then going straight to the net. He also demonstrated a strong desire to score, and his shot was deadly — nobody else could pick the far side of the net the way Staal did throughout the 2005–06 season. Staal finished the year seventh in league scoring with an even 100 points (45 goals and 55 assists). He was 24 points better than any of his teammates (Justin Williams with 76 was second), indicating just how valuable he was to Carolina.

Staal's great performance did not end with the close of the regular season. He scored the overtime winner in the third game of the playoff series against Montreal after his team had dropped the first two games at home. That turned out to be a big goal, as the Hurricanes swept the Habs out of the post-season with four consecutive wins.

In the following matchup, as New Jersey was about to tie the series after scoring a late goal in the second game, it was Staal who planted himself in front of the Devils' net to score the tying goal with just three seconds remaining. This sent the game into overtime, where the Hurricanes won it.

It is difficult to believe that Staal is so young and has won a Stanley Cup already, leading all playoff scorers, with 28 points. It's hard to imagine that he will get even better, but that's what is likely to happen, especially as he fills out a little. A star has been born.

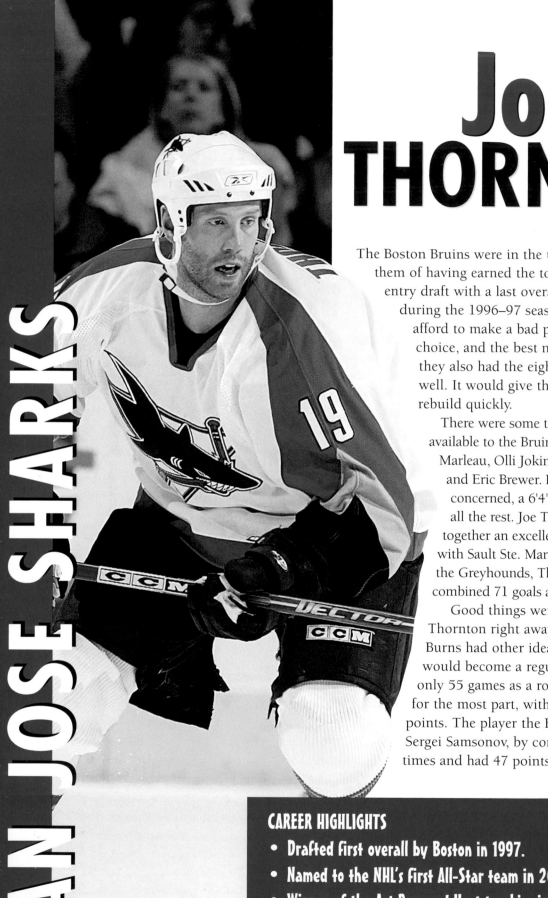

Joe THORNTON

SAN JOSE SHARKS

The Boston Bruins were in the unusual position for them of having earned the top pick for the 1997 entry draft with a last overall finish in the NHL during the 1996–97 season. They could not afford to make a bad pick with the first choice, and the best news of all was that they also had the eighth overall pick as well. It would give the team a chance to rebuild quickly.

There were some tantalizing choices available to the Bruins, including Patrick Marleau, Olli Jokinen, Roberto Luongo and Eric Brewer. But as far as Boston was concerned, a 6'4" center stood out from all the rest. Joe Thornton had put together an excellent major junior career with Sault Ste. Marie. In his two years with the Greyhounds, Thornton had scored a combined 71 goals and 198 points.

Good things were expected from Thornton right away, though coach Pat Burns had other ideas before Thornton would become a regular. Thornton got into only 55 games as a rookie and was average for the most part, with three goals and seven points. The player the Bruins chose eighth, Sergei Samsonov, by comparison scored 22 times and had 47 points in 81 games.

CAREER HIGHLIGHTS
- Drafted first overall by Boston in 1997.
- Named to the NHL's First All-Star team in 2006.
- Winner of the Art Ross and Hart trophies in 2006.
- Has scored 189 goals and 546 points in 590 NHL career games.

Immaturity was holding Thornton back. He needed to understand that dedication is required to be a full-time NHL player.

Thornton's second season was a little better – with 16 goals and 41 points in 81 games – as the Bruins crawled back into the playoffs. Thornton improved further in 1999–2000, with 23 goals and 60 points in 81 games played. The Bruins' investment was starting to pay off as they had hoped, with Thornton leading the team in goals, assists, points and penalty minutes (82). Thornton was also showing a more mature attitude.

The biggest improvement to Thornton's game was the rise in his intensity level. He is the type of player who needs to get involved physically. His big, strong body is imposing; and when he is in the mood, Thornton can make life very difficult for any defenseman who tries to check him. He does have good vision on the ice, which makes him a strong playmaker, but he is most effective when he goes to the net and causes havoc in front of the goal.

An enthusiastic, upbeat sort of person, Thornton showed great leadership potential, and the Bruins knew he would eventually be their captain.

When Mike Keenan was brought in to take over the team he challenged Thornton even more. Thornton responded with his best year to that point in 2000–01, scoring 37 times and recording 71 points. He had 68 points in six fewer games the next year. But Thornton really broke out in 2002–03, his first year as captain. He finished third in NHL scoring with 36 goals and 101 points, the first Bruin to surpass 100 in nine seasons. Despite the loss of sniper linemate Sergei Samsonov to injury for four months, Thornton was second in the NHL with 65 assists. Without Bill Guerin, Byron Dafoe and Kyle McLaren, Thornton's resolve and tough work led Boston to a 19-4-3-1 start. The team then slumped badly, eventually fired coach Robbie Ftorek and barely made the playoffs.

Thornton wore out his welcome in Boston with poor playoff performances and then general manager Mike O'Connell sent him to San Jose in a blockbuster deal (three players were sent to the Bruins but O'Connell was soon fired). Thornton thrived in San Jose and learned that he could carry and control the puck in the new style of NHL game. He led the league in points with 125 and got the Sharks into the '06 playoffs after they had started the season poorly. The Sharks won the first round of the playoffs by beating Nashville but could not contain Edmonton despite a 2–0 lead to start the series.

PLAY MAKERS!

Players with great vision, great hands and great hockey sense. They use their skills to set up or score highlight goals.

Patrice BERGERON

Boston fans were surprised when Patrice Bergeron made the Bruins' roster just two months after his 18th birthday. But nobody was more shocked than Patrice Bergeron. He had fully expected to return to the Quebec junior league to hone his skills for another season. However, Bergeron makes a habit of accomplishing things earlier than anticipated.

The Bruins had selected the center from Acadie-Bathurst in the second round of the 2003 entry draft (45th overall) after he had showed promise with a 73-point season as a 17-year-old rookie in the Quebec league. He played so well in his first NHL training camp, and his game was so mature, that there was no sending him back. And there has been nothing since then to indicate that the Bruins made even the slightest mistake in promoting him so rapidly. He is a quick learner with superior skating, shooting and playmaking skills and is becoming adept at shielding the puck with his increasingly muscular body.

Bergeron adjusted quickly to the NHL, and registered 16 goals and 23 assists in the final low-scoring season before the lockout. The 39 points ranked Bergeron fifth among all NHL rookies that year and his assist total was fourth best, the highest totals of any

BOSTON BRUINS

CAREER HIGHLIGHTS
- Drafted 45th overall by Boston Bruins in 2003.
- Gold medal winner with Team Canada at 2004 world championship.
- Gold medal winner with Team Canada at 2005 world junior championship.
- Has scored 47 goals and 112 points in 152 NHL career games.

player drafted in 2003. He also finished at plus five, in an era when rookies were usually victimized defensively. Had he not lost the last 11 games due to a shoulder injury, he would have been a Calder Trophy contender.

The Bruins were upset by the Canadiens in the opening round of the 2004 playoffs, but Bergeron was solid with four points in seven games, and continued to gain the coach's confidence. His ice time went up nearly a minute to 17:13 minutes per game in the play-offs. After the Bruins were eliminated in '04, Bergeron flew to Prague in the Czech Republic and helped Canada win a gold medal at the world championships. Still only 18, he was the third-youngest player ever to play for Canada at the worlds, and the third-youngest to score a goal. He went home for the summer and dedicated himself to a regimen of weight training, running and skating, six days a week, and returned a much stronger player for 2004–05.

While most NHL players were locked out, Bergeron was eligible to play in the AHL and scored 23 goals and 73 points for Providence in 70 games, adding another 15 points in the playoffs. He also spent time with Brad Boyes, another promising youngster, whom the Bruins had obtained from San Jose the previous spring. In the middle of that AHL season, Bergeron joined Canada's national junior team and won another world championship medal, led all scorers and was named the tournament MVP. When NHL play resumed in the fall of '05, Bergeron was playing extremely well, but the Bruins were not. As playoff possibilities grew more distant, the Bruins shocked the hockey world by trading All-Star Joe Thornton to San Jose in late November. For Bergeron, the Thornton trade meant two things: He stepped into Thornton's role and became team leader at the age of 20; and he found a new winger among the three players who came to the Bruins. Marco Sturm, a 26-year-old with a scoring touch, moved onto a line with Bergeron and Boyes. The exciting troika immediately became the Bruins' top unit, providing most of the offensive punch in an otherwise dismal season in which the club missed the playoffs.

Bergeron finished the year with 31 goals and 41 assists for 72 points, leading the Bruins in all three categories. And on April 13, 2005, against Montreal, at the age of 20 years and 262 days, he became the youngest player in Bruins history to score his 30th goal. The previous record holder, Barry Pederson, was 73 days younger when he scored his 30th in 1982.

Daniel BRIERE

BUFFALO SABRES

It took awhile, but center Daniel Briere has finally made a name for himself in the National Hockey League. Like most smaller players (generously listed as 5'10", 178 pounds in the *NHL Guide and Record Book*), Briere had to find his niche and understand how he had to play the game for his size. During the last two seasons, Briere has come on to be a very effective playmaker and goal scorer for the Buffalo Sabres. In 2003–04 he scored a career-high 28 goals and 65 points and was on pace to set new marks in 2005–06, but a sports hernia injury held his season to just 48 games, although he managed 58 points (25 goals, 33 assists). However, he was ready for the playoffs and helped the Sabres get past Philadelphia and Ottawa in the early rounds before losing to Carolina.

Briere was born in Gatineau, Quebec, and his father had him on skates by the age of two. Robert Briere was a junior player in his day, and he wanted Daniel to learn the game as soon as possible. The backyard was flooded during the winter, giving Briere a chance to play hockey whenever he could. Daniel took to the game very quickly and, while he was almost always the smallest player on his team, he was also the most creative and usually the leading point producer. Eventually he was noticed by teams in the

CAREER HIGHLIGHTS
- Drafted 24th overall by Phoenix in 1996.
- Named Rookie of the Year in the AHL in 1998.
- Traded to Buffalo by Phoenix on March 10, 2003.
- Has scored 130 goals and 281 points in 402 NHL career games.

Quebec Major Junior Hockey League and played for Drummondville for three seasons. Briere's first year saw him win the Rookie of the Year award (51 goals and 123 points) and his second year (1995–96) had him leading the league in goals (67), assists (96) and points (163). It was good timing for Briere, who was eligible for the 1996 NHL entry draft, and the Phoenix Coyotes made him a first-round selection.

For the next number of years Briere was shuffled between the minors and the Coyotes. He suffered a concussion one year, which wrecked his game for some time, and he lost some confidence as well. But he told his minor-league coach that the 2000–01 season was going to be different, and he kept his word, with 21 goals and 46 points in just 31 games. That performance got him back up with the Coyotes, and the next season saw him finish with 32 goals and 28 assists, earning a new contract in the process. It appeared Briere's minor league days were over, but late in the 2002–03 season, he was dealt to Buffalo for Chris Gratton, a much larger (6'4", 220 pounds) but older player. The Coyotes might now wish they had a chance to make that deal over again.

ICE CHIPS

Goal-scoring has always been rather high in the Quebec Major Junior Hockey League and Daniel Briere was no exception, scoring 51, 67 and 52 goals in his three years with Drummondville. His point totals were 123, 163 and 130, respectively.

Briere has been dynamic since he arrived in Buffalo. He works hard at his game at both ends of the ice (although he still needs to work on his defense) and is a talented goal scorer with a nose for the net. His stature does not stop him from getting in the thick of the action which, combined with his good shot, makes him a dangerous attacker. Briere is a very good skater with a nice burst of speed and a deft passer as well.

Dedicating himself to getting fitter, he instituted a strongman type of weight-training program (he would lift large boulders, for example) as part of his prepara-

tion regimen. This seems to be working out for him very well. He now feels he is able to compete against larger players and still thrive, although he must be careful because he is not going to overpower anyone, and he does have a bit of an injury history.

The Buffalo squad was built for speed and skill for the '05–'06 season as general manager Darcy Reiger seriously took the NHL edict about how the game was going to be called. Players like Briere can now be stars in the NHL, and his performance in the playoffs (17 points in 14 games) is further proof of that fact.

Rod BRIND' AMOUR

Every year, around NHL trade deadline time, the name of center Rod Brind'Amour comes up as a possibility for a late-season swap. While it may be flattering that so many teams covet his services, Brind'Amour must wonder why his name comes up at all, considering his long years of good service at the big-league level. Somehow, the hard-nosed Brind'Amour manages to keep it all in perspective and continues to go about being one of the very best two-way players in the game. In the 2005–06 season, he added one more duty to his impressive hockey résumé when he took on the captaincy of the Carolina Hurricanes.

Brind'Amour was a first-round draft choice of the St. Louis Blues in 1989 after playing one year of college hockey at Michigan State (27 goals and 59 points in 42 games). He attended Michigan after spending two seasons with the famous Notre Dame school in Saskatchewan.

His rookie season saw him score 26 goals and record 61 points in 79 games, but he was dealt by the Blues to Philadelphia prior to the start of the 1991–92 season. He thrived in Philadelphia with three seasons of 30 or more goals, but once again found himself on the move after eight full years in the City of Brotherly Love.

If truth be told, Brind'Amour did not want to go

CAREER HIGHLIGHTS
- Drafted 9th overall by St. Louis in 1989.
- Named to the NHL's all-rookie team in 1990.
- Named winner of the Selke Trophy in 2006.
- Has scored 382 goals and 981 points in 1,185 NHL career games.

to Carolina when he was dealt there in January of 2000. He was perfectly happy to be a Philadelphia Flyer – a team he helped lead into the finals in 1997 with 21 points in the playoffs – but the team wanted to bring Keith Primeau (who was having a contract dispute with the Carolina club) into the fold and was not reluctant to throw Brind'Amour into the package. Flyers coach Roger Neilson seemed to get it into his mind that Brind'Amour had trouble keeping up as a second-line center, so the deal was made. The quiet Brind'Amour was devastated by the news, but he did report and finished a poor season (only nine goals in 45 games played) in Carolina. He bounced back in the 2000–01 season to score 20 goals and total 56 points, and the next year saw him score 26 times and record 55 points. The 2001–02 season was the year the Hurricanes surprised the entire hockey world by going all the way to the Stanley Cup finals (before losing to Detroit) and Brind'Amour chipped in with 12 points in 23 playoff games. By this point the native of Ottawa, Ontario, was comfortable playing in Carolina and was seen as a team leader.

When Ron Francis announced his retirement prior to the start of the 2005–06 season, it meant that the classy veteran would not be returning to Carolina.

Francis had been captain of the team until he was dealt to Toronto late in the 2003–04 season, and the Hurricanes turned to the 35-year-old Brind'Amour and planted the "C" on his sweater. It was a fitting reward for a very hard-working player who takes great pride in being consistent (10 seasons of 20 or more goals).

The strength of Brind'Amour's game is that he can be thrust into any situation and be trusted to perform his duties. He does not possess any one great skill, but he is a determined player who will fight for the puck any way he can. Defensemen have a difficult time handling Brind'Amour because he is very strong (his off-ice workouts are marveled at by anyone who knows him) and is always in top condition. He is extremely reliable defensively and is one of the best face-off men in the league, ready to stand in the slot and take his best shot with a quick release.

The 2006 season was a memorable one for both the Hurricanes and Brind'Amour. He scored 31 goals and had 79 points playing for a team that embraced the new style of play in the NHL. The Hurricanes rallied to beat the Montreal Canadiens in the first round of the playoffs and then knocked off the New Jersey Devils in the next before taking out Buffalo and Edmonton to win the Stanley Cup.

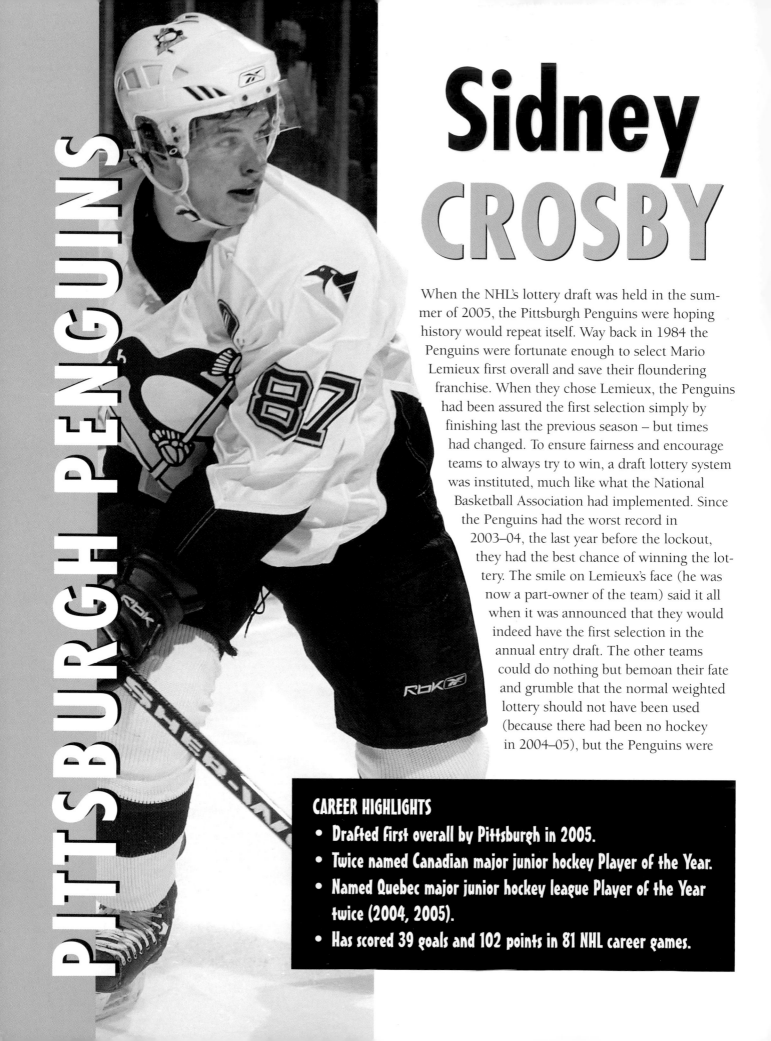

PITTSBURGH PENGUINS

Sidney CROSBY

When the NHL's lottery draft was held in the summer of 2005, the Pittsburgh Penguins were hoping history would repeat itself. Way back in 1984 the Penguins were fortunate enough to select Mario Lemieux first overall and save their floundering franchise. When they chose Lemieux, the Penguins had been assured the first selection simply by finishing last the previous season – but times had changed. To ensure fairness and encourage teams to always try to win, a draft lottery system was instituted, much like what the National Basketball Association had implemented. Since the Penguins had the worst record in 2003–04, the last year before the lockout, they had the best chance of winning the lottery. The smile on Lemieux's face (he was now a part-owner of the team) said it all when it was announced that they would indeed have the first selection in the annual entry draft. The other teams could do nothing but bemoan their fate and grumble that the normal weighted lottery should not have been used (because there had been no hockey in 2004–05), but the Penguins were

CAREER HIGHLIGHTS

- Drafted first overall by Pittsburgh in 2005.
- Twice named Canadian major junior hockey Player of the Year.
- Named Quebec major junior hockey league Player of the Year twice (2004, 2005).
- Has scored 39 goals and 102 points in 81 NHL career games.

through the hockey ranks, Crosby decided to attend Shattuck–St.Mary's, a private school in the hockey-mad state of Minnesota, for one year. He scored a remarkable 72 goals and 162 points in the 57 games he played that year.

Crosby returned to Canada for the rest of his junior career, joining the Rimouski Oceanic of the Quebec junior league for two seasons, leading the league in points in both years. In his final year of junior he scored 66 times and totaled 166 points in 62 games. His team represented the Quebec league at the Memorial Cup tournament but, in the final contest, were no match for the London Knights of the Ontario league. Crosby led all scorers in the tournament and his draft stock kept rising as more and more people spoke of him as "the next one."

Media-savvy Crosby knows how to handle all the attention and still keep his focus on the ice. He joined the NHL as an 18-year-old and managed a point in his first contest by setting up Mark Recchi for the lone goal in a 5–1 loss to New Jersey. The Penguins' home opener was attended by 17,132 fans, who saw Crosby score his first NHL goal against the Boston Bruins (just as Lemieux had done years earlier), although the game ended 7–6 for the visitors. He had five points in his first three games and the Penguins looked poised to be a competitive team.

While Crosby might have met the incredibly high expectations placed on him (recording 102 points), the Penguins quickly disintegrated, starting with the retirement of Lemieux. Soon coach Eddie Olczyk was fired, and at the end of the year, longtime general manager Craig Patrick (who had signed many veteran players as free agents to surround Crosby in his first year) was also dismissed. Crosby had difficulty keeping his comments in check when he spoke to referees, and they quickly let him know who was in charge (he had 110 penalty minutes during the 2005–06 season). Crosby's youth and inexperience were evident at times, but maturity and a better team will take care of those problems.

ICE CHIPS

The Pittsburgh Penguins made the mistake of thinking they could ride superstar Sidney Crosby to a playoff berth in his first year in the NHL. By the end of the season they realized they had to build with youth, and started using young players like Colby Armstrong, Ryan Malone, Ryan Whitney, Michel Ouellet and Marc-André Fleury more often. The Penguins' future will look even brighter when Evgeni Malkin arrives from Russia.

ecstatic to select Sidney Crosby, a native of Cole Harbour, Nova Scotia, first overall. They had a new savior for their team and maybe for the entire National Hockey League.

Son of parents Troy and Trina, Crosby was like most other kids as he grew up. He enjoyed playing with pogs and loved the Teenage Mutant Ninja Turtles. He was also a very good student who enjoyed reading about the Second World War (not long ago he had an opportunity to visit Normandy, the scene of the biggest and most important battle of the war). Young Sidney was also a hockey player (the first ever story about him was published when he was seven) and he wanted to be a netminder like his father when he played hockey. But when Troy (who was drafted by the Montreal Canadiens) saw how good a skater Sidney was and how quickly he understood how to play the game, he told his son he needed to give up the idea of being a goalie. As he rose

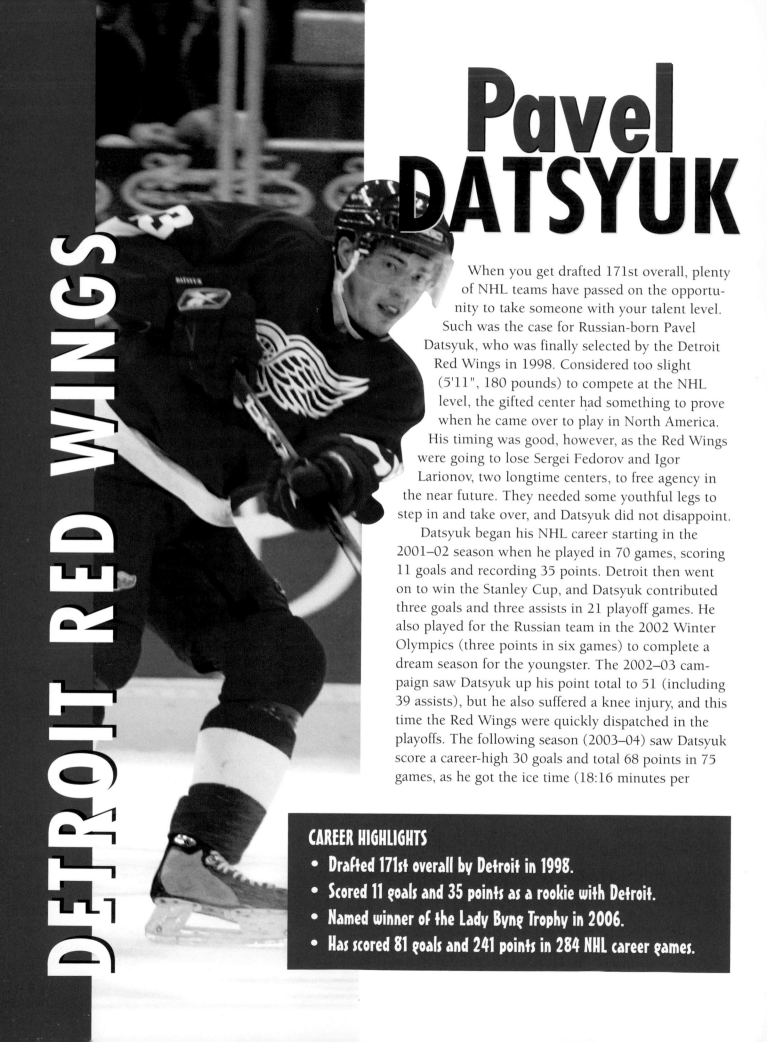

DETROIT RED WINGS

Pavel DATSYUK

When you get drafted 171st overall, plenty of NHL teams have passed on the opportunity to take someone with your talent level. Such was the case for Russian-born Pavel Datsyuk, who was finally selected by the Detroit Red Wings in 1998. Considered too slight (5'11", 180 pounds) to compete at the NHL level, the gifted center had something to prove when he came over to play in North America. His timing was good, however, as the Red Wings were going to lose Sergei Fedorov and Igor Larionov, two longtime centers, to free agency in the near future. They needed some youthful legs to step in and take over, and Datsyuk did not disappoint.

Datsyuk began his NHL career starting in the 2001–02 season when he played in 70 games, scoring 11 goals and recording 35 points. Detroit then went on to win the Stanley Cup, and Datsyuk contributed three goals and three assists in 21 playoff games. He also played for the Russian team in the 2002 Winter Olympics (three points in six games) to complete a dream season for the youngster. The 2002–03 campaign saw Datsyuk up his point total to 51 (including 39 assists), but he also suffered a knee injury, and this time the Red Wings were quickly dispatched in the playoffs. The following season (2003–04) saw Datsyuk score a career-high 30 goals and total 68 points in 75 games, as he got the ice time (18:16 minutes per

CAREER HIGHLIGHTS
- Drafted 171st overall by Detroit in 1998.
- Scored 11 goals and 35 points as a rookie with Detroit.
- Named winner of the Lady Byng Trophy in 2006.
- Has scored 81 goals and 241 points in 284 NHL career games.

game) that goes with being a regular center. He was now an established NHL player.

Much of Datsyuk's game is built around his outstanding skating ability. His exceptional lateral movement makes Datsyuk a very dangerous one-on-one player, and his moves with the puck can dazzle the crowds at the Joe Louis Arena. He can tease a defenseman with the puck and then quickly get around that opponent, who is suddenly looking for Datsyuk – who has "disappeared." It seemed he would be a typical Russian player, always looking to dish the puck off (he already has 160 assists in just four seasons) rather than shoot it himself, but his 30-goal season appears to have dispelled that notion. The slick center is very patient with the puck, and his top playmaking skills are due to his good vision on the ice. He is not very physical, but that does not stop him from excelling as an offensive player.

Datsyuk spent the lockout year back in Russia playing in 47 games for Moscow Dynamo, and recording 32 points during the regular season. He added nine points in the playoffs for Dynamo, including six goals. His performance in Russia had him poised and ready for the 2005–06 season, which proved to be an interesting one

for both Datsyuk and the Red Wings. He led the team in points with 87 (28 goals, 59 assists) and showed that his past performance in the NHL was no fluke. He enjoyed showing off his great stickhandling skills during the shootouts that were instituted to settle tied games. Datsyuk made more than one goalie look like he was coming out of his equipment (Tomas Vokoun of Nashville and Dwayne Roloson of Edmonton were a couple of netminders he beat with great moves during shootouts). The Detroit club captured the Presidents' Trophy for having the best regular-season record in the league, and many expected the Red Wings to romp through the playoffs and perhaps recapture the Stanley Cup. However, the Edmonton Oilers stomped on those dreams by knocking out the Red Wings in six games and, for the first time, Datsyuk's performance was subpar, with no goals to show for the series. He has not scored a goal in 27 consecutive playoff games – a fact the Red Wings will want to see change, given that Datsyuk was rewarded with a two-year $7.8 million contract prior to the start of '05–'06.

In spite of the poor playoff showing in 2006, Datsyuk should be an effective player in the new NHL for many years.

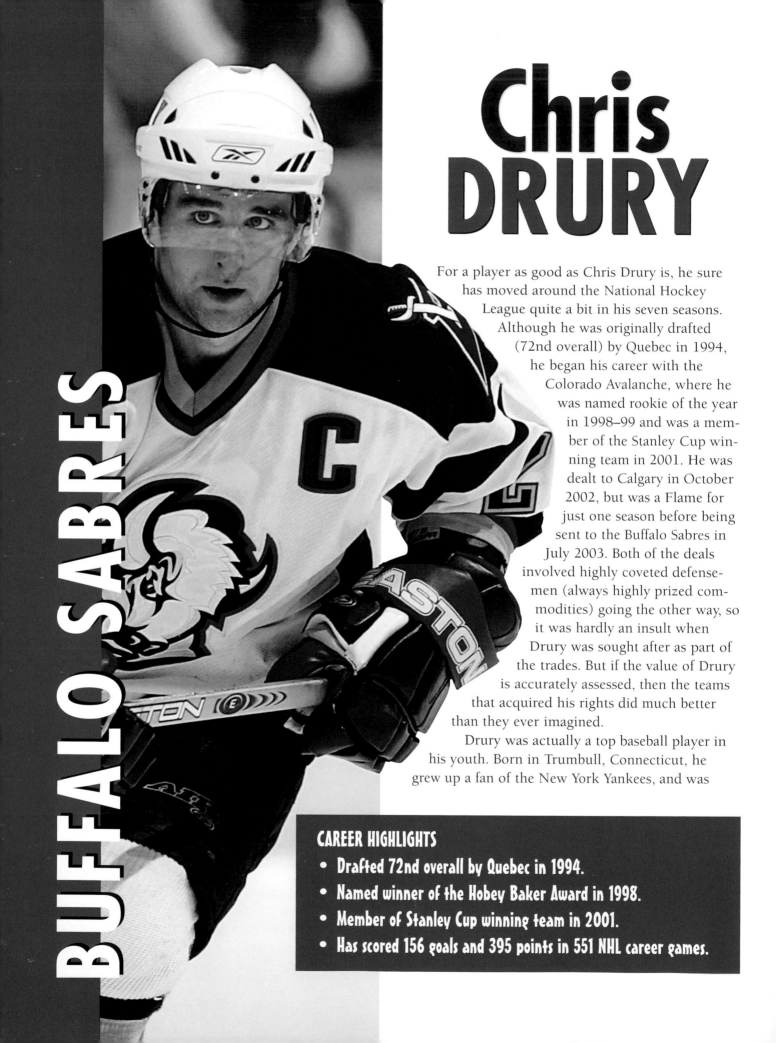

Chris DRURY

BUFFALO SABRES

For a player as good as Chris Drury is, he sure has moved around the National Hockey League quite a bit in his seven seasons. Although he was originally drafted (72nd overall) by Quebec in 1994, he began his career with the Colorado Avalanche, where he was named rookie of the year in 1998–99 and was a member of the Stanley Cup winning team in 2001. He was dealt to Calgary in October 2002, but was a Flame for just one season before being sent to the Buffalo Sabres in July 2003. Both of the deals involved highly coveted defensemen (always highly prized commodities) going the other way, so it was hardly an insult when Drury was sought after as part of the trades. But if the value of Drury is accurately assessed, then the teams that acquired his rights did much better than they ever imagined.

Drury was actually a top baseball player in his youth. Born in Trumbull, Connecticut, he grew up a fan of the New York Yankees, and was

CAREER HIGHLIGHTS
- Drafted 72nd overall by Quebec in 1994.
- Named winner of the Hobey Baker Award in 1998.
- Member of Stanley Cup winning team in 2001.
- Has scored 156 goals and 395 points in 551 NHL career games.

ICE CHIPS

Chris Drury is quickly developing a reputation for being a clutch goal scorer by scoring overtime winners. He scored three overtime goals while he was with the Colorado Avalanche (two versus Detroit and one against Dallas). His goal that beat Ottawa in the first game of their 2006 playoff series gives him a total of four overtime winners. All have come in the month of May.

the winning pitcher when his team won the Little League World Series in 1989 against a powerful Taiwan team. Luckily, he also played hockey and advanced through the ranks to the point where he helped Boston University Terriers win the NCAA title in 1995. He was also named the winner of the Hobey Baker Award as the best U.S. college hockey player in 1998. Drury scored a remarkable 101 goals and 187 points for the Terriers in his final three years at the university. After four years at Boston U., he was clearly ready to give the NHL a shot. He was quite impressive, scoring 20 goals and totaling 44 points for Colorado while beating out Marian Hossa of Ottawa for the Calder Trophy as the best rookie of 1998–99. Colorado coach Bob Hartley noted that Drury was very intense and competitive for a first-year player. He followed up his good start with 67 points in his second year and looked to have a secure place on the Avalanche for years to come.

When Colorado won their second Stanley Cup in '01, Drury racked up 65 points (24 goals, 41 assists) and then had 11 goals and 16 points in the playoffs. His overall production slipped a little the following season (46 points) and the Colorado club really wanted to add Calgary blueliner Derek Morris to the team. Drury did not complain and had a good season with the Flames, scoring 23 goals and adding 30 assists. The Flames wanted to add defenseman Rhett Warrener to their club and Drury soon found himself playing for the Sabres. He scored a career low in goals in 2003–04

when he managed just 18 tallies, but he did have 35 assists for a team not known for its goal scoring.

Drury is all about being a consistent and versatile performer. He has scored 20 or more goals six times in his career (including a career high of 30 in 2005–06) and can play wing or center. A very good skater, he knows the direct route to the net. Drury is certainly not the biggest player in the league (5'10", 180 pounds), but he is sturdy and can take the heavy going. He is more likely to be setting up a goal (239 career assists) than scoring one, but he is a threat from just about anywhere in the offensive zone. Drury gives it his all every time he is out on the ice and that approach makes him a leader for the revamped Buffalo club. The Sabres took the right approach to building their roster for the new NHL in the 2005–06 season and won 52 games, recording 110 points, behind only Ottawa and Carolina in the Eastern Conference. Drury led the team in goals scored as well as powerplay goals (16) and tied for team lead in game-winning goals (five).

The Sabres dismissed Philadelphia in six games in the opening round of the '06 post-season playoffs and defeated Ottawa in five games, with Drury scoring a lightning-fast overtime winner (just 18 seconds into extra time) to take the first contest 7–6. The Sabres were then defeated by Carolina in the third round.

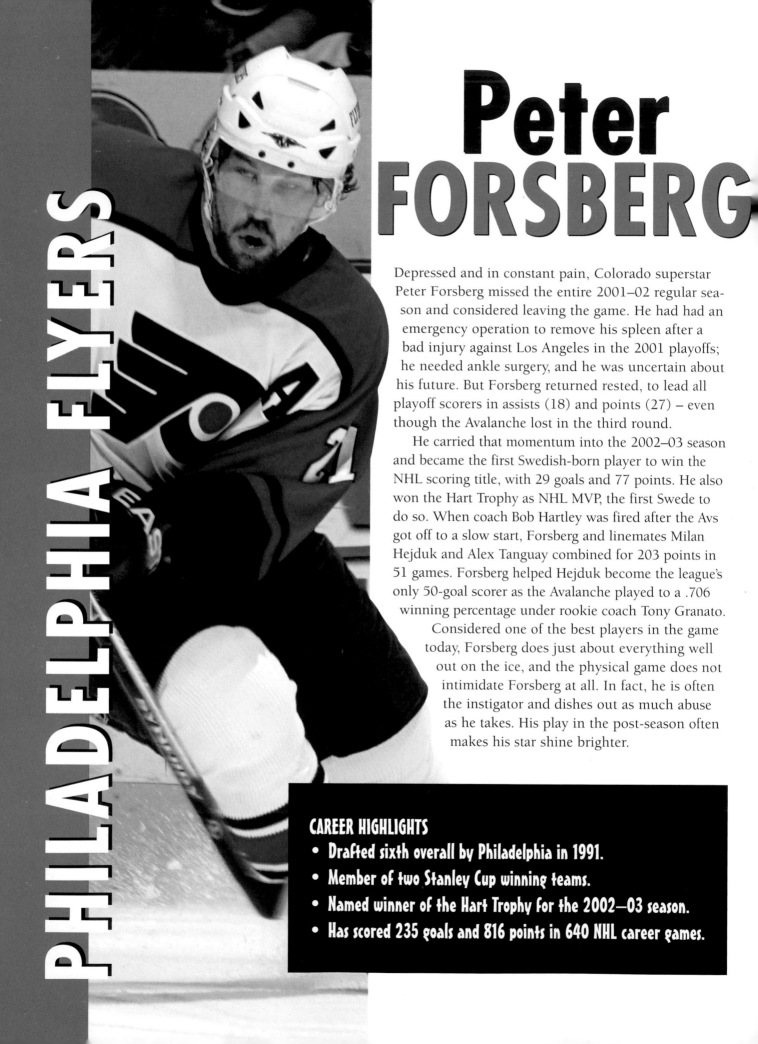

Peter FORSBERG

Depressed and in constant pain, Colorado superstar Peter Forsberg missed the entire 2001–02 regular season and considered leaving the game. He had had an emergency operation to remove his spleen after a bad injury against Los Angeles in the 2001 playoffs; he needed ankle surgery, and he was uncertain about his future. But Forsberg returned rested, to lead all playoff scorers in assists (18) and points (27) – even though the Avalanche lost in the third round.

He carried that momentum into the 2002–03 season and became the first Swedish-born player to win the NHL scoring title, with 29 goals and 77 points. He also won the Hart Trophy as NHL MVP, the first Swede to do so. When coach Bob Hartley was fired after the Avs got off to a slow start, Forsberg and linemates Milan Hejduk and Alex Tanguay combined for 203 points in 51 games. Forsberg helped Hejduk become the league's only 50-goal scorer as the Avalanche played to a .706 winning percentage under rookie coach Tony Granato. Considered one of the best players in the game today, Forsberg does just about everything well out on the ice, and the physical game does not intimidate Forsberg at all. In fact, he is often the instigator and dishes out as much abuse as he takes. His play in the post-season often makes his star shine brighter.

CAREER HIGHLIGHTS
- Drafted sixth overall by Philadelphia in 1991.
- Member of two Stanley Cup winning teams.
- Named winner of the Hart Trophy for the 2002–03 season.
- Has scored 235 goals and 816 points in 640 NHL career games.

PHILADELPHIA FLYERS

No one in hockey today would trade Peter Forsberg for Eric Lindros. But in 1992 the Philadelphia Flyers gave up a boatload of players, including Forsberg, whom they had drafted sixth overall in 1991.

Forsberg joined the Quebec Nordiques for the shortened 1994–95 season and made a great splash by winning the Calder Trophy with 50 points (15 goals, 35 assists) in 47 games played. The next season saw the team move to Colorado, where Forsberg produced an amazing 116-point season (30 goals, 86 assists) – with 21 points in 22 post-season contests as the Avalanche won the cup.

ICE CHIPS

The rights to Peter Forsberg along with Ron Hextall, Mike Ricci, Kerry Huffman, Steve Duchesne, Chris Simon, two draft choices (which turned out to be Jocelyn Thibault and Nolan Baumgartner) and $15,000,000 were sent by Philadelphia to Quebec in exchange for the rights to Eric Lindros on June 30, 1992.

Forsberg missed 17 games the next season and his point production slipped to 86, but he returned the next year to record 91 points in 1997–98. In 1998–99, Forsberg's consistency continued with a club-leading 97 points. He also recorded over 100 penalty minutes (108) for the first time in his career, indicating he was as feisty as ever, and was selected to the first All-Star team for the second consecutive season.

Forsberg had another great year in 2000–01, with a 27-goal, 62-assist performance. He was terrific again in the playoffs (when he usually excels), but suffered a serious injury on May 10 and had to have his spleen removed. The Avalanche looked to be in trouble without their star player. But the team had such a deep

lineup (which included defenseman Ray Bourque, a late addition to the Colorado roster) that they were able to overcome Forsberg's injury to beat St. Louis and New Jersey in the last two rounds. They were a better team when Forsberg returned in late 2002, and the Avs won their ninth straight division title in 2003.

The 2003–04 season was another injury-plagued year for Forsberg, who got into only 39 games due to groin and hip problems. He did chip in 11 points in the playoffs, but the Avalanche were knocked out by San Jose in the second round. After spending the lockout in Sweden, Forsberg signed as a free agent in Philadelphia (the team that originally drafted him) for the 2005–06 campaign. The Flyers and their fans were thrilled to have such a talented player, but once again injuries limited Forsberg to 60 games (although he recorded 75 points, including 56 assists, which showed he was still a dangerous playmaker). He was effective at times in the playoffs versus Buffalo, but he revealed that ankle problems slowed him down considerably. The question now becomes whether Forsberg can stay healthy enough to be the dominating player hockey fans are used to seeing every night.

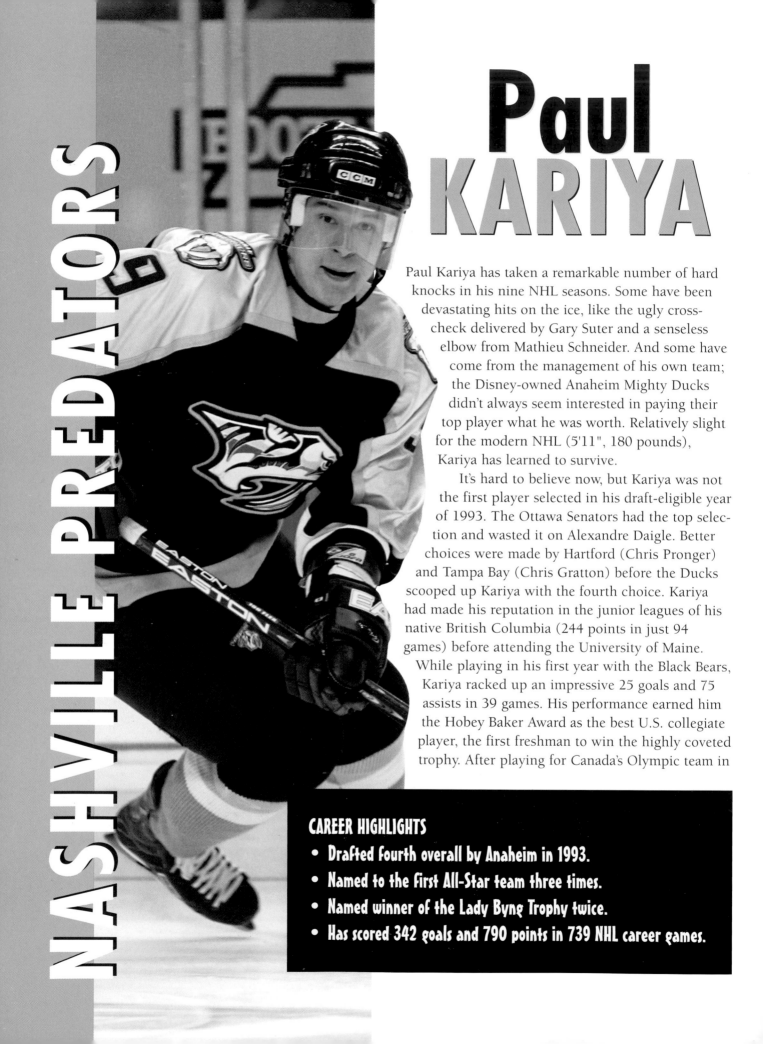

Paul KARIYA

Paul Kariya has taken a remarkable number of hard knocks in his nine NHL seasons. Some have been devastating hits on the ice, like the ugly cross-check delivered by Gary Suter and a senseless elbow from Mathieu Schneider. And some have come from the management of his own team; the Disney-owned Anaheim Mighty Ducks didn't always seem interested in paying their top player what he was worth. Relatively slight for the modern NHL (5'11", 180 pounds), Kariya has learned to survive.

It's hard to believe now, but Kariya was not the first player selected in his draft-eligible year of 1993. The Ottawa Senators had the top selection and wasted it on Alexandre Daigle. Better choices were made by Hartford (Chris Pronger) and Tampa Bay (Chris Gratton) before the Ducks scooped up Kariya with the fourth choice. Kariya had made his reputation in the junior leagues of his native British Columbia (244 points in just 94 games) before attending the University of Maine. While playing in his first year with the Black Bears, Kariya racked up an impressive 25 goals and 75 assists in 39 games. His performance earned him the Hobey Baker Award as the best U.S. collegiate player, the first freshman to win the highly coveted trophy. After playing for Canada's Olympic team in

CAREER HIGHLIGHTS
- Drafted fourth overall by Anaheim in 1993.
- Named to the First All-Star team three times.
- Named winner of the Lady Byng Trophy twice.
- Has scored 342 goals and 790 points in 739 NHL career games.

1994 and helping the team win a silver medal, Kariya was ready for the NHL.

When he entered the NHL in 1994–95, Kariya displayed all the talents necessary for a great career. A superb skater with a terrific sense of anticipation, Kariya also demonstrated a great shot that goalies had to respect. Kariya is always near the top of the list for shots on goal, and in 1998–99 he led all players with 429. But Kariya can do more than shoot, and he has the assists to prove it. In 1995–96, Kariya scored 50 goals and added 58 assists in just his first full NHL season. He came back with 44 goals and 99 points the next year to show he was for real. The following season was one to forget for young Kariya. First he had a long contract dispute with the Ducks, then a hit to the head kept him out of the Olympic Games.

The 1998–99 season was much better for Kariya, who played in all 82 contests and recorded 101 points (39 goals, 62 assists). A throwback to a style of play that recognizes you don't have to take a penalty to be effective, Kariya has won two Lady Byng trophies. Kariya is also dedicated to the game and is willing to spend the necessary time needed for conditioning.

In 2001–02, the Ducks missed the playoffs for the fourth time in five years, and although he scored 32 goals, Kariya's assists slipped to 25, his lowest total for a full season. But although the Ducks were for sale, they brought in some help for their franchise player in 2002–03. Peter Sykora, Adam Oates, Sandis Ozolinsh and Rob Niedermayer helped the Ducks increase their point total from 69 to 95. Kariya had only 25 goals, but his 56 assists ranked eighth in the NHL.

The Ducks, named after a Disney movie, wrote a script of their own by reaching the Stanley Cup finals, beating powerhouses Detroit Red Wings and Dallas Stars. Paul Kariya finally had that long NHL spring he'd waited nine years for. The Ducks took New

Jersey all the way to the seventh game of the Stanley Cup final before losing 3–0. Kariya is the Anaheim all-time leader in goals (300), assists (369) and points (669).

In a shocking move, Anaheim let Kariya become an unrestricted free agent. He signed with the powerful Colorado Avalanche for one season – at 20 percent of his former salary – to play alongside his good friend Teemu Selanne, who joined the Avalanche in a package deal. It did not work out so well for either player (only 11 goals and 36 points in 51 games played for Kariya) and neither returned to Colorado after the lockout.

Kariya took the lockout year off completely and returned refreshed to play for the upstart Nashville Predators in 2005–06, signing a two-year deal for $9 million. The Predators had their best year in the NHL to date (49 wins, 106 points) but were steamrolled by San Jose in five games during the playoffs. Nonetheless, Kariya showed his teammates a good example of how to prepare for games and how important it is to have a strong work ethic. A healthy Kariya will help keep the Predators a contender for the foreseeable future.

ICE CHIPS

Paul Kariya was able to play in all 82 games during the 2005–06 season and set Nashville franchise records for most points in one season (85) and for most assists in one year (54). His 31 markers tied the team record (also held by Steve Sullivan) for most goals in a season. Kariya also tied single season marks for most powerplay points (45) and most multipoint games (25) by a Predator.

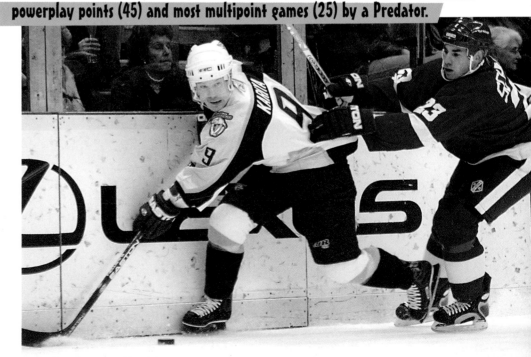

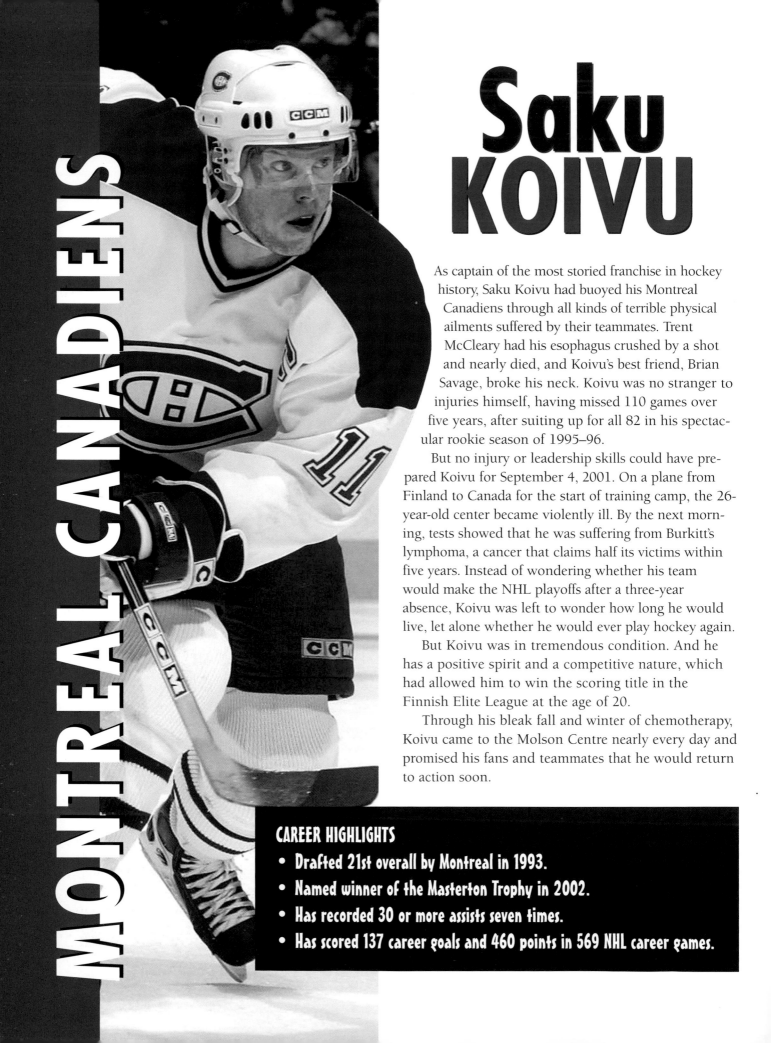

MONTREAL CANADIENS

Saku KOIVU

As captain of the most storied franchise in hockey history, Saku Koivu had buoyed his Montreal Canadiens through all kinds of terrible physical ailments suffered by their teammates. Trent McCleary had his esophagus crushed by a shot and nearly died, and Koivu's best friend, Brian Savage, broke his neck. Koivu was no stranger to injuries himself, having missed 110 games over five years, after suiting up for all 82 in his spectacular rookie season of 1995–96.

But no injury or leadership skills could have prepared Koivu for September 4, 2001. On a plane from Finland to Canada for the start of training camp, the 26-year-old center became violently ill. By the next morning, tests showed that he was suffering from Burkitt's lymphoma, a cancer that claims half its victims within five years. Instead of wondering whether his team would make the NHL playoffs after a three-year absence, Koivu was left to wonder how long he would live, let alone whether he would ever play hockey again.

But Koivu was in tremendous condition. And he has a positive spirit and a competitive nature, which had allowed him to win the scoring title in the Finnish Elite League at the age of 20.

Through his bleak fall and winter of chemotherapy, Koivu came to the Molson Centre nearly every day and promised his fans and teammates that he would return to action soon.

CAREER HIGHLIGHTS
- Drafted 21st overall by Montreal in 1993.
- Named winner of the Masterton Trophy in 2002.
- Has recorded 30 or more assists seven times.
- Has scored 137 career goals and 460 points in 569 NHL career games.

The Canadiens hung around the edges of the '02 playoff chase until April 9, when they played host to Ottawa. If the Canadiens won, they would make the playoffs for the first time in four years. It was also the game in which Saku Koivu returned to the Canadiens' lineup.

When his name was announced, the overflow crowd at the Molson Centre leaped to their feet and clapped and cheered and cried for eight solid minutes. The Senators stood on their bench and tapped their sticks on the boards in respect. Koivu played 13 shifts that night, mostly on the fourth line, as the Canadiens won 4–3 and snuck into the playoffs.

With spectacular goaltending from José Theodore, the Canadiens upset Boston in the first round of those 2002 playoffs and led Carolina two games to one in the next round, before falling apart in the third period of game 4. Koivu continued to defy the odds by tying for the team lead in scoring with 10 points in 12 playoff games.

The Canadiens missed the playoffs in 2003 with weak special teams and too many small forwards who weren't effective. But that didn't include Koivu, who is only 5'10" and 181 pounds. In an inspirational comeback, Koivu centered the first line and led the Canadiens in scoring with 21 goals, 50 assists and 71 points, all personal bests.

It was the kind of season that the

Canadiens predicted for Koivu when they made him their first choice, and 21st overall, in the 1993 draft, just a few weeks after winning their last Stanley Cup. After two more years of seasoning in Finland, he arrived in the NHL and finished fourth among NHL rookies, with 20 goals and 25 assists. A superb passer, he was leading the league in scoring with 13 goals and 25 assists in his sophomore year when he injured his knee in early December, and missed 32 games.

During the 2003–04 season, Koivu managed a respectable 55 points (including 41 assists) in 68 games played and the Habs returned to the Stanley Cup playoffs. The team fell behind three games to one to Boston but rallied to beat the Bruins in seven games (the last coming right in Boston). The Tampa Bay Lightning wiped the Canadiens out during the next round on their way to winning the Cup, but Koivu could be proud of his performance, which included 11 points in 11 post-season games.

Koivu played just 20 games in his native Finland during the lockout but returned for the 2005–06 season determined to keep his team in the playoffs (he had 62 points in 72 games played). The Habs got off to a great start but when they faltered, head coach Claude Julien was let go and replaced by general manager Bob Gainey.

Montreal recovered to make the post-season and were up two games on Carolina when Koivu suffered a bad eye injury (forcing him out of the playoffs) as a result of an errant high stick. The Hurricanes went on to win the series in six games. Clearly the Canadiens missed their captain, who is the emotional leader on the team.

Koivu, who does it all on the ice, is also very active off the ice. He has established the Saku Koivu Foundation to raise money for cancer-diagnostic equipment in Montreal area hospitals. The work of the foundation will remind everyone of how Koivu won the biggest battle of his life.

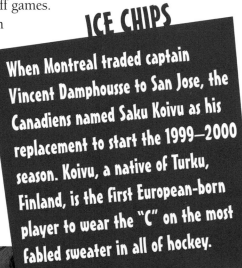

ICE CHIPS

When Montreal traded captain Vincent Damphousse to San Jose, the Canadiens named Saku Koivu as his replacement to start the 1999–2000 season. Koivu, a native of Turku, Finland, is the first European-born player to wear the "C" on the most fabled sweater in all of hockey.

MONTREAL CANADIENS

Alexei KOVALEV

Alexei Kovalev is one of those frustrating players who dot all the NHL rosters. Enormously gifted and blessed with terrific hockey sense, players like Kovalev just don't bring their top game every night. Eventually, people in management get fed up and deal these talented players to new clubs, which often turns out to be a big mistake. All you have to do is ask the New York Rangers about Kovalev. They dealt him away in late 1998, only to deal to get him back again in February 2003.

Kovalev has excellent size at 6'2", 215 pounds, and that caught the eye of the Ranger scouts in 1991 when they selected him 15th overall at the entry draft. He became the first Russian to be selected in the first round. A skilled puckhandler who is very strong on his skates, Kovalev came over to North America for the 1992–93 season. He split that season between New York in the NHL (20 goals and 38 points in 65 games) and Binghamton of the AHL (13 goals and 11 assists in 13 games), adjusting quickly to the game as played here. He improved to 23 goals and 33 assists in 1993–94 and then tasted the ultimate success with a Stanley Cup win in the 1994 playoffs as the Rangers won for the first time since 1940. Kovalev certainly made a strong contribution with 21 points (nine goals, 12 assists) in 23 games played. He appeared to be on the verge of a major breakout the next year. But it did not happen for Kovalev.

The lockout-shortened 1994–95 season saw Kovalev produce just 28 points in 48 games. He bounced back

CAREER HIGHLIGHTS
- Drafted 15th overall by NY Rangers in 1991.
- Member of Stanley Cup winning team in 1994.
- Member of Soviet gold medal-winning team at 1992 Olympics.
- Has scored 315 goals and 745 points in 918 NHL career games.

with a decent year in 1995–96, with 24 goals and 58 points for the Rangers. It was his last good year in New York as he settled into the 50-point range. With some reluctance, Kovalev was dealt to Pittsburgh in November 1998. Kovalev quickly produced 20 goals and 26 assists in 63 games and then improved his point total to 66 (26 goals, 40 assists) in 1999–2000. It once again looked like Kovalev was about to deliver more, only this time he did not disappoint. In 2000–01 he had his best season, with 44 goals and 95 points, which was good timing on his part. His contract was up, with restricted free agency on the horizon. The Penguins re-signed him, but traded away Jaromir Jagr in a cost-cutting move.

Kovalev has a dangerous shot and shows a willingness to crash the net to get what he wants. He takes his share of abuse (Kovalev also has a temper and has earned suspensions in the past), but now shows a maturity that goes along with some brilliant talent and keeps himself under control. Kovalev had 32 goals and 44 assists in 2001–02, but with the Penguins in financial trouble, Kovalev's future with the team was in jeopardy.

When Kovalev came on the market after he had 27 goals and 64 points in the first 54 games of 2002–03, the Rangers picked him up for their playoff drive. The Rangers missed the playoffs again, but Kovalev made an impact with 10 goals in 24 games.

The Rangers decided to go in a completely different direction and general manager Glen Sather shipped Kovalev to Montreal, which was looking for talented goals scorers. He helped the Canadiens make the 2004 playoffs and pull off one upset, and then he re-signed with Montreal after the lockout. In 2005–06 he led the Habs in scoring with 65 points (23 goals, 42 assists) in 69 games, but he had trouble finding the range in the playoffs and the Canadiens were out in the first round. Kovalev must play at a high level if the Canadiens are to succeed.

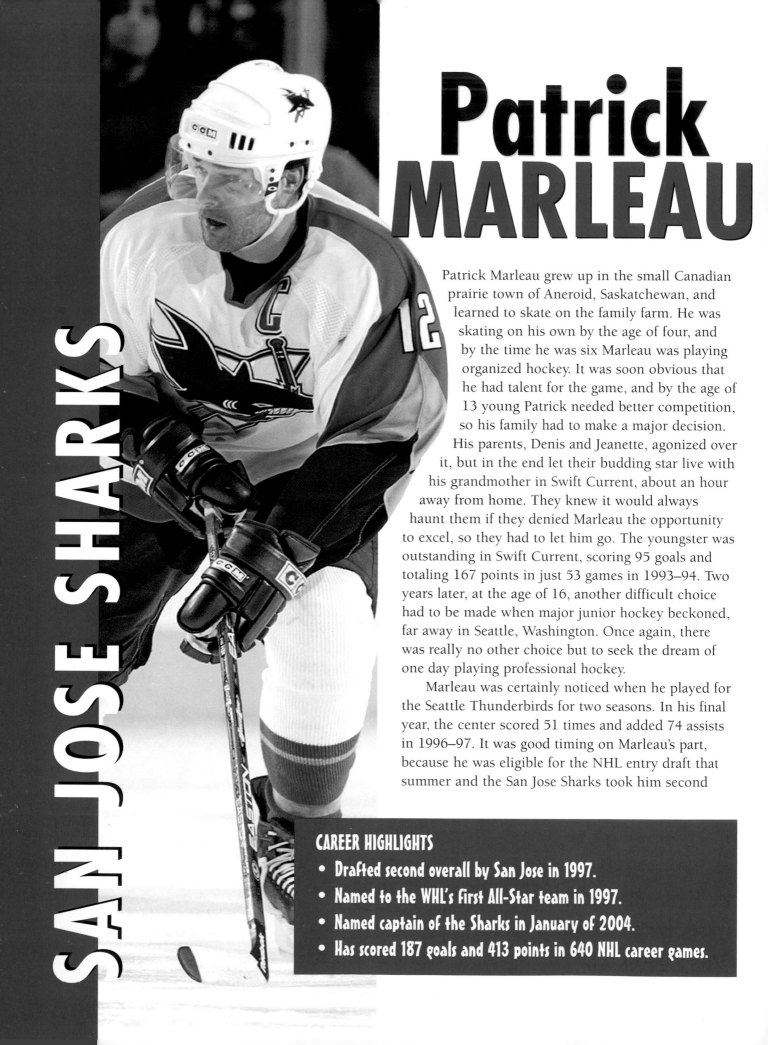

Patrick MARLEAU

SAN JOSE SHARKS

Patrick Marleau grew up in the small Canadian prairie town of Aneroid, Saskatchewan, and learned to skate on the family farm. He was skating on his own by the age of four, and by the time he was six Marleau was playing organized hockey. It was soon obvious that he had talent for the game, and by the age of 13 young Patrick needed better competition, so his family had to make a major decision. His parents, Denis and Jeanette, agonized over it, but in the end let their budding star live with his grandmother in Swift Current, about an hour away from home. They knew it would always haunt them if they denied Marleau the opportunity to excel, so they had to let him go. The youngster was outstanding in Swift Current, scoring 95 goals and totaling 167 points in just 53 games in 1993–94. Two years later, at the age of 16, another difficult choice had to be made when major junior hockey beckoned, far away in Seattle, Washington. Once again, there was really no other choice but to seek the dream of one day playing professional hockey.

Marleau was certainly noticed when he played for the Seattle Thunderbirds for two seasons. In his final year, the center scored 51 times and added 74 assists in 1996–97. It was good timing on Marleau's part, because he was eligible for the NHL entry draft that summer and the San Jose Sharks took him second

CAREER HIGHLIGHTS
- Drafted second overall by San Jose in 1997.
- Named to the WHL's First All-Star team in 1997.
- Named captain of the Sharks in January of 2004.
- Has scored 187 goals and 413 points in 640 NHL career games.

ICE CHIPS

With the acquisition of Joe Thornton, the San Jose Sharks now have the first two players chosen in the 1997 entry draft on their team — Patrick Marleau is the other. There are many quality NHL players who were also selected in the first round of the '97 draft, including Olli Jokinen, Roberto Luongo, Eric Brewer, Sergei Samsonov, Marian Hossa, Brenden Morrow and Scott Hannan (also with the Sharks).

overall. Most people anticipated that Marleau would return to junior for more seasoning, since he was only 18 at the time; however, (former) Sharks coach Darryl Sutter liked what he saw of the team's top draft choice, and felt there was no reason for him to go back to Seattle. Sutter did his best to protect Marleau by not overplaying him, but the rookie still managed to score 13 goals and total 32 points in the 74 games he played in 1997–98. He never did play junior again and has never played a single game in the minors. Marleau is now living his dream.

The strength of Marleau's game is built around his superb skating abilities. He can kick into overdrive when he sees a break and can be a scoring threat from just about anywhere on the ice, getting a shot off quickly and with pinpoint accuracy. He has very soft hands, with a nice finishing touch and a flair for playmaking.

Although Marleau is not a very aggressive player (only 219 career penalty minutes), he is not afraid of heavy traffic and has a thick body (6'2" and a superbly conditioned 220 pounds) that allows him to take or give hits as needed. He is still polishing his

game and needs to be more alert defensively, but he is rapidly becoming one of the best two-way players in the NHL. He has always had a quiet confidence about himself without being boastful and likes to be challenged in a positive way.

Marleau has been San Jose's best and most consistent player for a number of years (five seasons with 20 or more goals), and he improved his numbers when management finally got him some help. A blockbuster deal during the 2005–06 season saw the Sharks reel in Joe Thornton, and one of the players who benefited most from that deal was Marleau. No longer facing the other team's best defensive player, the slick center scored a career best 34 goals and 86 points. The new style of game implemented by the NHL in 2005–06 suits Marleau perfectly, allowing him to demonstrate his ample offensive skills (he scored 20 powerplay goals). Marleau is now captain of the Sharks and will likely follow the style of Joe Sakic, letting his play do all the talking.

Marleau's play in the '06 playoffs certainly spoke loudly as he led his team past Nashville in the first round (scoring a hat trick in one game), but a loss to Edmonton in the second round ended a dream season.

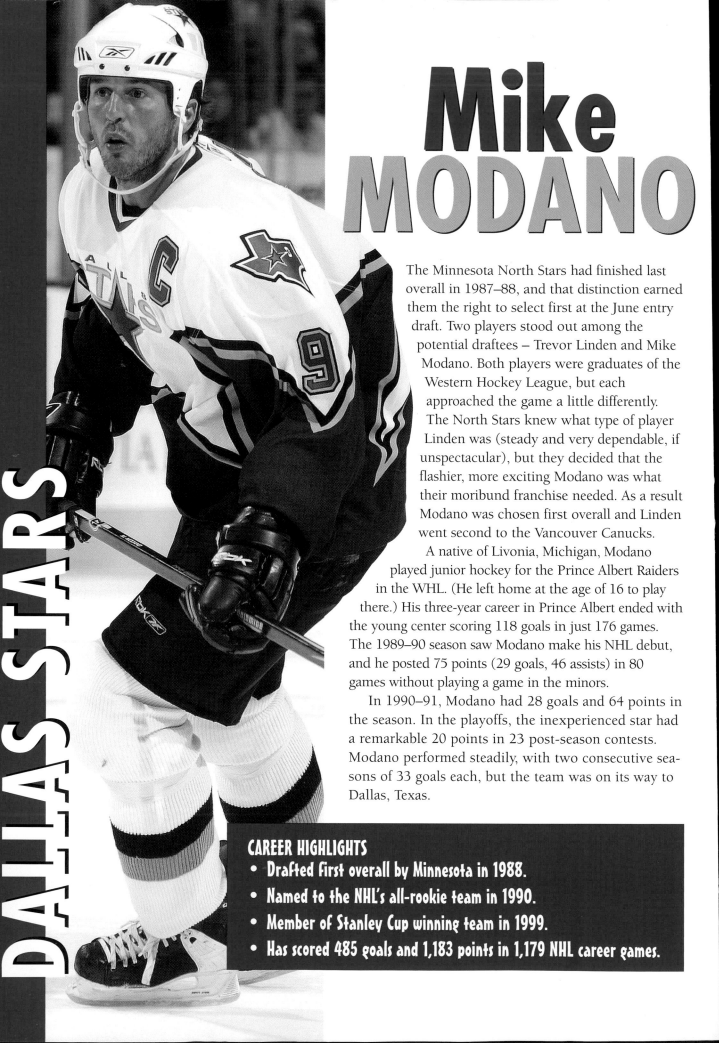

Mike MODANO

The Minnesota North Stars had finished last overall in 1987–88, and that distinction earned them the right to select first at the June entry draft. Two players stood out among the potential draftees – Trevor Linden and Mike Modano. Both players were graduates of the Western Hockey League, but each approached the game a little differently. The North Stars knew what type of player Linden was (steady and very dependable, if unspectacular), but they decided that the flashier, more exciting Modano was what their moribund franchise needed. As a result Modano was chosen first overall and Linden went second to the Vancouver Canucks.

A native of Livonia, Michigan, Modano played junior hockey for the Prince Albert Raiders in the WHL. (He left home at the age of 16 to play there.) His three-year career in Prince Albert ended with the young center scoring 118 goals in just 176 games. The 1989–90 season saw Modano make his NHL debut, and he posted 75 points (29 goals, 46 assists) in 80 games without playing a game in the minors.

In 1990–91, Modano had 28 goals and 64 points in the season. In the playoffs, the inexperienced star had a remarkable 20 points in 23 post-season contests. Modano performed steadily, with two consecutive seasons of 33 goals each, but the team was on its way to Dallas, Texas.

CAREER HIGHLIGHTS
- Drafted first overall by Minnesota in 1988.
- Named to the NHL's all-rookie team in 1990.
- Member of Stanley Cup winning team in 1999.
- Has scored 485 goals and 1,183 points in 1,179 NHL career games.

Modano has top passing skills (698 career assists to date) and loves to go on the attack. He is one of the top powerplay specialists in the NHL, but is now a more reliable two-way player. When he first broke into the league, Modano was viewed as a soft performer who could be rattled, but he has since become more willing to take the pounding that star players get. Also, by understanding the value of good defensive play, he has posted seasons where his plus-minus stats have reached as high as a plus 43 (in 1996–97). He has also been a plus player for eight out of his last nine seasons (missing only in 2003–04, when he had a terrible year and ended up a minus 21).

The Stars still want Modano to score and he has not disappointed, with a 50-goal season the first year in Dallas, and subsequent years where he has scored 36, 35, 34, 38, 33, 34 and 28 goals.

As well as Modano has done, the Stars realized he needed some offensive help. Their best move was to acquire center Joe Nieuwendyk from Calgary to take some pressure off Modano and allow their young star to develop with a good role model on the team. The combination worked, as the Stars have finished first overall in the NHL two times and the team won their first Stanley Cup in 1999. Modano played hurt in the finals and showed a grit and determination not previously seen from the superstar. Nieuwendyk was then dealt to New Jersey for Jason Arnott, who absorbed some of the opposition checking. The addition of Bill Guerin also helped Modano. His 57 assists were the second most of his career, and with 85 points he finished in the NHL

top 10 in 2002–03. His leadership, and Dallas' recovery from a terrible 2001–02 season, earned Modano some MVP consideration in '02–'03. He was named team captain in July 2003.

Modano had a very difficult time during the '03–'04 season, as rumors swirled about his personal finances. Many thought he was done (although he was pursued strongly by both Boston and Chicago as a free agent) but the Stars wanted him back and signed him to a new long-term deal (a $17.5 million contract over five years). The year off due to the lockout seemed to do wonders for Modano, who got the distractions off the ice in order and changed his diet to prepare for the new NHL. He came back in 2005–06 to lead his team with 77 points, and the Stars won 53 contests during the season. Nobody on the Stars had a good playoff in '06, but in many ways it was a year of redemption for Mike Modano.

TAMPA BAY LIGHTNING

Brad RICHARDS

When Brad Richards was three years old, he learned to skate on a pond behind his grandfather's house on Prince Edward Island. Twenty years later, Brad Richards carried the Stanley Cup to that very same house so his grandfather could have his picture taken with the cup and the grandson who had just won it. Not only did Richards' Tampa Bay Lightning win the 2004 Stanley Cup, the creative center was named the winner of the Conn Smythe Trophy as the MVP of the NHL playoffs. In late June, he was also elected the winner of the Lady Byng Trophy for sportsmanlike and effective play.

Although the Lightning were known more for Vincent Lecavalier, Martin St. Louis and captain Dave Andreychuk, hockey fans came to realize during the 2004 post-season that Richards is the real deal – the kind of player who can carry a team. He has a fine all-around game: he's one of the best playmakers, if not the best playmaker, in the NHL, but is not afraid to let fly at the net either, logging over 250 shots a season. He can block shots, defuse a point man on the powerplay and generate spectacular set-ups off the rush. And he's durable, missing just two games in the first five years of his NHL career. He has proven his durability, but there was a time when Richards wasn't considered big enough to make the NHL, and some scouting reports wondered if he would wear down when exposed to larger, physical centers. He hasn't yet, and it's unlikely that he will in the new, free-skating NHL.

CAREER HIGHLIGHTS
- Drafted sixth overall by Tampa Bay in 1998.
- Named Canadian Junior Player of the Year in 2000.
- Named winner of the Conn Smythe Trophy in 2004.
- Has scored 107 goals and 368 points in 408 NHL career games.

Richards' father, Glen, is a third-generation lobster fisherman, but his son was never attracted to the profession. Instead, Richards ended up as far away from the ocean as you can get, playing hockey for Saskatchewan's Notre Dame College Hounds. When he was 14, he met another young Hound player the same age – Vincent Lecavalier – and the two became roommates. When Lecavalier headed back to Quebec in 1996 to play for the Rimouski Oceanic, Richards stayed at Notre Dame for a season of tier II junior A, and was named Rookie of the Year. A year later (1998), Richards also joined the Oceanic, and after that season both were drafted by Tampa Bay (Lecavalier first overall, Richards 64th).

When Lecavalier went to the NHL, Richards spent two more years with Rimouski, scoring 72 goals and setting up 115 others in 1999–2000, leading the entire league and carrying his team to the Memorial Cup championship. Foreshadowing his 2004 NHL hardware haul, in the spring of 2000 Richards was the Canadian major junior Player of the Year, Quebec regular season and playoff MVP, the MVP of the Memorial Cup tournament, and the league's leading scorer. He then joined the Lightning for the 2000–01 season and led all NHL rookies in goals (21), assists (41) and points (62), making him the second youngest player in the NHL (20 years, nine months) to lead his team in scoring and finishing second to Evgeny Nabokov in the Calder Trophy balloting for NHL Rookie of the Year.

His scoring totals were almost exactly the same in his sophomore season of 2001–02 (20 goals and 62 points), but a higher skill level was emerging and he was among the top 10 NHL scorers after the Olympic break. In 2002–03, Richards established career highs with 74 points and 57 assists, helping the Lightning to their first post-season appearance in seven years. But he managed just five points (all assists) in 11 games, and Tampa Bay was ousted in the second round. In '03–'04, he scored 22 goals and 38 assists over the final 51 games and stormed

ICE CHIPS

In the Tampa Bay Lightning's magical Stanley Cup season of 2004–05, the team did not lose a game when Brad Richards scored a goal. Overall, the team had 32 wins and two ties when he scored, and they were a perfect 9–0 in the playoffs.

into the playoffs with a head of steam. Richards stole the show in the post-season, setting an NHL record with seven game-winning goals, breaking the record of six held by his boyhood idol Joe Sakic.

The post-lockout season of 2005–06 was not a good one for the Lightning as the defending champions struggled to make the playoffs and were eliminated in the first round. However, Richards recorded a career-best 91 points to lead the Lightning again, and fashioned a career-high 68 assists (fifth best in the league). Tampa Bay, recognizing Richards' consistency, re-signed him to a five-year deal worth $39 million ($7.8 million per year) in May 2006.

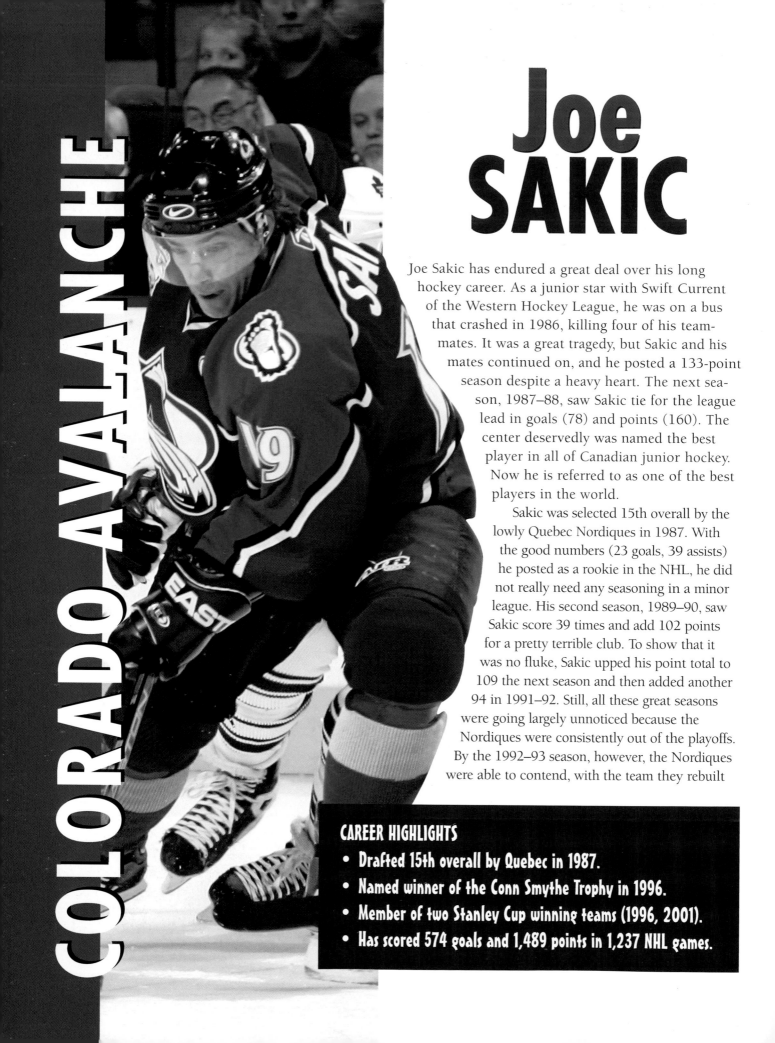

COLORADO AVALANCHE

Joe SAKIC

Joe Sakic has endured a great deal over his long hockey career. As a junior star with Swift Current of the Western Hockey League, he was on a bus that crashed in 1986, killing four of his team-mates. It was a great tragedy, but Sakic and his mates continued on, and he posted a 133-point season despite a heavy heart. The next season, 1987–88, saw Sakic tie for the league lead in goals (78) and points (160). The center deservedly was named the best player in all of Canadian junior hockey. Now he is referred to as one of the best players in the world.

Sakic was selected 15th overall by the lowly Quebec Nordiques in 1987. With the good numbers (23 goals, 39 assists) he posted as a rookie in the NHL, he did not really need any seasoning in a minor league. His second season, 1989–90, saw Sakic score 39 times and add 102 points for a pretty terrible club. To show that it was no fluke, Sakic upped his point total to 109 the next season and then added another 94 in 1991–92. Still, all these great seasons were going largely unnoticed because the Nordiques were consistently out of the playoffs. By the 1992–93 season, however, the Nordiques were able to contend, with the team they rebuilt

CAREER HIGHLIGHTS

- Drafted 15th overall by Quebec in 1987.
- Named winner of the Conn Smythe Trophy in 1996.
- Member of two Stanley Cup winning teams (1996, 2001).
- Has scored 574 goals and 1,489 points in 1,237 NHL games.

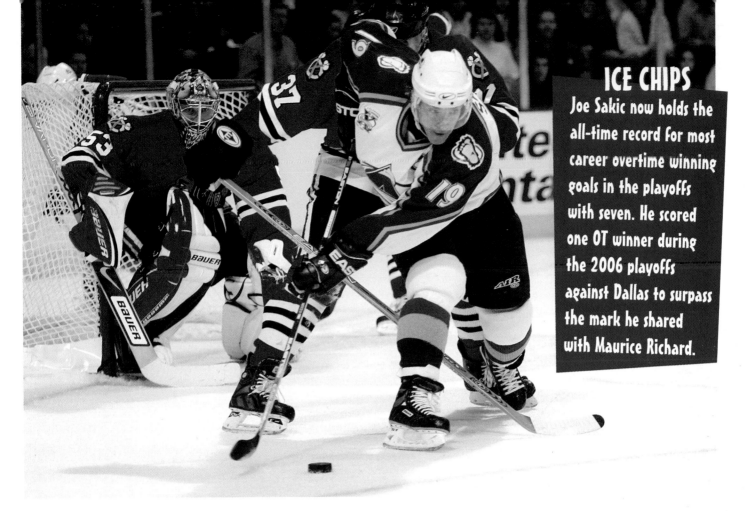

through the entry draft and by trading the rights to Eric Lindros for a large package of players. Sakic produced 105 points that year, and the Quebec squad made the post-season for the first time in six years.

Even though Sakic's team lost many games in the early years of his pro career, he did have a chance to develop his game with little pressure. Sakic has a great snapshot that he gets off with lightning quickness. He sees the entire ice very well and his passes are pinpoint in precision. Sakic has become a great special-team player and can even handle the point on the power-play. He is not overly physical, but he isn't afraid to be hit and knows how to roll off those he has to take. Sakic keeps his legs moving all the time, which allows him to get to many loose pucks. In close to the opponent's net, his quick hands make him deadly accurate and very dangerous every time he touches the puck.

After he enjoyed two more great seasons in Quebec (in 1993–94 he recorded 92 points), the Nordiques were moved to Colorado. The first season there proved an auspicious one for Sakic, who had a career-high 120 points. Then he had a superb playoff with 34 points in 22 games and won the Conn Smythe Trophy as the best player in the post-season. He won the Stanley Cup as team captain, and his long suffering was finally over.

After that, Sakic produced point totals of 74, 63, 96, 81 and 118 in 2000–01, when he led his team back to the cup (he was the leading playoff scorer in 2001, with 26 points made up of 13 goals and 13 assists). He was named winner of both the Hart Trophy and the Lester B. Pearson Award in 2001, for his outstanding season. He was tied for fifth in NHL scoring in 2001–02 with 79 points and was also one of Canada's best players in its 2002 Olympic victory. Injuries limited him to 58 games in 2002–03, but still he recorded 58 points.

One of the classiest players in the game of hockey, he let teammate Ray Bourque hoist the cup over his head first when it was presented to the Avalanche in 2001, even though Sakic was the undisputed team leader.

Sakic has been his usual consistent self the last two seasons, recording 87 points in both 2003–04 and 2005–06. He still leads by example and his work ethic is unquestioned. His play is inspiring to his teammates and he is known for playing the game on an even keel. Colorado coach Joel Quenneville came to realize that his captain is not a player who will be outworked. Sakic takes care of himself physically (he will be 37 prior to the start of the 2006–07 season), which should allow him to add a few more years to what will certainly be a Hall of Fame career.

TORONTO MAPLE LEAFS

Mats SUNDIN

When the Toronto Maple Leafs lost their second consecutive conference final in 1994, the management decided they'd better start rebuilding. Cliff Fletcher, then general manager, was never afraid to pull the trigger on a big deal if he thought it would help his team. He and coach Pat Burns knew the Leafs needed to score more goals. They targeted Mats Sundin, then with Quebec, as the young player they could build an attack around.

Getting Sundin in the June 1994 trade would prove to be very costly, as the Leafs were forced to include captain Wendel Clark (shocking Toronto fans) and blueline stalwart Sylvain Lefebvre in the package. Some said the Leafs paid too high a price. The first payoff for landing the big center was not to come until 1998–99, and Fletcher and Burns were long gone by then.

Sundin first became known to North American hockey fans when he was selected first overall by the Quebec Nordiques in the 1989 entry draft. He was the first-ever European-born player to be taken as the first choice. Sundin quickly proved the Quebec club had made a good choice by scoring 23 goals and 59 points as a rookie in 1990–91. The next year saw Sundin's numbers improve to 33 tallies and 76 points. Then in 1992–93, the big Swede scored 47 goals and 114 points as the Nordiques became a club on the move. The talented but young hockey club fizzled out in the playoffs, and after a 1993–94 season that saw Sundin drop his point total to 85, the Nordiques believed their club

CAREER HIGHLIGHTS
- Selected first overall by Quebec in 1989 entry draft.
- Scored five goals in one game on March 5, 1992.
- Named captain of the Maple Leafs on September 30, 1997.
- Has scored 496 goals and 1,156 points in 1,167 career games.

needed some veteran leadership and thus became interested in making a deal with Toronto for Clark.

It is easy to see why the Leafs would be interested in Sundin. A large man (6'4", 228 pounds), Sundin is one of the best skaters in the NHL. He has a fluid stride and can turn on the speed burners quickly. Sundin uses his long reach effectively and has the soft hands to work in close. His touch allows him to score goals and he has a strong shot, as well as the best backhand in the league. But he often tries to make that one extra pass when he should shoot. Despite his size, Sundin does not usually play with a physical edge but is often more effective when he does throw his weight around.

Sundin has been captain of the Leafs since 1997 and he enjoys playing in a city where hockey reigns supreme. He is comfortable being the main spokesperson for a team that has many ups and downs, but he has proven to be a consistent performer since he became a Leaf by posting seasons of 83, 94, 74, 83, 73, 76, 80, 72, 75 and 78 points (he had led the team in points a club record nine times since his arrival in Toronto). However, the Leafs had little success in Sundin's early years with the club, but things turned around when coach Pat Quinn installed an attack-oriented style starting in 1998-99 (the Leafs led the NHL in goals scored that year). The Leafs made it to the conference finals in '99 and again in 2002, but the Stanley Cup still remains elusive.

Although still not as popular in Toronto as he should be (a fact that bothers many hockey observers), Sundin

ICE CHIPS

Mats Sundin has now scored 363 goals as a Maple Leaf, behind only Dave Keon (365) and Darryl Sittler (389). As of the end of the 2005–06 season, only Sittler has recorded more career points (916) as a Leaf than Sundin (846).

has quietly fashioned a career that will leave him as one of the all-time great Leafs. During the 2001–02 season he scored 41 times (tied for second in the entire league) and was named to the NHL's second All-Star team – the first time a Leaf made a post-season team in 22 years. He was named to the second All-Star squad again in 2003–04 and has achieved many of his accolades while playing with less than all-star caliber wingers. The Leaf organization has failed to give Sundin top notch talent to work with, which makes his play all the more amazing. Sundin started the 2005–06 season on the injured list but came back to lead Sweden to a gold medal at the Winter Olympics and then nearly took the Leafs to a playoff spot almost by himself. His performance after the Olympics was outstanding, and he recorded a six-point night (four goals, two assists) against the Florida Panthers in April as a regular-season highlight. In his mid-30s, Sundin needs to speak out more about the direction of the team, but that is simply not his style. Leaf fans can only hope management will do what is right for the team and the long-suffering captain.

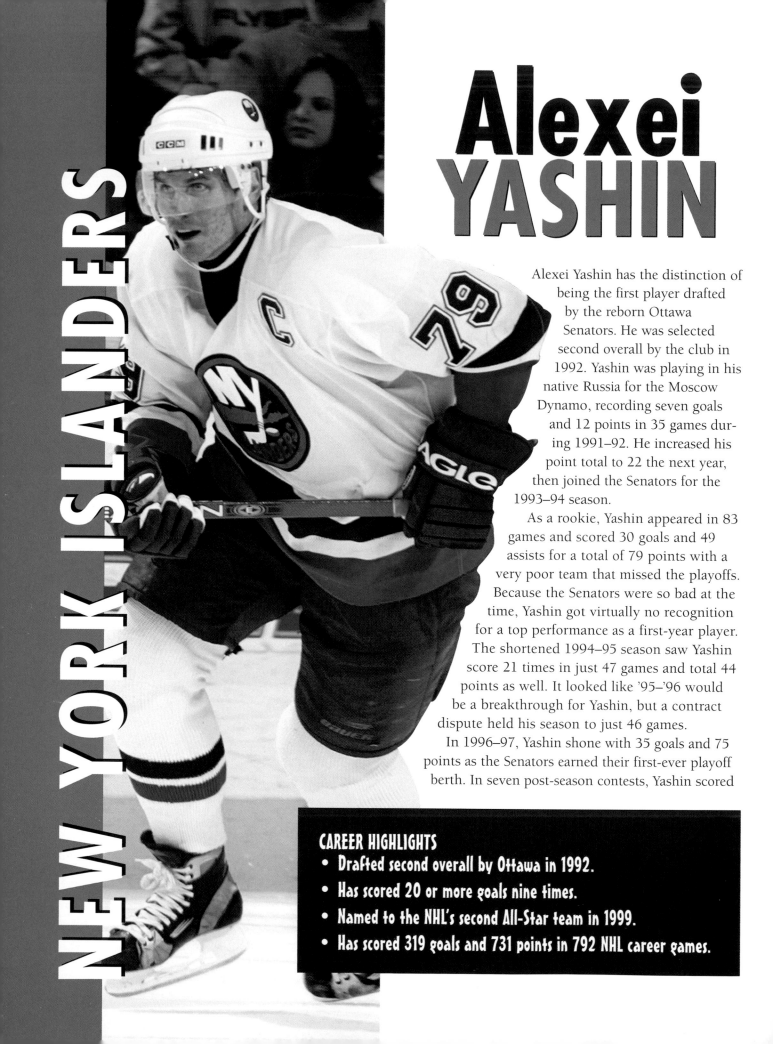

NEW YORK ISLANDERS

Alexei YASHIN

Alexei Yashin has the distinction of being the first player drafted by the reborn Ottawa Senators. He was selected second overall by the club in 1992. Yashin was playing in his native Russia for the Moscow Dynamo, recording seven goals and 12 points in 35 games during 1991–92. He increased his point total to 22 the next year, then joined the Senators for the 1993–94 season.

As a rookie, Yashin appeared in 83 games and scored 30 goals and 49 assists for a total of 79 points with a very poor team that missed the playoffs. Because the Senators were so bad at the time, Yashin got virtually no recognition for a top performance as a first-year player. The shortened 1994–95 season saw Yashin score 21 times in just 47 games and total 44 points as well. It looked like '95–'96 would be a breakthrough for Yashin, but a contract dispute held his season to just 46 games.

In 1996–97, Yashin shone with 35 goals and 75 points as the Senators earned their first-ever playoff berth. In seven post-season contests, Yashin scored

CAREER HIGHLIGHTS
- Drafted second overall by Ottawa in 1992.
- Has scored 20 or more goals nine times.
- Named to the NHL's second All-Star team in 1999.
- Has scored 319 goals and 731 points in 792 NHL career games.

one goal and added five assists, but the Senators lost in seven games to the Buffalo Sabres. The 1997–98 season saw Yashin score 33 times and record 72 points, but this time the team knocked off the highly favored New Jersey Devils before losing to the Washington Capitals in the second round. (The center contributed eight points in 11 contests.) By 1998–99 Yashin's talents were in full bloom when he recorded 44 goals and 94 points for a team that was now a power in the Eastern Conference, finishing second overall. Yashin, who had been named captain, was a big disappointment in the playoffs, with no goals (and no leadership skills either, at least according to some critics).

Ottawa fans were quick to criticize Yashin, but he was the team's best player. He has a great shot and soft hands that are helping him to become a consistent goal scorer. Yashin is big (6'3", 195 pounds) and strong and will take a beating to get a shot off. His outstanding work was noticed with a Hart Trophy nomination for 1998–99 and a second-team All-Star selection.

Yashin made himself very unpopular by sitting out the entire 1999–2000 season even though he had a signed contract. The Senators struck a blow for all teams (and fans) by making Yashin honor the last year of his deal. He did come back to post a fine season with 40 goals and 88 points in 2000–01. Once again a dud in the play-offs, he was dealt to the New York Islanders at the June draft.

In 2001–02, Yashin and Mike Peca helped the Islanders into the playoffs for the first time in eight years. Although he had seven points in a seven-game loss to Toronto, Yashin's performance was considered a failure. By the middle of 2002–03, Yashin had been demoted to the fourth line because of indifferent play.

Yashin did not play much hockey (injuries and the lockout) in the two years prior to the 2005-06 season but he started off strong by recording 23 points in his first 30 games. He took over as captain of the Islanders with Michael Peca gone to Edmonton, and the club

stayed in contention for the early part of the year. A slide down the standings meant coach Steve Stirling was history (replaced by Brad Shaw) and eventually general manager Mike Milbury was booted upstairs, making way for Neil Smith in '06–'07. Yashin tied for the club lead in points (66, the same number as Miro Satan) but his ridiculously high salary ($6.9 million) could not be justified even in the new NHL.

Everything looks even worse when you consider what the Islanders gave up to get Yashin (defenseman Zdeno Chara and a draft choice that turned out to be Jason Spezza) from the Senators. The 10-year contract was given to him by the owner, and it could still be terminated with a buyout, but it will affect the Isles' salary cap for the next five seasons. If they keep him, the Islanders better hope new coach Ted Nolan can get more production out of the enigmatic Yashin.

When the New York Islanders named Alexei Yashin as team captain for the 2005–06 season, he became just the second non-Canadian to have the "C" on his sweater. The other was defenseman Kenny Jonsson (who was captain for just one season, in 1999–2000). The longest-serving captain of the Isles was Hall of Fame defenseman Denis Potvin, who held the role from 1979–80 to 1986–87.

SNIP

Accurate shooters who get into the right position to snap or slap a shot into the net.

OTTAWA SENATORS

Daniel
ALFREDSSON

There is no player who personifies the Ottawa Senators' puzzling, frustrating history of contrasts more than Daniel Alfredsson. The classy right-winger is the only Senator who has been involved in all 79 games of the 14 playoff series that Ottawa has played during a remarkable nine straight years in the post-season. And, as the Senators' captain since 2001, he has been forced to explain how he and his team always seem to find a way of coming up short in the post-season. He does not like that part of the job, but credit must be given, because he shows up after every game, win or lose, to speak for the team.

Alfredsson is another one of those gems over-looked by other teams, but unearthed and nurtured by the superb Ottawa scouting staff, when the club was still missing the playoffs regularly. The Sens chose him as a 21-year-old (133rd overall in the 1994 entry draft), and after another season with Frolunda of the Swedish League, he made an immediate impact in the NHL. The Senators missed the playoffs in his first year, but Alfredsson scored 26 goals and won the Calder Trophy as the league's top rookie.

Playing a lesser role to the likes of Alexei Yashin, Alfredsson grew steadily as an NHL player, and in the post-season was often more physically aggressive than during the regular season, perhaps because there were so many criticisms about the Senators being too "soft." After scoring 24 goals and increasing his points total by 10 for

CAREER HIGHLIGHTS
- Drafted 116th overall by Ottawa in 1994.
- Named winner of the Calder Trophy in 1996.
- Named captain of the Senators in 1999.
- Has scored 262 goals and 671 points in 706 NHL career games.

71 points in his sophomore season of '96–'97, Alfredsson's climb toward elite status leveled off for four seasons when he missed a total of 90 games because of injuries. But, in that span, he still potted 73 goals and tallied 207 points.

Alfredsson really broke into the NHL's upper echelon in 2001–02. He had shown grit and tremendous leadership qualities the previous season, when he was made temporary captain after Yashin held out for the year. Yashin returned in 2001, but the Sens retained Alfredsson as captain, and Ottawa became his team. He responded by scoring 37 goals and 71 points and logging 20:19 minutes in ice time (the only time in his career, other than playoffs, when he's averaged more than 20 minutes). His goal total dropped to 27 in 2002–03, but his points total rose to a career-best 78. He upped that to 80 points (with 32 goals) in 2003–04, signing a new five-year contract near the end of that season.

Alfredsson is the Senators' all-time leader in regular season points, goals and assists, and he leads all three categories in the playoffs, too. But despite winning four regular-season division titles with superior teams, it's the failure to advance to the Stanley Cup finals that haunts the Senators and their captain. Yet Alfredsson also exemplifies the positives of the Ottawa franchise. With his stickhandling mastery, speed, velvet hands and vision on the ice, he's always a threat to score or set up a highlight-reel goal.

During the lockout, Alfredsson propelled Frolunda to the Swedish championship (he led all scorers, with 12 goals and 18 points in the playoffs). In a cruel irony for Ottawa fans, he was the leading scorer for Team Sweden on its way to the 2006 Olympic gold medal.

Alfredsson had a career year in 2005–06, in the new, speed-oriented NHL, which seemed to be created specifically for his team. He turned in a stellar 103-point regular season, tying for fourth place in the scoring race. Scoring over 100 points for the first time, he recorded career highs in goals (43) and points (103). And his plus 29 was more than double his previous best.

Unfortunately, his superb regular season is not what most hockey fans will remember about Alfredsson's 2005–06 year. Unfairly or not, they will always recall Buffalo's Jason Pominville skating around him for the short-handed overtime goal that eliminated the Sabres in round 2. And they will also remember that a 43-goal shooter managed just one goal against Buffalo (scored on a two-man powerplay), during a series in which all five games were decided by a single goal.

ICE CHIPS

Daniel Alfredsson scored the NHL's first-ever game-winning goal on a shootout, on opening night October 15, 2005, against Toronto. He also scored both of Ottawa's goals during regulation time in that game.

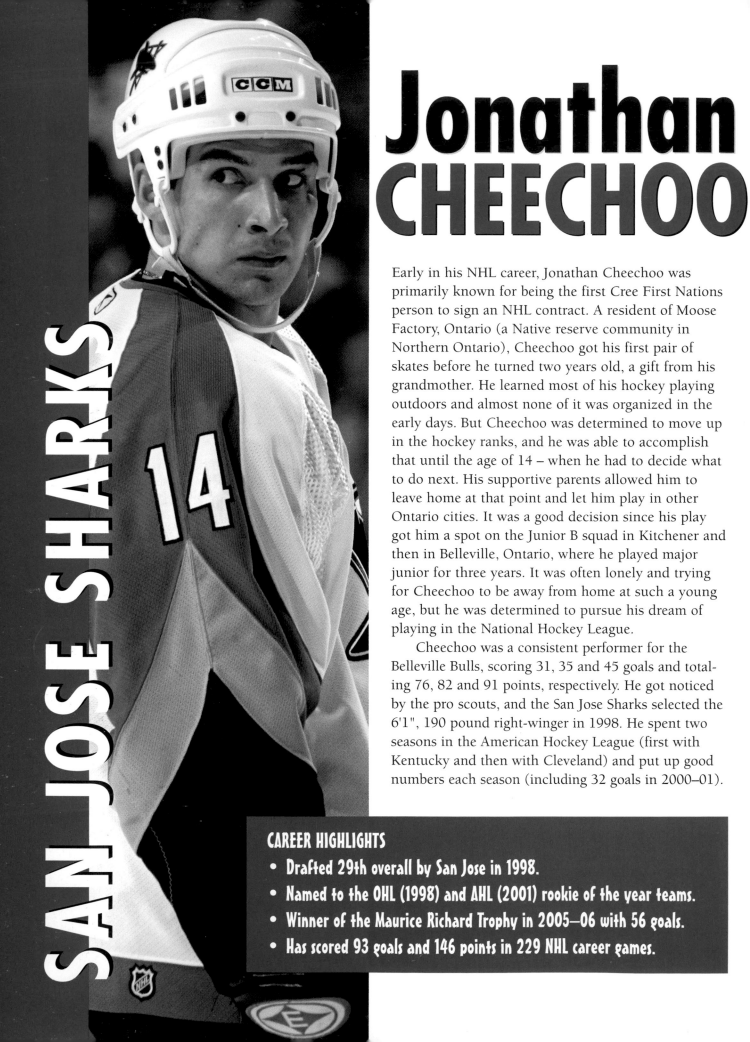

Jonathan CHEECHOO

SAN JOSE SHARKS

Early in his NHL career, Jonathan Cheechoo was primarily known for being the first Cree First Nations person to sign an NHL contract. A resident of Moose Factory, Ontario (a Native reserve community in Northern Ontario), Cheechoo got his first pair of skates before he turned two years old, a gift from his grandmother. He learned most of his hockey playing outdoors and almost none of it was organized in the early days. But Cheechoo was determined to move up in the hockey ranks, and he was able to accomplish that until the age of 14 – when he had to decide what to do next. His supportive parents allowed him to leave home at that point and let him play in other Ontario cities. It was a good decision since his play got him a spot on the Junior B squad in Kitchener and then in Belleville, Ontario, where he played major junior for three years. It was often lonely and trying for Cheechoo to be away from home at such a young age, but he was determined to pursue his dream of playing in the National Hockey League.

Cheechoo was a consistent performer for the Belleville Bulls, scoring 31, 35 and 45 goals and totaling 76, 82 and 91 points, respectively. He got noticed by the pro scouts, and the San Jose Sharks selected the 6'1", 190 pound right-winger in 1998. He spent two seasons in the American Hockey League (first with Kentucky and then with Cleveland) and put up good numbers each season (including 32 goals in 2000–01).

CAREER HIGHLIGHTS
- Drafted 29th overall by San Jose in 1998.
- Named to the OHL (1998) and AHL (2001) rookie of the year teams.
- Winner of the Maurice Richard Trophy in 2005–06 with 56 goals.
- Has scored 93 goals and 146 points in 229 NHL career games.

The 2002–03 season saw Cheechoo play in 66 games for San Jose and the rookie had a respectable nine goals and 16 points that year (although he was briefly demoted to the AHL). The 2003–04 season was the first year Cheechoo got noticed by scoring 28 goals and adding 19 assists, and then ringing up 10 points in 17 playoff games. As much as he had improved, there was little to suggest he was one day going to lead the NHL in goals scored.

The Sharks were struggling badly when hockey resumed for the 2005–06 season. They were in serious need of a shake-up, and luckily for them the Boston Bruins were in much the same position. San Jose landed superstar center Joe Thornton in the deal, and no one benefited more than Cheechoo. The two were put together as soon as Thornton joined the team and an instant chemistry was formed. The big center decided he could hang onto the puck much more than he ever had before (mostly because of the new rules), and the first player he would look for, to hit with a pass, was the right-handed shooter Cheechoo. The Sharks' winger was much like Thornton's old linemate in Boston, Glen Murray. Both could pick corners, and each had a deadly accurate shot. Cheechoo has a high, hard drive and because he is a little smaller, he can beat defensemen one-on-one with the puck. By the end of the 2005–06 season, Cheechoo had scored a league-leading 56 goals and Thornton led the NHL in points with 125. Those numbers were not the only amazing statistics for the Sharks. The San Jose club raised itself out of the depths to finish fifth in the Western Conference with 44 wins and 94 points. It was a season-long battle to get into the playoffs, but at the end of the year the Sharks were one of the hottest teams in hockey.

Cheechoo is solidly built and is very willing to check and go into the corners. He will sacrifice to battle in front of the net (which is now a little easier with the rules as they are now interpreted – a fact Cheechoo readily admitted was a huge part of his success in '05–'06) and he has

the quick hands to convert his opportunities. Now it is up to Cheechoo to become a consistent performer. But he has beaten long odds to get where he is – one of the best goal scorers in the NHL.

ICE CHIPS

Jonathan Cheechoo set a new team record for the San Jose Sharks with 56 goals in one season. The previous mark was held by Owen Nolan (44). Cheechoo scored 24 goals on the powerplay and he led the team with 11 game-winning markers in 2005–06.

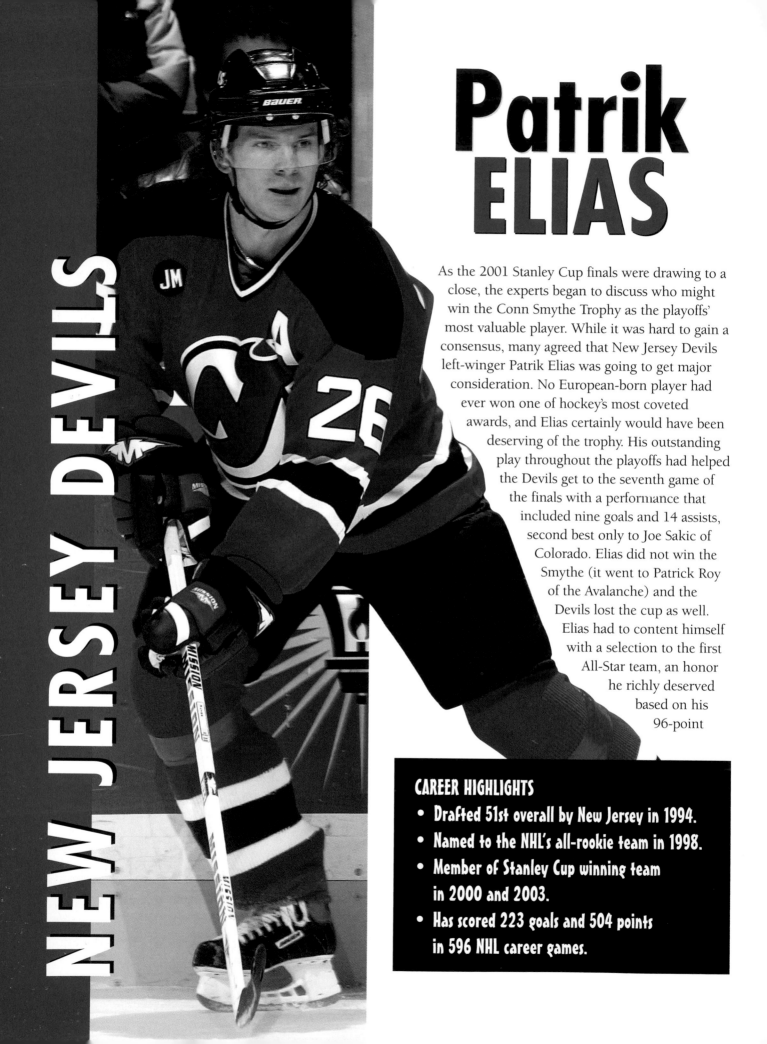

Patrik ELIAS

NEW JERSEY DEVILS

As the 2001 Stanley Cup finals were drawing to a close, the experts began to discuss who might win the Conn Smythe Trophy as the playoffs' most valuable player. While it was hard to gain a consensus, many agreed that New Jersey Devils left-winger Patrik Elias was going to get major consideration. No European-born player had ever won one of hockey's most coveted awards, and Elias certainly would have been deserving of the trophy. His outstanding play throughout the playoffs had helped the Devils get to the seventh game of the finals with a performance that included nine goals and 14 assists, second best only to Joe Sakic of Colorado. Elias did not win the Smythe (it went to Patrick Roy of the Avalanche) and the Devils lost the cup as well. Elias had to content himself with a selection to the first All-Star team, an honor he richly deserved based on his 96-point

CAREER HIGHLIGHTS
- Drafted 51st overall by New Jersey in 1994.
- Named to the NHL's all-rookie team in 1998.
- Member of Stanley Cup winning team in 2000 and 2003.
- Has scored 223 goals and 504 points in 596 NHL career games.

season (40 goals, 56 assists) that placed him third in NHL scoring, behind only Jagr and Sakic, during 2000–01.

There is certainly no reason to feel sorry about Elias missing out on a trophy, since he has had a very successful career to date, including being on a Stanley Cup winner with the Devils in 2000 in just his fourth year. He spent his first full year in the NHL in 1997–98 when he scored 18 goals and added 19 assists, earning all-rookie team honors. Elias produced a second good season in 1998–99 when he scored 17 times and upped his point total to 50. During the 1999–2000 campaign, he had 35 goals and 37 assists and then added 20 points in 23 post-season games, including a tie for the most assists (13) as the Devils won their second cup in team history. The speedy winger was selected by the Devils 51st overall in 1994 but played a little with Albany of the AHL, where the Devils have wisely decided to groom their best prospects for the pro game. Elias learned his lessons well by producing 27 goals and 36 assists for the River Rats in 1995–96. He split the next season with Albany (24 goals in 57 games) and New Jersey (two goals in 17 games) before sticking with the big team for good.

For two-and-a-half seasons Elias was on one of the top lines in the NHL, joining center Jason Arnott and right-winger Petr Sykora. The line was a perfect blend of size, skill, toughness and determination. But at the trade deadline in 2002, Arnott was traded to Dallas, and that summer, Sykora was dealt to Anaheim. The players they got in return – Jamie Langenbrunner, Joe Nieuwendyk, Jeff Friesen, Oleg Tverdovsky – helped reshape the Devils for 2002–03. New Jersey won the Stanley Cup and, for the fourth year in a row, Elias was their leading scorer. But his goal totals dropped to 28 and 29 as the Devils became more defense oriented. Elias developed his will to succeed in his native Czech Republic, where he waited until he was 14 years of age before getting his older brother's skates – the first pair he ever actually owned. His father, Zdenek, was a truck driver in the construction

industry; his mother, Zdena, had suffered a serious injury, ironically enough at a hockey rink where she worked. These circumstances made Elias appreciate his lot in life.

Elias is one of the top skaters in hockey and is a very creative player. He can do everything at top speed and can unleash a powerful shot. Elias is not big enough (six feet, 195 pounds) to be a power forward, but he will stick his nose in there to dig out a puck and can take the heavy slugging required to survive in the NHL as a goal scorer and playmaker. Many have tried to intimidate the Devils winger, but Elias will use his stick to gain himself some space. He played an integral part in the Devils' cup win in the 2003 play-offs, scoring five goals and adding eight assists.

Elias had a superb season in 2003–04 with 81 points (38 goals, 43 assists) in 81 games and spent the lockout year playing in the Czech Republic and Russia. It was there that Elias contracted hepatitis B, which kept him out of the 2005–06 Devils' lineup until early January. As soon as he was back playing, the Devils went out on a nine-game winning streak with Elias recording 16 points in 12 games. His performance led the Devils out of the doldrums and into the playoffs. The Devils knocked off the New York Rangers in the '06 playoffs, and Elias was superb throughout the series (recording six points in the opening contest, including five assists). A healthy Elias is obviously a very valuable player in the NHL.

Marian GABORIK

Whatever they're putting in the water in Trencin, they should export it to the rest of the hockey world. The Slovakian city produces some of the finest players ever to come out of Europe. Ziggy Palffy (now retired), Pavol Demitra, Miroslav Satan, Zdeno Chara, the Hossa brothers – all of them were raised in Trencin.

So was Marian Gaborik, who might turn out to be the best of all of them. In the middle of the 2002–03 season, when Gaborik was still two months shy of his 21st birthday, no less an authority than Mario Lemieux said that the 6'1" Minnesota Wild winger was already among the top five players in the NHL. He shoots hard, and often; he was the fastest skater in the super skills competition at the 2003 All-Star Game; and he can read a developing play like a book. And, unlike most young offensive stars, he understands defensive responsibility.

When the expansionist Wild made Gaborik their first-ever choice, and third overall, in the 2000 draft, their first in the NHL, they could not have imagined that he would make such an immediate impact. But they knew he was precocious. At the age of 16 he scored three goals in six games at the world under-18 championship, a tough tournament at which even 17-year-olds struggle to cope. The same year, he began

CAREER HIGHLIGHTS
- Drafted third overall by Minnesota in 2000.
- Has scored 30 or more goals three times in his career.
- Has recorded 65 or more points three times in his career.
- Has scored 134 goals and 274 points in 360 NHL games played.

playing in the Slovakian Elite League. And in his final season in the league, for most of which he was 17 years old, he scored 25 goals in 50 games.

Many teams had him pegged as a first-overall choice, but Rick DiPietro and Dany Heatley went ahead of him. The Wild hadn't even planned to start him off in the NHL, figuring he'd need a year in the minors to become familiar with the different rules and tighter ice surface of North American hockey. In fact, at the prospects' camp his first summer, he was so accustomed to having no center red line, he went offside on nearly every play.

The Wild also felt Gaborik would need to work on defense. But what the team, and everybody else, had not understood was what a quick study he is. By the end of his first training camp, he had adjusted to the new rules and rink dimensions, had overcome his distaste for North American food and had bought into coach Jacques Lemaire's stifling trap game. So he was never sent to the minor leagues.

From the first whistle, Gaborik began creating history. He scored the Wild's first preseason goal. He scored their first regular-season goal, in the team's first game, and was chosen the third star. He scored the first game-winning goal in franchise history. In just his third NHL game, he scored twice. He took a whopping 19 shots in his first five NHL games. On a young team that thought about defense long before offense, he finished with 18 goals and 18 assists in his rookie season.

Lemaire and general manager Doug Risebrough kept a careful watch on their franchise player and repeatedly deflected attention away from him. As a result, for more than a year Gaborik was one of the best-kept secrets in the NHL.

But the anonymity couldn't last, not the way Gaborik was playing. He nearly doubled his offensive output in his sophomore season, scoring 30 goals and notching 36 assists to again lead the Wild, who moved up to 73 points. When the NHL decided to crack down on neutral-zone interference for the 2002–03 season, many observers felt the Wild would suffer the most.

But Lemaire's trap was built on speed and discipline, not illegal moves, so Minnesota thrived under the new system and improved dramatically in their third season. By mid-December, the Wild were in first place and Gaborik led the NHL with 19 goals.

The expected slide came after Christmas, but Minnesota did make the playoffs and made it all the way to the Western Conference finals. Gaborik had another brilliant season, with 30 goals and 35 assists. He notched six points in an October game against Phoenix and, at 20, became the youngest player in 10 years to score a half-dozen points in one game.

A contract squabble and injuries have hampered Gaborik's development over the last two seasons. He scored only 18 times in 2003–04 but bounced back nicely in 2005–06 to lead the team with 38 goals (a franchise single season record) and recorded 66 points (his second best total to date). Lemaire believes Gaborik is learning to accept the ups and downs of pro hockey better as he matures but experts wonder if the winger might be better off playing for another coach, especially with the rule enforcement now prevalent in the NHL. The Wild recognized Gaborik's value to their team by signing him to a new three-year contract, thus avoiding losing him as a free agent.

ICE CHIPS

Marian Gaborik scored a goal in seven straight games between December 13, 2005, and January 3, 2006. He finished the 2005–06 season with 10 powerplay goals and seven game-winning tallies, but despite the impressive performance by Gaborik, the Wild still missed the playoffs for the second consecutive year.

PHILADELPHIA FLYERS

Simon GAGNE

For the two NHL seasons prior to the 2005–06 campaign, Simon Gagne had not produced to the level expected of him. In 2002–03 he had only nine goals and 27 points in an injury-shortened, 46-game season. He played 80 games in 2003–04 but scored only 24 times and totaled 45 points – good numbers for most players but not for the multi-talented Gagne, who should have been able to score 30 goals easily. He took the lockout year off completely and returned to find the new NHL very much to his liking – and potted a team-high 47 goals and 79 points (both career bests for Gagne). The swift left-winger was now exceeding expectations, and he had the good fortune to do it in a year when his contract was up for renewal.

Growing up in Ste-Foy, Quebec, allowed Gagne to play hockey at every turn. He was on skates at the age of two and was playing organized hockey by the time he was four. People marveled at his skating ability, much of it learned on the family's backyard rink.

Gagne was mentored through minor hockey by his father, Pierre. The senior Gagne was a good minor-pro player in Quebec as was his father, Roger, a terrific player in the American Hockey League during the 1940s. As a third generation hockey player in his family, Gagne had both the background and the desire to play pro hockey. He played in the prestigious Quebec Pee Wee tournament on two occasions, and his skills got noticed to the point where he was selected to play

CAREER HIGHLIGHTS
- Drafted 22nd overall by Philadelphia in 1998.
- Named to the NHL's all-rookie team in 2000.
- Selected for the Canadian Olympic team in 2002 and 2006.
- Has scored 136 goals and 324 points in 426 NHL career games.

ICE CHIPS

in the Quebec Major Junior Hockey League for the Beaufort club.

His last two years of junior saw Simon play for the Quebec Remparts, where he had a 30-goal, 69-point season in 1997–98. On the recommendation of former Flyer Simon Nolet (who was very familiar with the Gagne family), Philadelphia selected Gagne in the first round of the 1998 entry draft.

Simon went back for one more year of junior and notched 50 goals and 120 points to lead the league in scoring. He made the jump to the Flyers for the 1999–2000 season and made the all-rookie team with 20 goals and 46 points. He followed that up with 27 markers the next year, and then in 2001–02 was outstanding with 33 goals and 66 points. He was also thrilled to be selected for the Canadian squad for the '02 Olympics held in Salt Lake City, where he helped the team capture a gold medal for the first time in 50 years. Gagne had four points in six games during that tournament, and everyone remembers the front page newspaper photo of him and Martin Brodeur celebrating the end of the gold medal game. Gagne was actually

surprised to be selected for the team, but general manager Wayne Gretzky wanted him there.

Gagne is not a huge player (six feet, 190 pounds), nor is he overly aggressive (his highest penalty-minute total in one season is 38), but his skill level is very high. The puck always seems to follow him around and he is deadly in close. He can get a blast off quickly and is blessed with a wickedly accurate wrist shot. Gagne is especially good on the powerplay (12 goals with the extra man in 2005–06), where he has a little more room to maneuver. His skating is Gagne's best asset, allowing him to simply skate away from checkers, and few can pivot and turn like he does. He can control the puck, move at full speed and is a very willing passer of the puck.

Gagne's unselfish style of play had the Flyers contemplating giving him the team captaincy, but he felt a more senior player on the team deserved the honor, so he passed on it for the time being. However, it seems inevitable that he will one day wear the "C" for the Flyers.

Gagne needs to avoid the injury bug and improve a little on his playoff performances before he reaches his maximum potential.

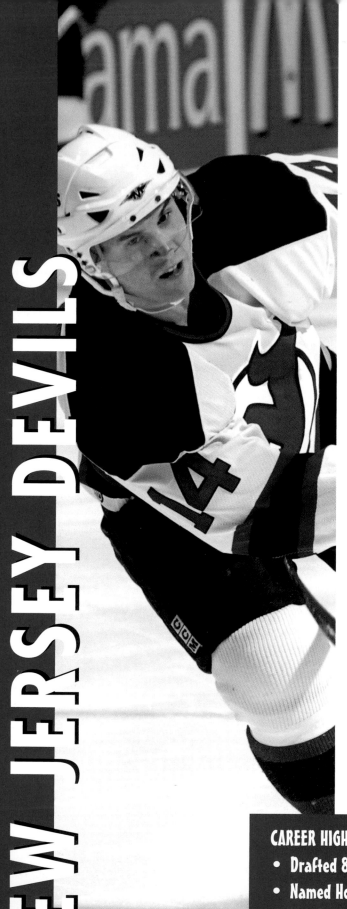

Brian GIONTA

The entire Gionta family of Rochester, New York, is small in stature: father Sam is just 5'4" and mother Penny barely hits the five-foot mark. Their children, three boys, Joe, Stephen and Brian, are all listed as 5'7" tall, but there is more than one way to measure a person, as the New Jersey Devils and the entire National Hockey League have found out. Brian Gionta has always heard that he is too small to be a professional hockey player and every year he has proven the skeptics wrong. Now that the NHL has changed the way the game is being played, it's Brian who is getting the last laugh.

Gionta never believed anything would come easy for him, but he was willing to work hard and he had confidence in his abilities. Growing up, he worked in his father's hardware store and learned to play hockey as well. He first played locally in Rochester and the 1994–95 season saw him score 52 goals in just 28 games. That performance got Gionta a place on the Niagara Scenics of the Metro Toronto Junior League, where he scored 57 goals and 127 points in 50 games, with 101 penalty minutes. Boston College recruited him and he played there for the next four seasons, helping his team make the Frozen Four each year he attended the school. In his last season, when he had 33 goals and 54 points in 43 games, he was named the Hockey East player of the year. He also got used to winning when Boston College won the NCAA championship in 2001.

The Devils were not quite sure how Gionta would

CAREER HIGHLIGHTS

- Drafted 82nd overall by New Jersey in 1989.
- Named Hockey East player of the year in 2001.
- Member of Stanley Cup winning team in 2003.
- Has scored 85 goals and 154 points in 348 NHL career games.

do at the NHL level, but they had done very well with U.S. college-trained players in the past, so they took the smallish star with the 82nd pick of the 1998 draft. They let him play out his college eligibility, and he turned professional for the 2001–02 season, which he split between New Jersey (11 points in 33 games) and Albany of the AHL (25 points in 37 games). He had big-league employment for the 2002–03 season, which saw him play 58 games for the Devils and record 25 points. Gionta played in 24 playoff games (recording one goal and nine points) and got his name on the Stanley Cup. He took the cup back home to the hardware store that summer and realized how lucky he was to have played on a championship team so early in his NHL career.

In 2003–04, Gionta broke the 20-goal barrier for the first time when he scored 21 in 75 games for New Jersey. He played just 15 games for Albany during the lockout year (he was still eligible to do so), but really started to excel during the 2005–06 season when the NHL reopened for business. Early in the year his performance allowed the Devils to hang around the playoff contenders

while they waited for star player Patrik Elias to return. Using his speed and agility to great effectiveness now that opposing players could no longer hold him up, Gionta led his team with 48 goals and 89 points. He was now able to do so much more, not having to worry about getting manhandled at every turn. Gionta may not be tall, but he has a stocky frame (175 pounds) and he is quite willing to throw himself into the high traffic areas if it means getting a goal. It seems like he can disappear for just a second, and when he reappears his arms are up signaling a goal. Gionta has learned how to gain proper body position, especially in front of the net, and if he keeps it up there is no telling how many goals he might be able to score in the revamped NHL.

Gionta's performance helped the Devils nail a playoff spot when it looked like they might miss for the first time in awhile. The team responded when general manager Lou Lamoriello took over behind the bench (greatly assisted by former Devils player John MacLean) and knocked off the rival New York Rangers in just five games.

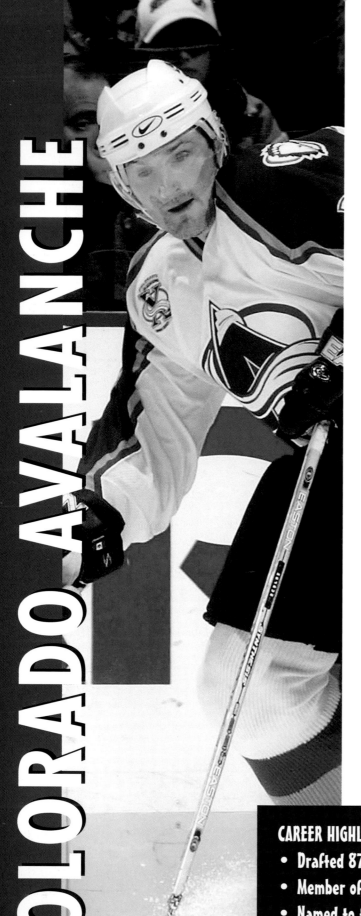

Milan HEJDUK

The success of the Stanley Cup winning teams that the Colorado Avalanche put together were rooted in the years preceding the team's move to the Denver area. As the Quebec Nordiques, the franchise made many great draft choices that would lead to two cups, in 1996 and 2001. A good drafting record allows you to make good trades (Adam Deadmarsh, Chris Drury and Owen Nolan are examples of this) and keep those who help your team win by staying with the organization. This includes quality players like Joe Sakic, Adam Foote and Milan Hejduk, who all played on the 2001 championship team.

The case of Hejduk is a particularly good example of how well the Avalanche scouts do their homework. Selected 87th overall in 1994, the right-winger has proven to be one of the best choices ever made by the franchise. In the 2001 playoffs, he finished tied for second among all scorers with 23 points (seven goals, 16 assists), putting him among the elite in the NHL.

He confirmed that status with a brilliant 2002–03 season. After missing 20 games with an abdominal injury in 2001–02, Hejduk stormed back to score 50 times and win the Maurice Richard Trophy (most goals). He finished fourth in NHL scoring with 98 points, was fourth in powerplay goals (8) and tied with linemate Peter Forsberg for the NHL's best plus-minus rating at a phenomenal plus 52.

Hejduk had been showing this potential for years.

CAREER HIGHLIGHTS
- Drafted 87th overall by Quebec in 1994.
- Member of Stanley Cup winning team in 2001.
- Named to the NHL second All-Star team in 2003.
- Has scored 221 goals and 474 points in 544 NHL career games.

COLORADO AVALANCHE

He came to North America from his native Czech Republic, where he had scored 53 goals in 99 games during his last two years while playing for HC Pardubice. He had a good background in sports, since both his parents were athletes – his father played hockey and his mother was a tennis player. He quickly showed a poise and maturity not seen in many young NHL players. Hejduk works very hard and one of his strengths is paying attention to detail, making him a defensively responsible player.

Not big at 5'11" and 185 pounds, Hejduk's strengths are his quick hands and his ability to finish off a nice play. Hejduk shows a willingness to go to the net and he is determined to score in spite of his smallish size. It always helps to be as speedy as Hejduk is, and his hockey sense takes him to all the right places on the ice. Off the ice, Hejduk had to make an effort to learn English but it has certainly paid off for the youngster.

Hejduk joined the Avalanche in 1998–99 and made a splash in his first NHL game by scoring a goal and an assist. He ended up with 14 goals and added 34 assists as a rookie. He was a finalist for the Calder Trophy, but that award went to teammate Chris Drury. Hejduk showed he could handle pressure, with 12 points in 16 playoff games, including three game-winners – of which two were in overtime! In his second season, Hejduk scored 36 times, leading the team, and raised his point total to 72. He had 13 powerplay markers and became a force to be reckoned with when the Avalanche had the extra man.

By his third season Hejduk was clearly feeling more comfortable, scoring 41 times and totaling 79 points in 80 games during the 2000–01 campaign. He was outstanding in the playoffs and scored a signature goal against Los Angeles when he broke in with Peter Forsberg on a two-on-one that he quickly converted into a shot past goaltender Felix Potvin. The Kings had been pressing, but Hejduk's goal quickly put an end to that.

Hejduk had another fine season in 2003–04 when he had 35 goals and 75 points in 82 games, and he spent a productive lockout year back home where he had 51 points in 48 games. He did not enjoy his best year when the NHL returned in 2005–06, missing eight games with an injury with his point total dropping to 58 (24 goals, 34 assists). Hejduk never really got untracked, although the Avalanche did make the playoffs and knocked off the Dallas Stars. His lightning-quick release and very high skill level should ensure that Hejduk will regain his goal scoring touch for the Avalanche, who will need his production to stay in playoff contention.

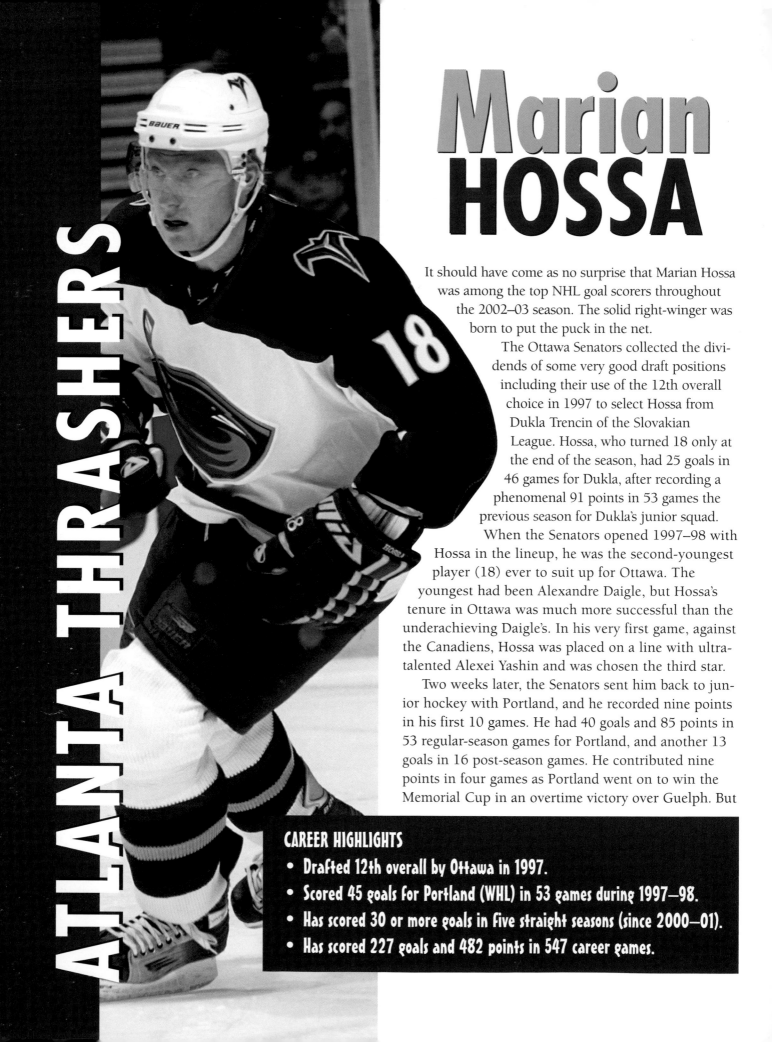

ATLANTA THRASHERS

Marian HOSSA

It should have come as no surprise that Marian Hossa was among the top NHL goal scorers throughout the 2002–03 season. The solid right-winger was born to put the puck in the net.

The Ottawa Senators collected the dividends of some very good draft positions including their use of the 12th overall choice in 1997 to select Hossa from Dukla Trencin of the Slovakian League. Hossa, who turned 18 only at the end of the season, had 25 goals in 46 games for Dukla, after recording a phenomenal 91 points in 53 games the previous season for Dukla's junior squad.

When the Senators opened 1997–98 with Hossa in the lineup, he was the second-youngest player (18) ever to suit up for Ottawa. The youngest had been Alexandre Daigle, but Hossa's tenure in Ottawa was much more successful than the underachieving Daigle's. In his very first game, against the Canadiens, Hossa was placed on a line with ultra-talented Alexei Yashin and was chosen the third star.

Two weeks later, the Senators sent him back to junior hockey with Portland, and he recorded nine points in his first 10 games. He had 40 goals and 85 points in 53 regular-season games for Portland, and another 13 goals in 16 post-season games. He contributed nine points in four games as Portland went on to win the Memorial Cup in an overtime victory over Guelph. But

CAREER HIGHLIGHTS
- Drafted 12th overall by Ottawa in 1997.
- Scored 45 goals for Portland (WHL) in 53 games during 1997–98.
- Has scored 30 or more goals in five straight seasons (since 2000–01).
- Has scored 227 goals and 482 points in 547 career games.

in the dying moments of regulation time in the finals, he tore ligaments in his left knee and was forced to have off-season surgery.

His knee operation and rehab kept him out of Ottawa's lineup until early December 1998. But in the remaining 60 games he served notice that he would be a force to be reckoned with. He scored 15 goals and 30 points, and, despite missing a quarter of the season, was named runner-up to Colorado's Chris Drury for the Calder Trophy.

As the injured knee strengthened, Hossa began to demonstrate his skating strength. Well-balanced, he is hard to knock off the puck. Ottawa's then-coach Jacques Martin compared his work along the boards to Peter Forsberg's. He has great hands and an excellent shot, and in his sophomore season he nearly doubled his goal total to 29, which tied for the Ottawa team lead. But in a game against Toronto late in the season, Hossa fired a shot at the net, and on the follow-through his stick caught Bryan Berard in the eye, virtually blinding the talented defenseman. The incident rattled Hossa and it stayed with him well after the season was over.

In 2000–01, Hossa jumped from being a good player into the NHL's upper ranks. Still only 21, he opened the season with a club-record nine-game point streak in which he rang up 13 points. He also had five assists in a game, set another club mark with two short-handed goals in one game against Florida, and was selected for the All-Star Game for the first time. He set career highs with 32 goals and 43 assists as the young Senators won their division and finished second overall in the NHL East.

But that excellent season was all but forgotten when the Senators were swept in the opening playoff round by Toronto, a team that had finished 19 points behind them. There was much finger-pointing about the Senators' lack of mental toughness in the post-season. And although most of the criticism went toward the invisible Yashin, it was noted that, as the Senators lost three straight years in the opening round, Hossa had managed only one goal in 14 games.

In 2001–02, Hossa's mercurial rise flattened out a bit, but he still scored 31 goals, recorded 66 points and showed a more aggressive streak with a career-high 50 penalty minutes. And he calmed concerns about his post-season production with five points in the opening round against Philadelphia and five more in a seven-game loss to Toronto.

Throughout the 2002–03 season, Hossa was locked in a tight battle for the Maurice Richard Trophy (for most NHL goals) with Markus Naslund, Todd Bertuzzi, Milan Hejduk and Glen Murray. When he was named to the All-Star Game in February, he led the league with 33 goals and had recorded two hat tricks and a four-goal game. He finally finished fourth with 45 goals, five behind leader Milan Hejduk. At just 24, he had developed into an NHL superstar.

Hossa had another good year in 2003–04 with 36 goals and 82 points and that helped earn him a lucrative new contract. However, the Senators had no intention of paying Hossa his rich three-year deal and promptly dealt him to Atlanta for Dany Heatley in late August. Although a little shocked at the turn of events, Hossa had his best year, recording a career-high 92 points (39 goals, 53 assists). Hossa was considered Atlanta's most consistent forward in 2005–06, but injuries hurt the Atlanta club and a late season run for the playoffs fell short. They may be a team to watch in the years to come with talented players like Hossa and Ilya Kovalchuk.

Jaromir JAGR

NEW YORK RANGERS

When Jaromir Jagr became eligible to be drafted into the NHL, nobody was sure if he was willing to leave his native Czechoslovakia. That may be why he lasted until the fifth pick overall in 1990. Penguins' general manager Craig Patrick took a bit of a gamble and selected the flashy winger, who would turn out to be the best player of the draft. New to North America and unable to speak English very well, Jagr was still able to score 27 goals and 30 assists as a rookie. In the playoffs, he added three goals and 13 points, helping the Penguins capture their first-ever Stanley Cup title. He followed that great start with a 69-point season (32 goals, 37 assists) in 1991–92, then had 24 points in 21 playoff games as the Penguins repeated as Stanley Cup champions. The team never reached such heights again, but Jagr went on to become the best player in hockey. That, however, didn't prevent the Penguins from having to trade him, for financial reasons, to the Washington Capitals in July 2001 in a horribly lopsided deal.

Jagr's game is built around his skating and tremen-

CAREER HIGHLIGHTS
- Drafted fifth overall by Pittsburgh in 1990.
- Member of two Stanley Cup winning teams.
- Has won the Art Ross Trophy five times.
- Has scored 591 goals and 1,431 points in 1,109 NHL career games.

dous physical strength. He can dominate by using his body to shake off any potential checkers, and his drive to the net is unparalleled today. He is well balanced on his skates, with moves that dazzle at full speed. He can do almost anything he wants on the ice and is not intimidated by anyone. Jagr's passing skills have become the equal of his scoring abilities, and his reading of the play is superb. When teamed with former Penguins superstar Mario Lemieux, the two were a joy to watch. They controlled the puck as if it were on a string between them, and there was almost nothing the other team could do about it. Many wondered whether Jagr would be the same when Lemieux retired, but there should have been no cause for concern.

Jagr was named captain of the Penguins in 1998 and became their undisputed leader on the ice. He has won the Art Ross Trophy five times (the last in the 2000–01 season, when he had 121 points) and has been a consistent member of the first All-Star team. At one point he was known as "Mario Jr." for his admiration of Mario Lemieux. Jagr had begun to tire of being the only star in Pittsburgh when his one-time friend and mentor came out of retirement to revive the team and its star captain. Jagr led the NHL in points, and the on-ice magic between the two was still quite evident. Off the ice was a different story; there were reports of a strained relationship between the two. Lemieux even challenged his former protégé to play better in the playoffs, a jibe that must have irked Jagr.

In the end it was money that drove the two apart. As owner of the team, Lemieux stated that he had to consider offers for Jagr because of his large contract. Jagr was traded, and his production slipped in Washington with seasons of 79 and 77 points – even with the addition of former Penguin teammate Robert Lang. Despite stretches of brilliance, Jagr was unable to lead the Capitals beyond the first round of the playoffs.

The Capitals felt Jagr was simply showing up and not giving his all. They decided to see if there was a taker for his huge contract and found the New York Rangers willing to do so, provided the Caps help pay for some of the money owed to Jagr. He went to the "Big Apple" in a deal that was completed in January 2003, and Jagr recorded 29 points in 31 games to close out the season. With the lockout looming, Jagr decided to play in the Czech Republic and Russia for the 2004–05 season, and that experience rejuvenated his love of hockey.

The Rangers went all-out to make Jagr comfortable and brought in many Czech-born players with NHL experience to aid their biggest star. They also added some younger players to their lineup, and Jagr responded with a great year by scoring 54 goals (second only to Jonathan Cheechoo) and totaled 122 points (second only to Joe Thornton). Given tremendous freedom by coach Tom Renney, Jagr did it all for the Rangers in every situation imaginable. Jagr does not really like to be coached, he just wants to get out there and go all-out. When he is determined, the large winger is virtually unstoppable and a threat to score on every shift. Only an injury in the playoffs against New Jersey brought his remarkable year to a premature end.

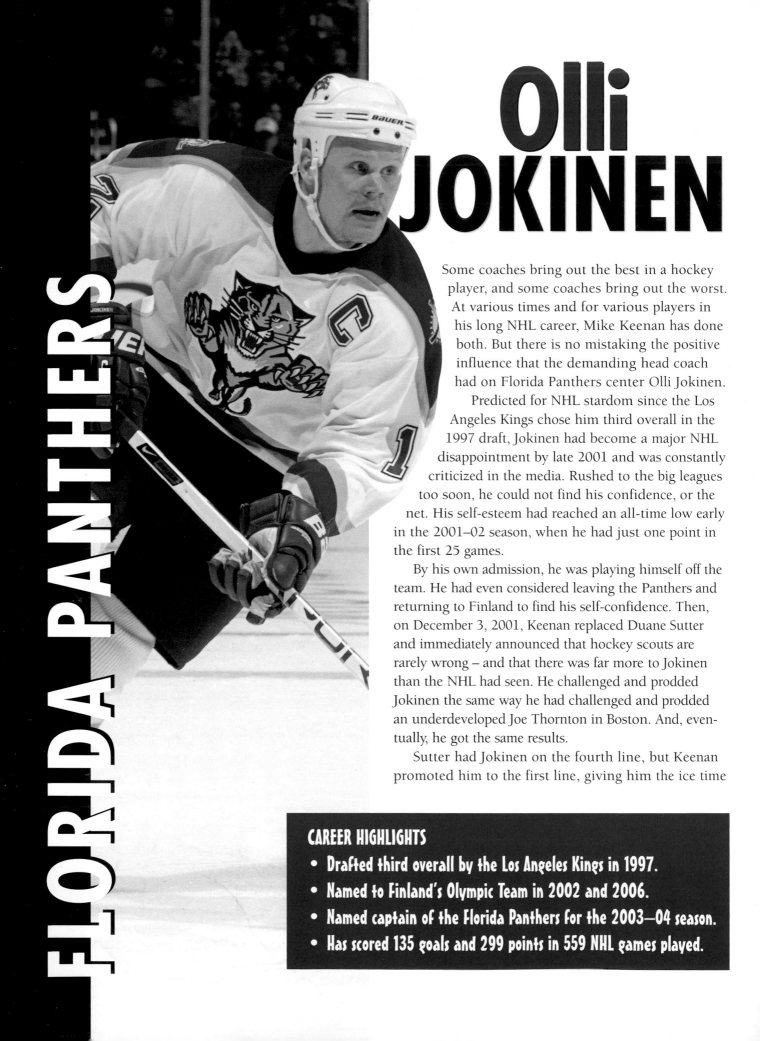

Olli JOKINEN

FLORIDA PANTHERS

Some coaches bring out the best in a hockey player, and some coaches bring out the worst. At various times and for various players in his long NHL career, Mike Keenan has done both. But there is no mistaking the positive influence that the demanding head coach had on Florida Panthers center Olli Jokinen. Predicted for NHL stardom since the Los Angeles Kings chose him third overall in the 1997 draft, Jokinen had become a major NHL disappointment by late 2001 and was constantly criticized in the media. Rushed to the big leagues too soon, he could not find his confidence, or the net. His self-esteem had reached an all-time low early in the 2001–02 season, when he had just one point in the first 25 games.

By his own admission, he was playing himself off the team. He had even considered leaving the Panthers and returning to Finland to find his self-confidence. Then, on December 3, 2001, Keenan replaced Duane Sutter and immediately announced that hockey scouts are rarely wrong – and that there was far more to Jokinen than the NHL had seen. He challenged and prodded Jokinen the same way he had challenged and prodded an underdeveloped Joe Thornton in Boston. And, eventually, he got the same results.

Sutter had Jokinen on the fourth line, but Keenan promoted him to the first line, giving him the ice time

CAREER HIGHLIGHTS
- Drafted third overall by the Los Angeles Kings in 1997.
- Named to Finland's Olympic Team in 2002 and 2006.
- Named captain of the Florida Panthers for the 2003–04 season.
- Has scored 135 goals and 299 points in 559 NHL games played.

that would either make him or break him. It made him. After recording just 35 goals and 87 points in 314 games over his first five NHL seasons, Jokinen scored 36 goals and notched 95 points in the 2002–03 season. He was named to the All-Star Game, which was held at the Panthers' home rink, and for much of the year he combined with Viktor Kozlov and Marcus Nilson to form one of the NHL's most dangerous forward lines (both those players are no longer with Florida).

This was the kind of season expected from Jokinen from the time he began playing in the Finnish Junior League at the age of 14. Less than a year after the Kings drafted him, he was in the NHL, playing in eight games at the end of the 1997–98 season. He registered nine goals the following season, a reasonable output for a 20-year-old making the adjustment to the North American pro game, but the Kings were desperate for more scoring and included him in a multiplayer trade to the New York Islanders for Ziggy Palffy and Bryan Smolinski. He spent just one year on Long Island, scoring 11 goals, but a large part of his job description with the Islanders was penalty killing.

Although he had great skating and stick skills, he was nowhere close to developing the scoring touch for which he had been drafted. Islanders' general manager Mike Milbury, who wanted to draft goalie Rick DiPietro, traded Jokinen and goalie Roberto Luongo to Florida for two players and the first choice in the 2000 draft. The Islanders did get DiPietro, but the Panthers ended up with their two key blocks for building strength down the middle. However, they didn't realize they had their No. 1 center until Keenan arrived.

In his first year in Florida, Jokinen scored only six goals and his self-belief continued to dive. Every time he'd have a bad game, it would affect him for the next five or six. Although he is 6'3", weighs 205 pounds and could play a physical game, Jokinen concedes that he wasn't mentally tough until he had to deal with Keenan every day. He responded well to Keenan's demands, and after playing well for Finland at the 2002 world championships he spent the off-season on

ICE CHIPS
Not only did Olli Jokinen lead the Florida Panthers in all the major scoring categories (51 assists as an example) in 2005–06, he also led the team with 14 powerplay goals and nine game-winning tallies.

a rigorous training program. He returned to Florida much stronger, particularly in the lower body, and previewed what was to come by scoring six goals in five pre-season games.

Keenan returned to Florida after some time away as the general manager of the team. The determined Keenan was intent on signing Jokinen to a new contract, and he was able to do so during the 2005–06 season, a year that saw the Panthers' captain score a career-best 38 goals and 89 points. Keeping Jokinen with the Panthers is a signal to the rest of the NHL that the Panthers are serious about contending with their young leader as the main forward. The Panthers had some terrible stretches during the '05–'06 campaign but their players (like Jay Bouwmeester and Nathan Horton) continued to develop. Post-season action for this group of talented performers should not be far off.

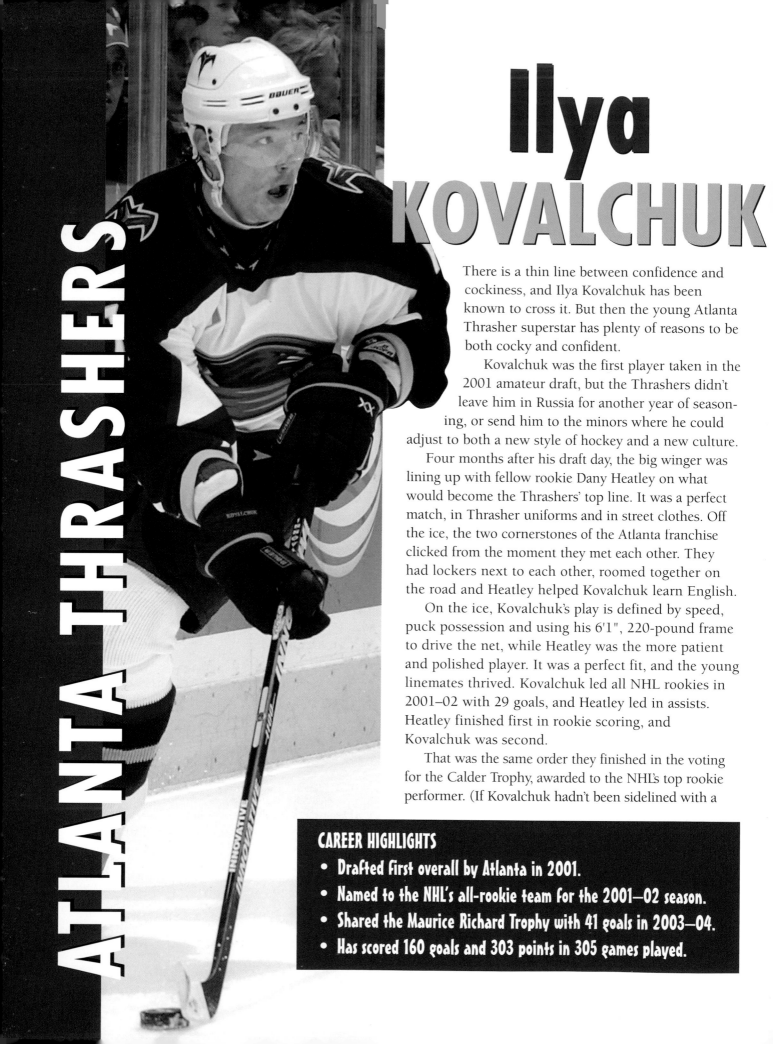

Ilya KOVALCHUK

ATLANTA THRASHERS

There is a thin line between confidence and cockiness, and Ilya Kovalchuk has been known to cross it. But then the young Atlanta Thrasher superstar has plenty of reasons to be both cocky and confident.

Kovalchuk was the first player taken in the 2001 amateur draft, but the Thrashers didn't leave him in Russia for another year of seasoning, or send him to the minors where he could adjust to both a new style of hockey and a new culture.

Four months after his draft day, the big winger was lining up with fellow rookie Dany Heatley on what would become the Thrashers' top line. It was a perfect match, in Thrasher uniforms and in street clothes. Off the ice, the two cornerstones of the Atlanta franchise clicked from the moment they met each other. They had lockers next to each other, roomed together on the road and Heatley helped Kovalchuk learn English.

On the ice, Kovalchuk's play is defined by speed, puck possession and using his 6'1", 220-pound frame to drive the net, while Heatley was the more patient and polished player. It was a perfect fit, and the young linemates thrived. Kovalchuk led all NHL rookies in 2001–02 with 29 goals, and Heatley led in assists. Heatley finished first in rookie scoring, and Kovalchuk was second.

That was the same order they finished in the voting for the Calder Trophy, awarded to the NHL's top rookie performer. (If Kovalchuk hadn't been sidelined with a

CAREER HIGHLIGHTS
- **Drafted first overall by Atlanta in 2001.**
- **Named to the NHL's all-rookie team for the 2001–02 season.**
- **Shared the Maurice Richard Trophy with 41 goals in 2003–04.**
- **Has scored 160 goals and 303 points in 305 games played.**

shoulder injury for the final 17 games, the Calder Trophy ballot could have resulted in a tie.) The last time two teammates had finished 1–2 in Calder Trophy voting was in 1976, when Bryan Trottier and Chico Resch did it for the Islanders. That duo went on to anchor an Islander dynasty, and Atlanta general manager Don Waddell was hoping for the same kind of progress from his two young wingers. The Thrashers didn't have much else to go along with their two rookies, however, and they finished 2001–02 with just 54 points. Kovalchuk and Heatley combined for a whopping 30 percent of the club's 187 goals.

Waddell and new coach Bob Hartley faced a challenge with Kovalchuk, though, because they wanted to increase his attention to defense while not cramping his spectacular offensive style. Early in the 2002–03 season, then-coach Curt Fraser benched him for a game in Toronto because he had the worst plus-minus record in the entire league. Near the end of the season Hartley, who took over in January, sat him down in the third period of another game. After both benchings, Kovalchuk's defensive play picked up for a couple of weeks. Waddell pointed out that, although Kovalchuk had played two NHL seasons, he was still only 19 years old. He also reminded critics that Kovalchuk had grown up in a Russian system, which was based on outscoring the opponent, not outdefending him.

That same system, the Thrashers say, also encouraged Kovalchuk's cockiness. North Americans had first seen a display at the 2001 world junior championship, when Kovalchuk scored an empty-net goal against Canada and skated down the ice pumping his fist. In a game against Edmonton in his rookie year, Kovalchuk was caught using an illegal stick. The Oilers didn't score on the powerplay, but Kovalchuk stormed out of the penalty box to take a pass with a stick he'd borrowed from a teammate, and scored the game-winning goal. He then enraged the Oilers by skating by their bench and pretending to check his stick for faults. There was a similar cocky incident against Florida in his sophomore season.

Kovalchuk is widely criticized for that kind of showing off, but he's also praised for his breathtaking

offensive plays. He was the talk of the 2002 All-Star Game weekend when he scored six goals in the young stars game.

He spent his first NHL off-season at home in Russia, adding extra muscle to improve his already hard shot and to withstand what was sure to be heavier checking in his sophomore season.

Kovalchuk not only avoided the sophomore jinx, he also improved his numbers by scoring 38 goals and adding 29 assists. He was still pretty bad on defense (a putrid minus 24) but for a team that had little going for it, the bad numbers can be overlooked. The next season, 2003–04, saw Kovalchuk score a league-best 41 goals (tied with Jarome Iginla and Rick Nash), which got him a share of the Maurice Richard Trophy. Still the Thrashers missed the post-season and then started the 2005–06 season without Heatley, who was traded to Ottawa after missing most of the previous year after a car accident. Kovalchuk was now being counted on more than ever, and he responded with a career-best 98 points (52 goals and 46 assists) and was a respectable defensive player. The new style of play suited him perfectly and he will undoubtedly take his team to the playoffs soon.

Vincent LECAVALIER

TAMPA BAY LIGHTNING

Talk about being under pressure! Try putting yourself in the shoes of young Vincent Lecavalier on draft day. Your hopes of becoming an NHL player are about to be fulfilled, and being selected first overall only adds to one of the greatest days of your life. Then, just before your name is about to be announced, the team owner announces you are going to be "the Michael Jordan of hockey"! Tampa Bay owner A.E. Williams made that rather audacious claim and then selected Lecavalier for his Lightning team, which was floundering badly.

Five years later, Williams was gone from the hockey scene and Lecavalier finally started to establish himself as an elite NHL player after struggling to find his niche. Eventually the entire Lightning team followed his lead and became Stanley Cup champions in 2004.

Lecavalier was groomed to be an NHLer by his father, Yvon, a firefighter and one-time junior player in his native Quebec. Well-learned lessons got Lecavalier playing against nine-year-old boys when he was just four.

CAREER HIGHLIGHTS
- Drafted first overall by Tampa Bay in 1998.
- Member of Stanley Cup winning team in 2004.
- Has scored 30 or more goals in three consecutive seasons.
- Has scored 181 goals and 402 points in 547 NHL career games.

Eventually, Lecavalier went to the famed Notre Dame prep school in Wilcox, Saskatchewan, for further development (52 goals and 104 points in 22 games during 1995–96), and then to Rimouski of the Quebec Major Junior Hockey League for two seasons of junior hockey (scoring 86 times and totaling 218 points) before becoming the top pick in the NHL entry draft in 1998. No matter where Lecavalier played, he knew he had to be a leader, and going to Tampa Bay was no different. So it was no shock when he was made captain of the team at 19 years, 11 months of age.

Lecavalier has shown the skill, talent and maturity that made him worthy of a first-overall selection. As a rookie in 1998–99, he scored 13 goals and recorded 28 points in 82 games. It was not a great start, but his second season quickly turned into a top performance with 25 goals and 67 points. His third year brought him back down to earth a little – with a drop in goals to 23 and points to 51. He was even benched for a time by new coach John Tortorella, but it was all part of the development process for the slick center. Tortorella also removed the "C" from Lecavalier's sweater and demoted him to assistant captain, mainly to take some pressure off the franchise cornerstone.

Lecavalier is a quiet leader, but his talent speaks volumes. With his outstanding puckhandling skills, Lecavalier will try to make moves on the ice that were once reserved for the likes of Wayne Gretzky or Mario Lemieux. He shows a good burst of speed and can make his move with the puck very quickly. Lecavalier takes great pride in his play and wants badly to excel. He certainly did that in 2002–03, when the Lightning jumped off to a quick start. A team that had made the

ICE CHIPS

Prior to the start of the 2005–06 season, Vincent Lecavalier re-signed with the Tampa Bay Lightning, giving up his first chance at free agency in one year's time. The Lightning wanted to get their key players from the Cup team signed to new deals and also signed forward Martin St. Louis, but were unable to keep goaltender Nikolai Khabibulin (who signed with Chicago). Lecavalier scored 35 goals (a career best) and totaled 75 points in the '05–'06 campaign.

playoffs only once in its history won the southeast division for the first time. Lecavalier had by far the best season of his career with 33 goals and 78 points. The Lightning lost in the second round to New Jersey in '03, but it appeared the Tampa Bay club was on its way to playoff glory.

Lecavalier was nearly dealt to Toronto, but incoming general manager Jay Feaster would have none of it and urged the trade to be vetoed. The slick center scored 32 goals and added 34 assists during the 2003–04 campaign and was outstanding in the playoffs. In 23 playoff games, Lecavcalier scored nine goals and totaled 16 points as the Lightning knocked off Philadelphia and Calgary in the last two rounds of the post-season to take home their first Cup. Lecavalier was so determined to succeed that he fought the very tough Jarome Iginla during the grueling seven-game final. It brought a new measure of respect for the Lightning star.

The 2005–06 season was not nearly so kind to the Tampa Bay club, which was quickly knocked out of the playoffs by a more talented Ottawa Senators squad in a short, five-game series. Once again Lecavalier gave his best (including a scrap with Senators giant defender Zdeno Chara) in the playoffs, but the Lightning clearly were lacking in the goaltending department.

Markus NASLUND

VANCOUVER CANUCKS

Craig Patrick was general manager of the Pittsburgh Penguins from 1989 to 2006. During that time, Patrick made many personnel moves – some good (he won two Stanley Cups with the Penguins) and some bad. All managers make mistakes and Patrick made a glaring one when he dealt Markus Naslund away. In 2002–03, Naslund became one of the NHL's premier players, leading the league in powerplay and game-winning goals and finishing second in goals (48) and scoring (104 points). He was also a finalist for the Hart Trophy as league MVP and won the Lester B. Pearson Award (players' choice as most outstanding player).

The right-winger was originally drafted by the Penguins in 1991 when they selected Naslund 16th overall at the entry draft. The Penguins noticed the 5'11", 195-pound Naslund after a good season with the MoDo junior team in Sweden in 1989–90, when he scored 43 goals and 78 points. It's too bad for them they did not give him more of a chance to find his game at the NHL level.

Naslund split his first two years (1993–95) in North America between Pittsburgh of the NHL and Cleveland of the IHL, although he mostly played with the Penguins. His production was fairly low, with only six goals in 85 games for

CAREER HIGHLIGHTS
- Drafted 16th overall by Pittsburgh in 1991.
- Named to the NHL's First All-Star team twice (2002, 2003).
- Named winner of the Lester B. Pearson Award in 2003.
- Has scored 322 goals and recorded 708 points in 871 NHL career games.

Pittsburgh, but he came to life in 1995–96 with 19 goals and 52 points in 66 games before he was inexplicably traded to the Vancouver Canucks for Alex Stojanov, also a former first-round selection in 1991 (seventh overall). Known more for his toughness, Stojanov was supposed to give the Penguins a missing element, but he made no impact in the NHL. On the other hand, Naslund has flourished in Vancouver. (In fairness to Patrick, Naslund did not mind being traded.)

As soon as Naslund arrived in Vancouver, his production started to increase. He scored 21 goals in 1996–97 and followed that up with seasons of 14, 36, 27, 41, 40 and, in 2002–03, 48. While not overly physical, Naslund has learned to use his shot effectively, and his soft hands allow him to hit the back of the net with regularity. He is strong on his skates and is so confident in handling the puck that he toys with many opposing defensemen. Naslund has developed a consistency that makes him a threat on a shift-to-shift basis. It has also helped that coach Marc Crawford has shown so much confidence in his star player.

The Canucks were facing a bit of a dilemma when Mark Messier was bought out of his contract option. When he was on the team, Messier (who played on a line with Naslund) was the natural choice to be captain. But now a decision had to be made as to who would take over the captaincy of the young team. Canucks management saw an emerging star in Naslund and designated him team leader for the 2000–01 season. It was a wise decision and Naslund responded with a great year and a trip to the NHL All-Star Game as well. The captain's role seemed to suit Naslund just fine, and the team made it to the playoffs for three straight years, after missing the post-season in all three of Messier's years on the west coast.

Naslund, Todd Bertuzzi and center Brendan Morrison were the NHL's best line in 2002–03 as the Canucks challenged for the Western Conference lead all season before finishing fourth. The unit combined for 272 points and was critical to the Canucks' superb powerplay, which was quarterbacked by their talented captain. It seemed like the Stanley Cup was well within the grasp of the Canucks.

However, the 2003–04 season ended badly when Naslund's close friend Todd Bertuzzi conducted a revenge attack on Colorado's Steve Moore and was promptly suspended, missing the playoffs. Calgary beat Vancouver in seven games and the disappointment around the Canucks was strong. Naslund returned for the 2005–06 season (signing a new contract in the process) and scored a team-best 32 goals and 79 points. But it was a bad year in Vancouver (Naslund was a poor minus 19 and the big line was broken up during the season) as the team missed the playoffs and Crawford was fired at the end of the season. The team hopes to regroup under new coach Alain Vigneault and hopefully enjoy a more injury-free season in 2006–07.

ICE CHIPS

Markus Naslund was named captain of the Vancouver Canucks in 2000 and has always been a rather quiet leader who leads by example. Recognizing that this might have to change for the good of the team, Naslund has offered to give up the coveted "C" at the end of the 2005–06 season if management thinks this would be best for the Canucks.

Alexander OVECHKIN

Rookie Alexander Ovechkin scored 51 goals for the Washington Capitals, but none was more spectacular than his tally against the Phoenix Coyotes on January 16, 2006. As he drove to the Coyotes' net with his usual gusto, Ovechkin was taken down and briefly lost control of the puck as he hit the ice. He did not lose sight of it, however, swinging his stick over his head and sweeping the puck into the net as he finished his sprawl on the ice. It became the goal of the year – merely one of many memorable efforts by the young Russian. Soon many were calling Ovechkin not only the best rookie but perhaps also the best player in the entire NHL. The 20-year-old sensation may not have achieved the latter distinction, but it might be only a matter of time.

Ovechkin is a right-hand-shooting left-winger who has blazing speed and an offensive flair rarely seen among players who love to tangle with defensemen. The 6'2", 215-pound Ovechkin would just as soon go through a defender than around him, and he can do either with great dexterity. He plays hard all the time and likes to get every ounce of his talent out on display. He also seems to find great joy in just playing the game and has a personality to go with that attitude. Most Russian-born players are rather reserved and tend to shy away from the media, especially in their early years in the league. But there seemed to be no interview that Ovechkin minded doing, and he usually had a big smile on his face. He came to North America to prove he was one of the best players in the world (Ovechkin

CAREER HIGHLIGHTS
- Drafted first overall by Washington in 2004.
- Scored 52 goals as rookie in the NHL.
- Winner of the Calder Trophy as the best rookie in 2005–06.
- Has scored 52 goals and 106 points in 81 NHL career games.

could easily have stayed at home and earned more than the roughly $984,000 allowed to NHL rookies), and he was going to relish every moment.

The ultra-talented Ovechkin may have inherited his mother Tatiana's athletic genes. She won two gold medals as an Olympic basketball player (in 1976 and 1980) for what was then the Soviet Union. But it wasn't all easy for Ovechkin, who, when he was just 10 years old, lost his older brother, Sergei, in a car accident. It was Sergei who had encouraged his younger sibling to go back to playing hockey, and every so often the pangs of loss would hit Alexander. But he has another brother, Mikhail, living with him in Washington (an area Ovechkin has come to really enjoy), and that has helped with the adjustment to North American life. In Russia he once predicted that he would score 50 goals in one season, but the most he ever scored there in one year was 20 (a combined total in 2001–02, when he played for two different teams in different Russian leagues). Ovechkin did, however, score 52 in his first year in the best league in the world, potting two in his very first NHL game against Columbus. Perhaps his prediction had been just a little off!

ICE CHIPS

When Alexander Ovechkin scored 52 times in 2005–06, he became just the fourth player in NHL history to score 50 or more goals in his rookie year. The others were Teemu Selanne (76 in 1992–93), Mike Bossy (53 in 1977–78) and Joe Nieuwendyk (51 in 1987–88).

What was most notable about Ovechkin's goal-scoring in the 2005–06 season was the variety of ways he could pot a goal. He could score on a breakaway, a tip-in near the crease or a rebound, snapping a shot with great velocity or simply picking a corner the goalie was giving him. He scored 21 goals on the powerplay – three markers while his team was short-handed – and five of his tallies were game-winners. He also found time to chip in with 54 assists to total 106 points. In short, he did it all without a great deal of help. The Capitals were not a very good team in 2005–06, winning just 29 games and finishing ahead of only the

Pittsburgh Penguins in the Eastern Conference. They were, however, a very hard-working club under coach Glen Hanlon and focused on using young players. They were not a pushover by any means, and conference rivals like Toronto and Atlanta felt the sting of losing games to the Caps that may have kept them from a playoff spot.

With Ovechkin clearly establishing himself as a superstar (he was named to the first All-Star team in 2006), the Washington club will be a force to be reckoned with for many years to come.

TAMPA BAY LIGHTNING

Martin ST. LOUIS

Long before the National Hockey League made life easier for smaller players, 5'9", 185-pound Martin St. Louis had learned to survive in a tough sport. He has always had people tell him he was far too little to play in the world's fastest league. St. Louis did not let all the negativity get to him, and turned it into a motivational tool to prove his detractors wrong. It was a long journey for St. Louis, but at the end of the 2003–04 season he was named the most valuable player in the league – an incredible feat given that he was never drafted by an NHL club!

The native of Laval, Quebec, was a good goal scorer and point producer in his development years in his home province, but St. Louis decided to try the U.S. college route and attended the University of Vermont for four years. On three occasions he was named as a finalist for the Hobey Baker Award (given to the NCAA's best hockey player), but he never won the trophy. In 1995–96, St. Louis had 29 goals and 85 points for

CAREER HIGHLIGHTS
- Signed as a free agent by Tampa Bay in 2000.
- Winner of the Art Ross Trophy in 2004 with 94 points.
- Winner of the Hart Trophy in 2004.
- Has scored 140 goals and 320 points in 444 NHL career games.

the Vermont club in just 35 games for his best college season. But no NHL club was willing to spend even a late-round draft choice on him. When he left Vermont, he had no immediate NHL option to pursue, so he signed to play in the International Hockey League and showed he could play pro hockey, with 50 points in just 56 games.

His performance with Cleveland of the IHL caught the attention of the Calgary Flames, who signed the diminutive right-winger as a free agent and assigned him to their farm team in Saint John, New Brunswick. St. Louis played in the AHL, getting 58 goals and 114 points in 95 games over three seasons, but he did not impress the Flames enough when he played 69 games in the NHL over the same time frame. They decided to let him go, making St. Louis a free agent once again. Discouraged, but not willing to quit by any means, he signed a contract with the Tampa Bay Lightning, who were hoping they might have found a diamond in the rough. Little did they know they had found a big piece of a larger puzzle that would one day land them the Stanley Cup.

Given the opportunity to play regularly, St. Louis started out with modest numbers in his first two years playing for the Florida club, but in 2002–03 he broke through with a 70-point season (33 goals, 37 assists) in 82 games. His play earned him a spot in the mid-season All-Star game, letting him realize for the first time that he was now considered among the best players in the NHL. The 2003–04 season was a dream season for St. Louis, who won the Art Ross Trophy as the league's leading scorer with 94 points (38 goals, 56 assists). His great play also got him the Hart Trophy and, perhaps more importantly, the Lester B. Pearson Award, which is voted on by all the players in the NHL. St.Louis was now recognized by his peers as the best player in the league, making his journey to the top all the sweeter.

Tampa Bay went on to win their first Stanley Cup with a seventh-game win over the Calgary Flames in the final. St. Louis had 23 points (including a playoff-leading 15 assists) in 24 games, which got him noticed by the Team Canada managers. He played for his country in the 2004 World Cup tournament and,

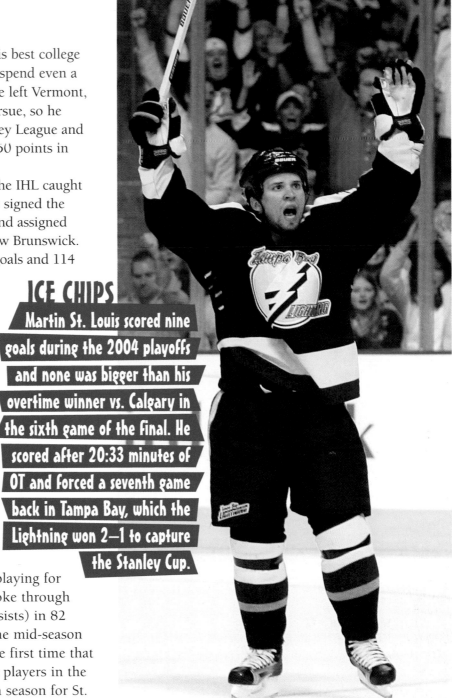

ICE CHIPS
Martin St. Louis scored nine goals during the 2004 playoffs and none was bigger than his overtime winner vs. Calgary in the sixth game of the Final. He scored after 20:33 minutes of OT and forced a seventh game back in Tampa Bay, which the Lightning won 2–1 to capture the Stanley Cup.

with four points, helped the Canadian side win the gold medal. The young man with the big heart has accomplished just about everything a hockey player can ever dream of and is an inspiration to all those who might hear the words "you are too small to play." (St. Louis also uses one of the longest sticks in the NHL for a player of his height!)

St. Louis and the rest of the Lightning had great difficulty defending their championship in the 2005–06 season, but he scored 31 goals and totaled 61 points in 80 games. Signed to a long-term deal, St. Louis figures in the Tampa Bay plans for the foreseeable future.

Teemu SELANNE

ANAHEIM DUCKS

If there is anything that defines Teemu Selanne as a hockey player, it would have to be his skating ability. Nobody in the NHL skates better than Selanne, and no player can start from a still position the way the Ducks' right-winger can. Selanne can blow by a defenseman with ridiculous ease, then unleash a deadly accurate shot that often results in a goal. He is difficult to stop because he has a big, strong body that he is very willing to use, especially when he smells a scoring opportunity. Selanne's arrival in the NHL was much anticipated, and the man known as the "Finnish Flash" did not disappoint when he joined the Winnipeg Jets in 1992–93.

Selanne was selected by the Jets 10th overall in the 1988 draft, but had a difficult time coming to contract terms with Winnipeg. The Calgary Flames jumped into the fray and offered a deal they hoped the Jets would not match. But Winnipeg general manager Mike Smith – one of the first NHL executives to realize the true value of European players' skills – knew he had drafted a gem. He was not about to let Selanne go to a division rival, or any other team for that matter.

Thus Selanne began his career in Manitoba, and he came out of the gate flying. He finished with NHL rookie

CAREER HIGHLIGHTS
- Drafted 10th overall by Winnipeg in 1988.
- Named winner of the Calder Trophy in 1993.
- Has scored 40 or more goals in a season six times.
- Has scored 492 goals and 1,041 points in 959 NHL career games.

records of 76 goals (smashing the previous first-year mark held by Mike Bossy) and 132 points. Selanne had always been a top scorer in his native Finland (four seasons of 30 or more goals), but nobody expected him to score at such a high rate in the much tougher NHL. His 76 tallies would normally lead the NHL, but that year Alex Mogilny of the Sabres had his great season and matched Selanne's mark.

The fast winger was looking to do more of the same in his second season with the Jets. He had 25 goals in 51 games when a skate sliced his Achilles tendon, and he was through for the year. The lockout-shortened season of 1994–95 saw Selanne showing he had recovered from serious injury, with 22 goals in 45 contests. The following year a trade was arranged between Winnipeg and the Anaheim Ducks. The deal (which happened after 51 games in 1995–96 and with Selanne having scored 24 goals) came about because the Jets were justifiably worried about the contract demands their star athlete would soon insist upon.

Selanne thrived when he was paired with the equally exciting Paul Kariya in Anaheim. He put together seasons of 51 and 52 goals in his first two years with the Ducks. In 1998–99, Selanne did not score 50, but he came very close, with 47 goals and 107 points (both team-high marks).

Eventually, the Ducks decided to trade Selanne to San Jose late in the 2000–01 season for a younger player in Jeff Friesen. Selanne was becoming less of a scorer, averaging only 30 goals a year, but at the same time he was becoming a better defensive player. With a thumb injury restricting him to just 54 points (29 goals) in 2001–02, he still helped the Sharks to their sixth straight season of improved point totals, and an appearance in the second-round of the playoffs. But San Jose had a disastrous 2002–03, firing the coach and GM and missing the playoffs. Selanne passed on his option for 2003–04, but his 28-goal, 64-point performance was still

good enough to land him a contract with the Colorado Avalanche for the 2003–04 season.

Even with Kariya at his side, things did not go very well in Colorado, which turned out to be a one-season experiment. Selanne took the lockout year off and had his knee repaired with surgery. He returned to Anaheim, and the Ducks were thrilled to see the Selanne of old with a 40-goal, 90-point season. He kept up his good play in the playoffs when the Anaheim club knocked off Calgary and Colorado. Selanne re-signed with Anaheim for the 2006–07 season.

ICE CHIPS
Teemu Selanne was the first-ever winner of the Maurice "Rocket" Richard Trophy when he led the NHL with 47 goals in 1998–99. Selanne has scored 50 or more goals in one season three times in his career. He won the Masterton Trophy in 2006.

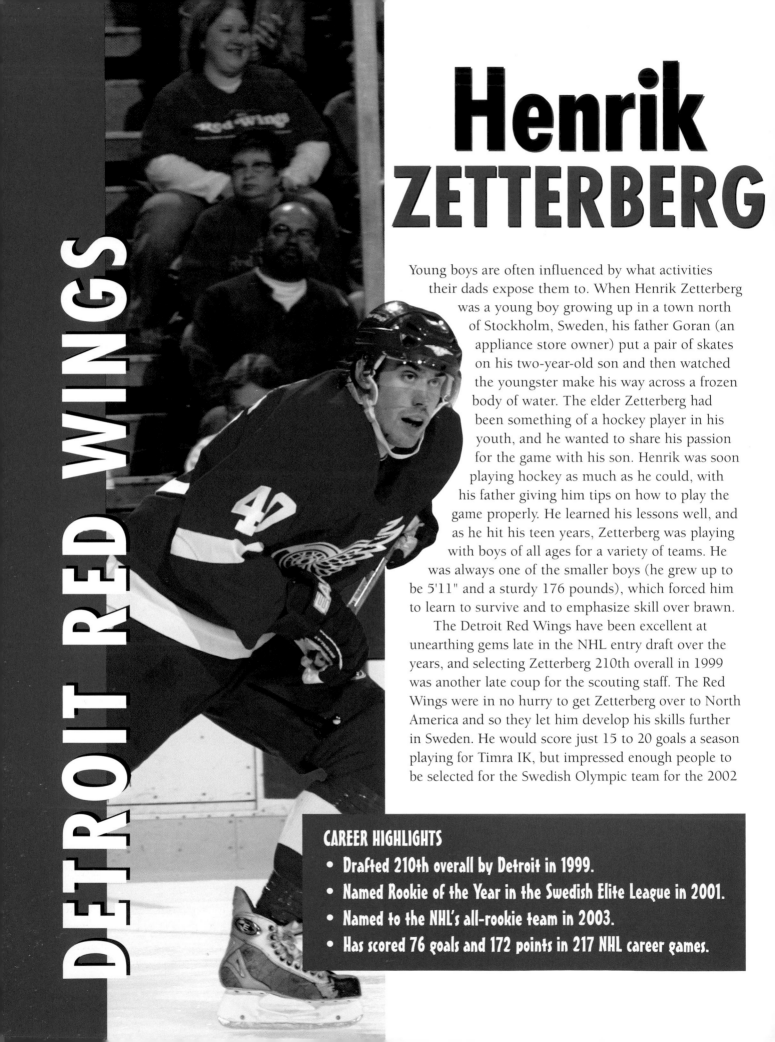

Henrik ZETTERBERG

DETROIT RED WINGS

Young boys are often influenced by what activities their dads expose them to. When Henrik Zetterberg was a young boy growing up in a town north of Stockholm, Sweden, his father Goran (an appliance store owner) put a pair of skates on his two-year-old son and then watched the youngster make his way across a frozen body of water. The elder Zetterberg had been something of a hockey player in his youth, and he wanted to share his passion for the game with his son. Henrik was soon playing hockey as much as he could, with his father giving him tips on how to play the game properly. He learned his lessons well, and as he hit his teen years, Zetterberg was playing with boys of all ages for a variety of teams. He was always one of the smaller boys (he grew up to be 5'11" and a sturdy 176 pounds), which forced him to learn to survive and to emphasize skill over brawn.

The Detroit Red Wings have been excellent at unearthing gems late in the NHL entry draft over the years, and selecting Zetterberg 210th overall in 1999 was another late coup for the scouting staff. The Red Wings were in no hurry to get Zetterberg over to North America and so they let him develop his skills further in Sweden. He would score just 15 to 20 goals a season playing for Timra IK, but impressed enough people to be selected for the Swedish Olympic team for the 2002

CAREER HIGHLIGHTS
- Drafted 210th overall by Detroit in 1999.
- Named Rookie of the Year in the Swedish Elite League in 2001.
- Named to the NHL's all-rookie team in 2003.
- Has scored 76 goals and 172 points in 217 NHL career games.

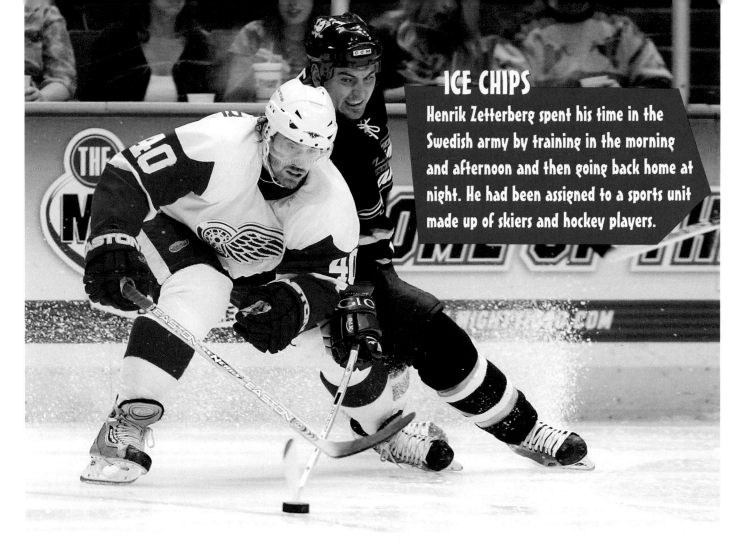

games. He enjoyed the experience (especially a 5–2 win over Canada in the preliminary round) and felt that he was now ready to play in the NHL.

Zetterberg joined the Red Wings for his first training camp in September 2002 and was quickly tested by the veteran players and the coaches. The defending Stanley Cup champions wanted to see if he was worthy of making their roster. He passed one test by taking all the physical punishment thrown at him and got to play in 79 games as a rookie in 2002–03, scoring 22 goals and adding 22 assists. He was indeed ready for the NHL.

Zetterberg's goal total dropped to 15 the next season in Detroit, but he did have six more assists than the previous year. He spent the lockout year playing in Sweden (recording 50 points in 50 games), and made loud noises about not returning to the NHL if he did not get the contract he wanted from the Red Wings. Detroit general manager Ken Holland handled the situation very adroitly, and soon Zetterberg was back in the fold for the 2005–06 season. He blossomed as a goal scorer with a team best 39 goals and a career high 85 points. The Red Wings had the best record in the NHL with 58 wins and 124 points, and Zetterberg dazzled

with his great stickhandling and picture goals. He was very prominent on the powerplay (17 goals with the extra man) and on the penalty-killing unit because he showed a devotion to playing an all-around game (he was a plus 29 for the season). The new style of NHL suited Zetterberg perfectly, and he should be able to produce better numbers in the future.

As the older Red Wings start to decline and retire, the Detroit club will count on the likes of Zetterberg, Pavel Datsyuk and Niklas Kronwall to lead the team in the future. Zetterberg has all the skills to be a great NHL player. He plays well in both ends of the rink, and he can make defensemen look silly with his shifty moves. Zetterberg docs not play an aggressive game, but he will protect the puck and he can take a hit to make something happen. His good shot should net Zetterberg between 30 and 40 goals a year. His playoff performance in the '06 playoffs (a bitter disappointment for the Red Wings, who lost to Edmonton in the first round – although Zetterberg had six goals) shows that he understands when he needs to shine the most. He was also a big part of Sweden's 2006 Olympic gold medal team with six points (three goals, three assists) in eight games.

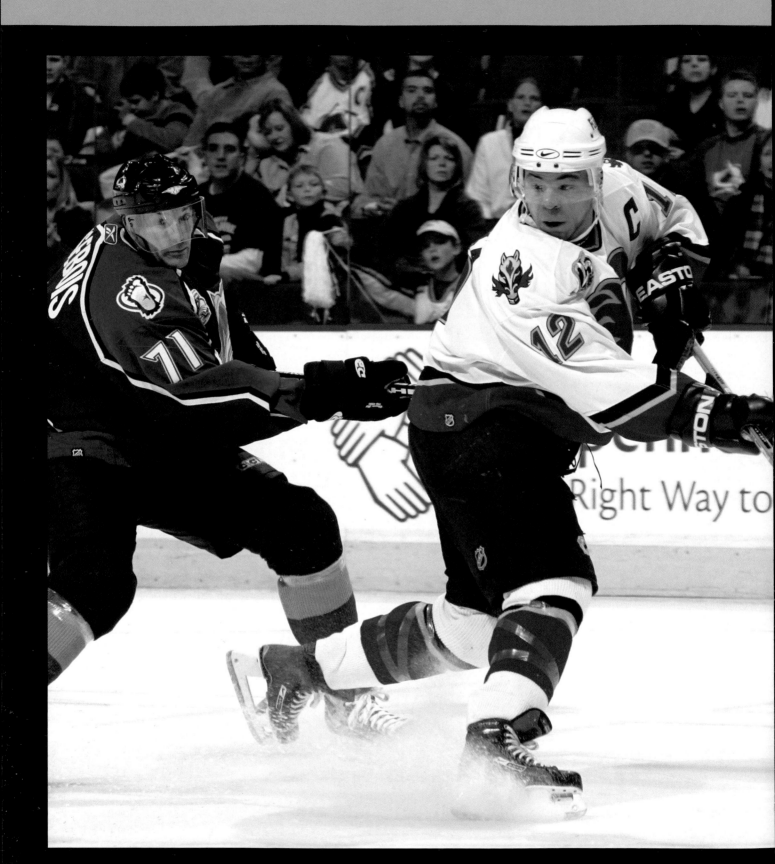

HIT MEN!

Physical players who hit, fight and score — always on the edge of the rulebook.

Shane DOAN

PHOENIX COYOTES

When one considers Shane Doan's family history, it's little wonder that the bruising right-winger is involved in professional sports. His sister Leighann did well in track and field and went on to play pro basketball in Europe, while many of the men in Doan's family excelled in rodeo. Even Doan's cousin got in on the act – his wife is Catriona LeMay Doan, the well-known Canadian speed skater. Shane's father Bernie was drafted 80th overall by the St. Louis Blues in 1971 (although he never played in the NHL) and played minor pro hockey (with Toledo in the old International Hockey League) for a while before deciding to take his life in another direction and raise a family. Shane was born in Halkirk, Alberta, and grew up on a ranch where he learned to ride horses and help move cattle. In addition, young Shane found lots of time for hockey and he learned his lessons well.

Doan was a junior star with the Kamloops Blazers of the Western Hockey League and he was named MVP of the 1995 Memorial Cup tournament (the Blazers won),

CAREER HIGHLIGHTS

- Drafted seventh overall by the Winnipeg Jets in 1995.
- Named MVP of the Memorial Cup Tournament in 1995.
- Named captain of the Coyotes for the 2003–04 season.
- Has scored 172 goals and 417 points in 730 career games.

finishing a great season that saw him score 37 goals and 57 assists. Drafted into the NHL by the Winnipeg Jets in 1995, who selected him seventh overall, he moved up to play for the Jets in their last season in Winnipeg (before the team moved to Phoenix), scoring seven goals and adding 10 assists. His play over the next few seasons was not especially distinguished, but he was learning the pro game at the NHL level. His lack of production got him sent to Springfield in the American Hockey League for half of the 1997–98 season, but he quickly proved he did not belong there by scoring 21 goals in just 39 games. The following year saw him get just six goals for the Phoenix Coyotes, and many wondered if Doan would ever find the range in the big league.

The 1999–2000 season proved to be a turning point for Doan, who broke through for a 26-goal season. He followed that up with 26-, 20-, 21- and 27-goal seasons, establishing himself as a consistent two-way performer. Doan's strength is his ability to be fast and physical, especially as he bears down on the opposing defensemen. His sculpted physique (listed at 6'2", 216 pounds) allows him to be a hard bodychecker and gives him the confidence to play with a little bit of an edge. Doan keeps his mean streak under control, but it can be roused in cer-

Shane Doan played very well for Team Canada during the 2004 World Cup tournament and scored the game-winning goal in the gold-medal game against Finland. During the 2005–06 season Doan scored 17 of his 30 goals on the powerplay.

tain circumstances, and he is very willing to stand up for a teammate. He can forecheck smartly, and when he is able to pry the puck loose he knows what to do with it. Doan is able to unleash a good wrist shot or a hard slapper if need be and does not just focus on checking alone anymore. His game has rounded into shape nicely and he has improved each and every year. The rest of the NHL took notice of the new Doan during the 2003–04 season when he had 68 points (41 assists to go along with his 27 goals) and played in the All-Star Game. His performance that year earned him an invitation to join Team Canada for the 2004 World Cup of hockey, where the Canadian squad won the title.

The Coyotes noticed the development in Doan's all-round game and named him captain of a very young team for the start of the 2003–04 season. Doan turned in another good season during the 2005–06 campaign, when he scored a career-high 30 goals (tied for team lead with Mike Comrie) and totaled 66 points. He also led the team with 123 penalty minutes, but the Coyotes missed the playoffs again. Coach Wayne Gretzky was pleased with his captain's play, but the lack of playoff experience is holding back the development of some very good younger players. Doan has played in only 32 playoff games to date and that number has to increase if he is going to be considered a truly elite player.

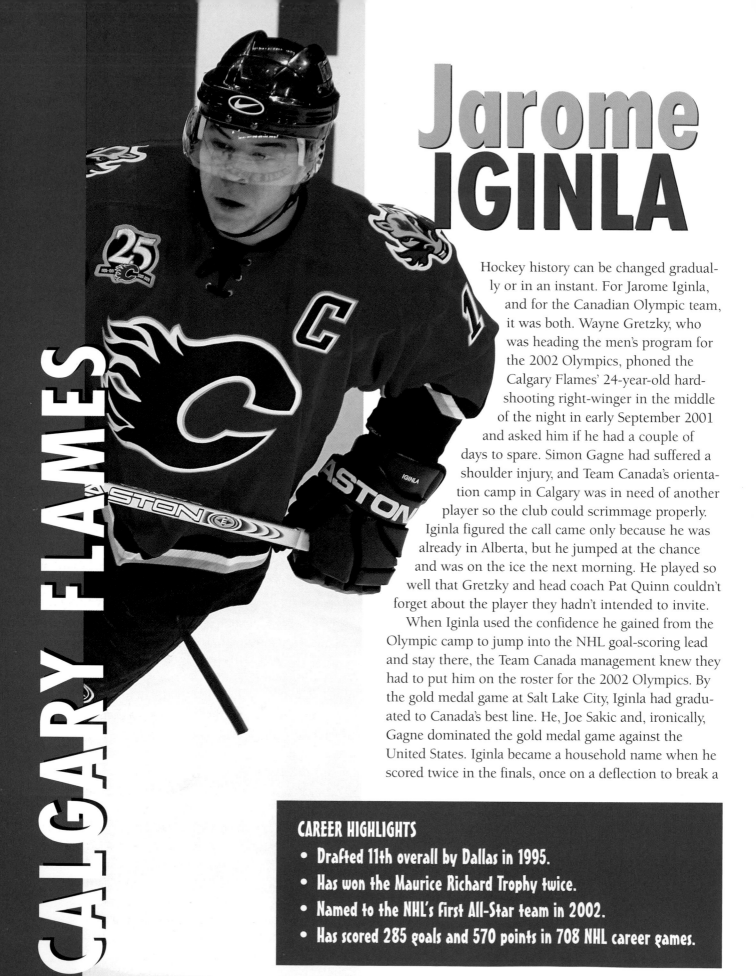

Jarome IGINLA

CALGARY FLAMES

Hockey history can be changed gradually or in an instant. For Jarome Iginla, and for the Canadian Olympic team, it was both. Wayne Gretzky, who was heading the men's program for the 2002 Olympics, phoned the Calgary Flames' 24-year-old hard-shooting right-winger in the middle of the night in early September 2001 and asked him if he had a couple of days to spare. Simon Gagne had suffered a shoulder injury, and Team Canada's orientation camp in Calgary was in need of another player so the club could scrimmage properly. Iginla figured the call came only because he was already in Alberta, but he jumped at the chance and was on the ice the next morning. He played so well that Gretzky and head coach Pat Quinn couldn't forget about the player they hadn't intended to invite.

When Iginla used the confidence he gained from the Olympic camp to jump into the NHL goal-scoring lead and stay there, the Team Canada management knew they had to put him on the roster for the 2002 Olympics. By the gold medal game at Salt Lake City, Iginla had graduated to Canada's best line. He, Joe Sakic and, ironically, Gagne dominated the gold medal game against the United States. Iginla became a household name when he scored twice in the finals, once on a deflection to break a

CAREER HIGHLIGHTS
- Drafted 11th overall by Dallas in 1995.
- Has won the Maurice Richard Trophy twice.
- Named to the NHL's First All-Star team in 2002.
- Has scored 285 goals and 570 points in 708 NHL career games.

1–1 tie and then on a hard shot to give Canada an insurmountable 4–2 lead.

Canada's first Olympic men's hockey gold in 50 years gave him further confidence, and he returned to the Flames to become the NHL's only 50-goal scorer in 2001–02.

The career year was a huge leap from 2000–01, when Iginla scored 31 goals, the first time he'd reached 30 in his five NHL seasons. But he'd been steadily improving his play since he joined the Flames for the 1996–97 season.

He had led the Kamloops Blazers to back-to-back Memorial cups and was named most outstanding forward when Canada won the 1996 world junior championship, just two weeks after he was traded to Calgary. As an NHL rookie in 1996–97, he had 21 goals and 29 assists and helped Canada to the world championship at the end of the season. He dipped to just 13 goals as a sophomore, but gradually increased his output to 28, 29 and 31 over the next three years.

In Calgary's first 52 games of the 2002–03 season, Iginla managed a disappointing 15 goals, but he confidently told everyone he would finish strongly in the final 30 games. He was true to his word, scoring 19 goals in the next 20 games, and ended up with 35. The '02–'03 season saw Darryl Sutter take over as coach of the Flames during the year, and he had his club ready to go for the 2003–04 campaign. Sutter named Iginla team captain and he responded to the challenge, pleasing a new coach with a share of the league lead in goals when he scored 41 times while totaling 73 points in 81 games. Iginla was outstanding in the '04 playoffs when he led his team to the Stanley Cup finals, scoring

ICE CHIPS

When the Calgary Flames signed Jarome Iginla to a new three-year, $21 million contract, it proved to many that the new salary-capped NHL was indeed going to work well for those clubs dubbed "small market." The Flames simply had to keep their best player and top ambassador for the organization. He is the only Calgary player to ever win the Lester B. Pearson Award (in 2002).

13 times and ringing up 22 points in 26 games. In the playoffs Iginla showed he could score, set up plays, hit and fight if necessary. He fought tough Derian Hatcher in the second round of the post-season, making a statement that the Flames were not going to be intimidated by the high-flying Red Wings. The Flames won that series and then beat San Jose to advance to the final for the first time since 1989, and then lost a tough contest to Tampa Bay in the seventh game of the final.

There was great expectation placed on Iginla's shoulders for the 2005–06 season, but he had trouble getting going after not playing any hockey during the lockout. He recovered nicely to score 35 times (17 on the power-play) and lead the team with 67 points, but it was clear he missed not having Craig Conroy as his center. The Flames had a terrific season with 103 points, but were dispatched by Anaheim in the first round of the playoffs. The Flames need to support Iginla with more players who can produce offensively, and that will be a challenge for Sutter. There is no question that Iginla is now the face of the Calgary Flames.

TORONTO MAPLE LEAFS

Michael PECA

Michael Peca is one of the softest-spoken and most articulate NHL players; he is also among the most tenacious two-way performers in the league. And he drives a hard bargain at contract time. After six seasons with the Sabres, most of them as their undisputed leader, Peca sat out the entire 2000–01 season rather than buckle under to what he considered an unfair offer from Buffalo management. Realizing he might sit out yet another season to prove his point, the Sabres had to trade him to the New York Islanders (for Tim Connolly and Taylor Pyatt) in June 2001. It took the Sabres a while to recover from the trade (although they were much happier about it after the 2005–06 season), which saw them lose their captain.

It wasn't the first time an NHL club had regretted trading Peca away. The Vancouver Canucks had him in the lineup for less than half a season before they swapped him to Buffalo in July 1995 for disenchanted superstar Alexander Mogilny, whom they wanted to put together with Pavel Bure. Four years later, the Canucks had played only one playoff round while the defensive-minded Sabres, led by the marvelous checking of Peca, had been to the Eastern Conference finals twice and the Stanley Cup finals once.

Along the way, Peca was always assigned to the opposition's top center and was well known for handing out stiff checks. At times he crossed the line and hit

CAREER HIGHLIGHTS
- Drafted 40th overall by Vancouver in 1992.
- Has captained the Buffalo Sabres and the NY Islanders.
- Named winner of the Frank Selke Trophy in 1997 and 2002.
- Has scored 160 goals and 394 points in 693 NHL career games.

opponents high, but generally the hits were clean and thunderous. The Canucks had a preview of this trait when, as a rookie, Peca broke the unwritten code that says that no superstar will be checked with force. Peca knocked superstar Teemu Selanne, then with the Winnipeg Jets, out of a game with a clean hit. The Jets were enraged and got into several brawls with the Canucks. But Peca had established his presence.

A native of Toronto, Peca played junior hockey in two other Canadian cities. He began in Sudbury during 1990–91, and recorded 41 points in 62 games. The next season was spent in Sudbury and Ottawa, where he combined for 75 points (including 24 goals). He was drafted by the Canucks 40th overall in June 1992. He spent most of the next two seasons with Ottawa and totaled 215 points over that period.

The 1994–95 season saw Peca start the year in the American Hockey League with the Canucks' farm team in Syracuse, scoring 34 points in 35 games. When the NHL started its season after a labor dispute, Peca was called up and got into 30 games, registering six goals and six assists. Then the Buffalo Sabres put Mogilny, a one-time 76-goal scorer, on the trading block. All the Sabres asked for was the unproven Peca, young defenseman Mike Wilson and a number one draft choice (who turned out to be Jay McKee). The Canucks could hardly believe their luck at the time and jumped at the chance to make the deal.

With the Sabres, Peca got plenty of ice time and, in his first complete NHL season, he produced 31 points in 68 games. In 1996–97, Peca became a better player and upped his point total to 49 (including 20 goals). His checking game was so good that he was named the winner of the Selke Trophy as the league's top defensive forward. The Sabres gave Peca the job of shadowing the best player on the other team. And not only would he shut down the opponent, but the centerman would often score a key goal himself.

When Peca joined the Islanders, he decided he wanted to contribute more offensively than he did during his time with the Sabres. He was made captain and, despite missing an entire year of competition, turned in a career high of 60 points in 2001–02 and won his second Selke Trophy. Under his leadership, the Islanders finished second in the Atlantic division and made the playoffs for the first time in eight years. But in the fifth game of a bitter, physical first-round series with the Toronto Maple Leafs, Peca took a straight-on hit from Darcy Tucker,

ICE CHIPS

Michael Peca is the type of player who can be an offensive threat while killing a penalty. He has scored 25 short-handed goals in his career.

which the Islanders claimed was a low blow. Peca missed the final two games with knee and shoulder injuries, and the Islanders lost in seven games.

After off-season surgeries, Peca was expected to be out of the lineup until at least Christmas of the 2002–03 season, but he returned in mid-November. By then, the Isles were floundering at 5-10-1. When Peca came back into the fold, they went on a 19-10-4-2 run and made the playoffs, causing coach Peter Laviolette to suggest his captain was an MVP candidate. Despite missing 16 games, overcoming two serious injuries and constantly drawing checking assignments, Peca finished with 42 points.

Peca struggled in his last two years as an Islander and was dealt to Edmonton prior to the 2005–06 season. He played poorly during the regular season (only nine goals and 23 points) but regained his confidence for the playoffs, scoring key goals and helping the Oilers get past Detroit, San Jose and Anaheim. Peca will try to stay on the upswing with the Maple Leafs in 2006–07.

Robyn REGEHR

CALGARY FLAMES

Robyn Regehr has developed into one of Canada's premier defensemen, a hard hitter who makes opponents think twice before venturing onto his side of the ice. But Robyn Regehr almost did not make it to the National Hockey League at all.

On July 4, 1999, just a few months after his junior career ended, Regehr's entire career could have ended. An oncoming vehicle crossed over to his side of the road and smashed head-on into his Chevy Nova. Two people in the other car were killed, and Regehr broke the tibias in both his legs. With his hockey future in serious jeopardy, he put himself through such intensive rehabilitation that only a few months after the accident he had recovered enough to join the Calgary Flames' AHL farm team in Saint John, New Brunswick. And by late October, after only five games there, he was back in the NHL to stay.

Regehr is the only player in the NHL who was born in Brazil. His parents were Mennonite missionaries, and he lived in Brazil and Indonesia until the family moved to Rothern, Saskatchewan, when he was 11. A strong work ethic, physical presence

CAREER HIGHLIGHTS
- Drafted 19th overall by Colorado in 1998.
- Named to the WHL West First All-Star team in 1999.
- Member of gold medal-winning team with Canada in 2004 World Cup tournament.
- Has scored 18 goals and 80 points in 431 NHL career games.

ICE CHIPS

On December 29, 2005, Robyn Regehr was able to attend a family reunion right on home ice. His younger brother Richie, a Flames prospect, was called up from Omaha for the siblings' first NHL game together. Richie got an assist on the game-winning goal.

and decent skating skills made Regehr a sought-after property among junior scouts, and after playing junior A for Prince Albert, he made the major junior Kamloops Blazers, arriving in the fall of 1996 – just after future teammate Jarome Iginla had left for the pros.

Regehr was drafted by the Colorado Avalanche in 1998, after his second year of junior hockey. The Avalanche had stockpiled draft picks and although he was taken in the third round (19th overall), he was Colorado's third choice in that draft. All that extra young talent made for attractive trade packages, and in February 1999 Regehr was swapped to Calgary with Rene Corbet, Wade Belak and two draft choices for Theoren Fleury and Chris Dingman. Five months later, he was involved in the horrible car crash. But the same work ethic that characterizes his on-ice play helped Regehr overcome his injuries more quickly than anyone predicted. By the first anniversary of the crash, he had played 57 games for the Flames.

Regehr scored his first NHL goal in his second week in the league, against San Jose's Mike Vernon, and totaled five goals (the most he scored until his sixth season). He was the Flames' nominee for the Masterton Trophy, the youngest nominee in the history of the award, recognizing his perseverance and dedication to hockey.

In Regehr's sophomore season (2001–02), he finished fourth on the team in penalty minutes, second in hits and first in blocked shots. Although the Flames were in the midst of a seven-year stretch out of the playoffs, Regehr was gaining notice and in his third season he played in the Young Stars game during the NHL All-Star weekend. On March 18, 2003, he scored what is referred to as a "Gordie Howe Hat Trick," recording a goal, an assist and a fight against Los Angeles.

Regehr, and his Flames, really came into prominence in the magical year of 2003–04, when Calgary went to the seventh game of the Stanley Cup final before losing to Tampa Bay. It was the team's first appearance in the playoffs since 1996, and Regehr made the most of the exposure, finishing third in scoring among defensemen, with nine post-season points. He got the underdog Flames heading in the right direction by scoring their first playoff goal in eight years, against Detroit, and he scored into an empty net for the clinching goal of the Western Conference final. Flames coach Darryl Sutter showed his confidence in Regehr by making him an assistant captain early in the season, and the defenseman went on to record career highs in assists (14), points (18) and games played (82) and was a plus 14 for the first time in his career.

His post-season play got him onto Canada's gold-medal World Cup team that fall, before the NHL shut down for a year. Regehr did not play during the lockout season, and a sprained knee kept him out of 14 games early in the 2005–06 season. But he increased his points total to a career-high 26, and was chosen for Canada's Olympic team.

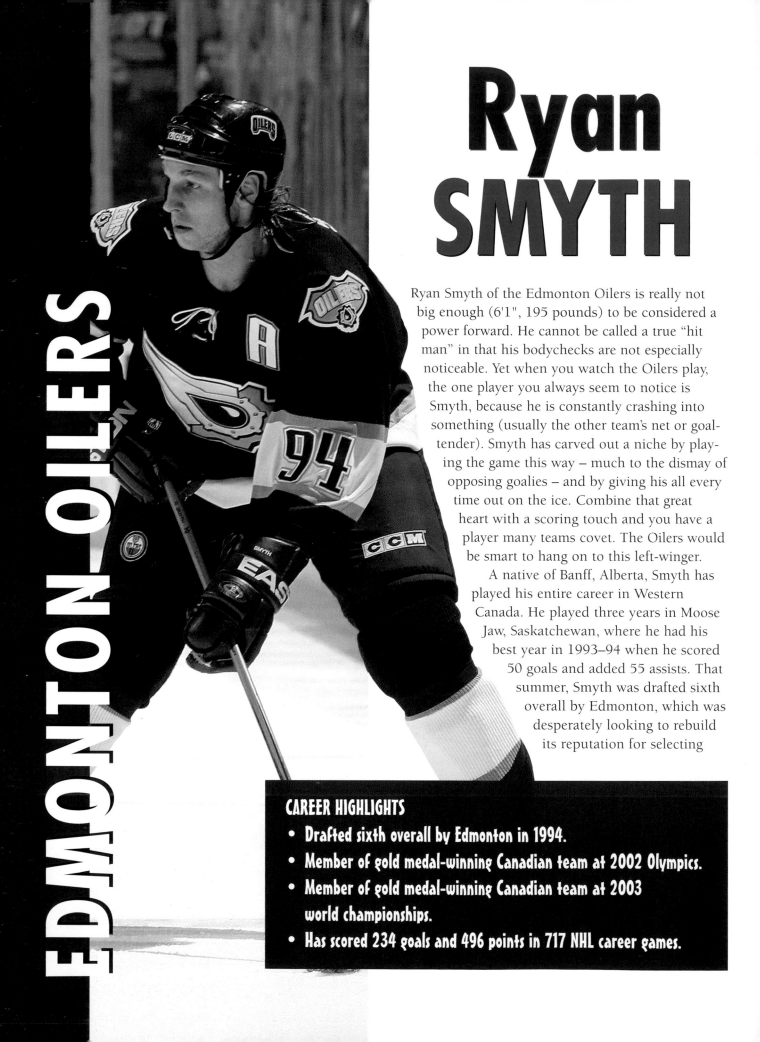

Ryan SMYTH

EDMONTON OILERS

Ryan Smyth of the Edmonton Oilers is really not big enough (6'1", 195 pounds) to be considered a power forward. He cannot be called a true "hit man" in that his bodychecks are not especially noticeable. Yet when you watch the Oilers play, the one player you always seem to notice is Smyth, because he is constantly crashing into something (usually the other team's net or goaltender). Smyth has carved out a niche by playing the game this way – much to the dismay of opposing goalies – and by giving his all every time out on the ice. Combine that great heart with a scoring touch and you have a player many teams covet. The Oilers would be smart to hang on to this left-winger.

A native of Banff, Alberta, Smyth has played his entire career in Western Canada. He played three years in Moose Jaw, Saskatchewan, where he had his best year in 1993–94 when he scored 50 goals and added 55 assists. That summer, Smyth was drafted sixth overall by Edmonton, which was desperately looking to rebuild its reputation for selecting

CAREER HIGHLIGHTS
- Drafted sixth overall by Edmonton in 1994.
- Member of gold medal-winning Canadian team at 2002 Olympics.
- Member of gold medal-winning Canadian team at 2003 world championships.
- Has scored 234 goals and 496 points in 717 NHL career games.

askew. Smyth is no fighter, but he will battle very hard along the boards for the puck and for every inch of ice. He will irritate goalies to distraction with his willingness to charge the net and often gets netminders to take penalties on him. He gets into trouble only when he plays too recklessly, and it often looks like he will kill himself out on the ice one day.

Smyth's bull-in-a-china-shop approach works well for him because of his soft hands in close. That's why he has scored over 30 goals three times in his career and why he might have more high-scoring seasons in the future. Smyth scored a typical goal during the 2001 playoffs in the series against Dallas, when he poked in a loose puck while down on the ice fighting off a defenseman and the goalie, Ed Belfour!

Being teamed with center Doug Weight worked well for Smyth. The two developed a certain chemistry that was unmistakable. During the 1999–2000 season, Smyth bounced back with a 28-goal effort and followed that up with a 31-goal season in 2000–01.

ICE CHIPS

Ryan Smyth was at his best on the powerplay during the 2005–06 season, scoring a team-high 19 goals with the extra man. He now has 103 career powerplay goals.

young talent. Previous Oiler drafts had produced precious little to sustain a team that enjoyed a dynasty in the 1980s.

Smyth finally changed the draft woes of the Oilers, but not until the 1996–97 season, when he scored 39 times and totaled 61 points in 82 games, his first full year in the NHL. He was motoring along the next season with 20 goals in 65 contests, but then suffered a serious knee injury that put an end to his year and cast doubts on his career. Smyth did return to play in 71 games in 1998–99, but scored only 13 goals and did not look to be the same player.

The Oilers wanted the young star to return to form because his style of play is so infectious. Smyth is fearless and his reckless approach is something Edmonton fans have not seen since kamikaze winger Glenn Anderson played in the glory days of the club. Smyth plays a confident game when he is on, and usually his helmet is flying off in every direction with his hair

But Weight was traded, for financial reasons, to St. Louis in July 2001, and Smyth became the team veteran. In 2001–02 he missed 21 games with an ankle injury and scored only 15 times. He returned in time to win an Olympic gold with Team Canada. He missed another 16 games in 2002–03 but contributed 27 goals, 61 points and solid leadership as the Oilers got back into the playoffs after a year on the outside. The Oilers have built up a very promising squad.

The Oilers kept drafting and adding young players through trades over the years, and it all paid off during the 2005–06 season when good veterans were added to the team. Smyth scored a career-best 36 goals and played his usual robust game in front of the net. The Oilers were back in the playoffs and upset Detroit, San Jose and Anaheim before losing to Carolina in seven games. Smyth took a puck to the face but kept playing – a typical performance by one of the grittiest players in the NHL.

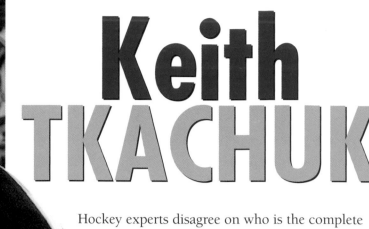

Keith TKACHUK

Hockey experts disagree on who is the complete hockey player, but one player who gets a lot of consideration is Keith Tkachuk of the St. Louis Blues. One of the few genuine power forwards in the NHL, Tkachuk's hero as he was growing up was retired Boston winger Cam Neely. Neely is an excellent role model for the Blues' power forward, and Tkachuk plays a very similar game. Talented and tough, Tkachuk can beat you with a goal or a great hit.

The rangy winger gets his hard-nosed work ethic from his Boston-area roots (he was actually born in Melrose, Massachusetts, and attended Boston University for a year). His working-class upbringing has given him a strong determination to succeed, a quality that's made Tkachuk one player most people would pick to build a team around. At times Tkachuk has met all expectations and at other times he has been something of a disappointment.

The big left-winger – he also plays at center – was the first selection of the Winnipeg Jets in the 1990 entry draft (19th overall), right out of high school, where he had become known for his goal scoring (42 in just 27 games). Tkachuk's one year in college saw him score 17 goals and 40 points in 36 contests before joining the U.S.

ST. LOUIS BLUES

CAREER HIGHLIGHTS

- Drafted 19th overall by Winnipeg in 1990.
- Named to the NHL's second All-Star team twice.
- Has scored 50 or more goals twice.
- Has scored 446 goals and 868 points in 897 NHL career games.

Olympic team for most of 1990–91. He joined the Jets full-time for the 1992–93 season and quickly established himself with 28 goals and 51 points to go along with 201 penalty minutes. In just his second season, Tkachuk scored 41 times and totaled 81 points. His penalty-minute total went up to 255, and his game was raising eyebrows all over the NHL. The final year the Jets played in Winnipeg, in 1995–96, saw the brash winger score 50 goals and add 98 points. He was now a star.

The strength of Tkachuk's game is his willingness to be physical. He will hand out a hit before he takes one and is usually over 100 minutes in penalties when he plays a full season. He seems to enjoy inflicting damage, if the grin on his face is any indication, and his aggressiveness has landed him in trouble on occasion. His unpredictability gives him the edge he needs to perform, but he may have to temper his approach a little, because his team needs him on the ice. In full flight, Tkachuk is very strong on his skates and can win almost all his one-on-one battles for the puck. He has a wicked wrist shot that is accurate and hard and allows him to score from virtually anywhere on the ice.

Tkachuk is especially good around the net and is not shy about introducing himself to the opposing goalies.

Off the ice, Tkachuk is just as unpredictable and is sometimes apt to say the wrong thing, especially to management. While he was with the Jets, Tkachuk signed a monster of a deal with the Chicago Blackhawks (millions in up-front money), but Winnipeg had to match it since the team could not afford to lose their best player. In 1997–98, the year after the Jets moved to Phoenix, Tkachuk led the entire league with 52 goals while totaling 86 points, and also found the time to serve 228 penalty minutes. He followed that great year with seasons of 40, 36, 22 and 29 goals for the Coyotes. A big contract forced a deal to St. Louis in 2000–01, when he scored 35 times and added 79 points. The next year he was 12th in NHL scoring with 75 points and seventh in goals with 38.

In 2002–03 he suffered a few injuries including one to his wrist late in the year, but he still managed to score 31 times in 56 games. His performance in the playoffs was not strong (only one goal in seven games), but Tkachuk bounced back to score 33 goals and 71 points in 75 games in 2003–04. Tkachuk did not play any hockey during the lockout, and it seemed all he did was get out of game shape. When he reported to the Blues for the start of the 2005–06 campaign he was suspended for being overweight (a fact he readily admits to) and then promptly got hurt and missed 15 games. The rebuilding Blues could have used his veteran savvy, but in one four-game segment he had six goals and 12 points.

He could not beat the injury bug and played in only 41 games, but he did score 15 goals and ended up with 36 points. The Blues liked the way Tkachuk finished the year and agreed to pick up the option on his contract (even though it will count $5.7 million against the St.Louis salary cap), a strong indication they want him to help lead the team back into the playoffs.

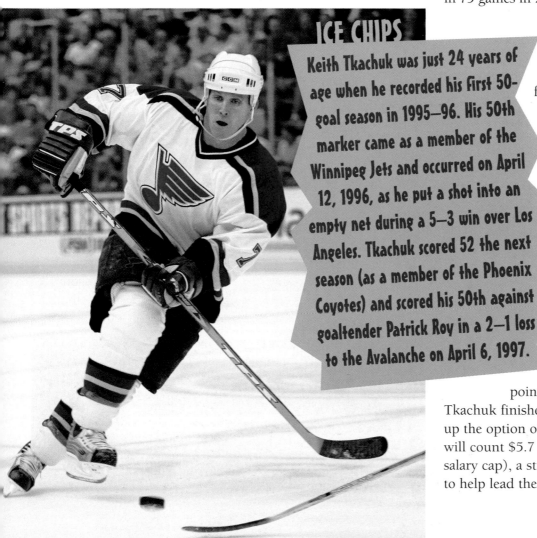

ICE CHIPS

Keith Tkachuk was just 24 years of age when he recorded his first 50-goal season in 1995–96. His 50th marker came as a member of the Winnipeg Jets and occurred on April 12, 1996, as he put a shot into an empty net during a 5–3 win over Los Angeles. Tkachuk scored 52 the next season (as a member of the Phoenix Coyotes) and scored his 50th against goaltender Patrick Roy in a 2–1 loss to the Avalanche on April 6, 1997.

TORONTO MAPLE LEAFS

Darcy TUCKER

As a youngster growing up in Castor, Alberta, left-winger Darcy Tucker idolized some of the greatest players in the history of the Edmonton Oilers. Photos adorning his wall included Wayne Gretzky, Mark Messier and Glenn Anderson. On a few occasions his father took young Darcy to Calgary to watch the fabled Oilers– Flames rivalry that dominated the game throughout the eighties. Those players and games made a strong impression on the young boy, who loved to play hockey. Tucker learned to skate and play the game outdoors for the most part, on a pond next to the family farm. Once the farm chores were done, it was off to the pond, where the snow had to be shoveled off before hockey could be played. It was often freezing, but that never bothered Tucker and his brother, who played as long as they could.

Coached in youth hockey by his father Dale, Tucker started getting noticed at a young age for his willingness to play the game. He left home at the age of 14 and, although it was difficult for him to leave his family, Tucker realized he had to if he wanted to pursue his dream of playing in the NHL. It may have helped to have an understanding mother who played hockey locally. Florence Tucker could play a rough-and-tumble brand of hockey, and her son was quite willing to play the same way. He played one season in Red Deer, Alberta, scoring 70 goals and 160 points in just 47

CAREER HIGHLIGHTS
- Drafted 151st overall by Montreal in 1993.
- Won the Memorial Cup three times with Kamloops (1992, 1994, 1995).
- Named Memorial Cup MVP in 1994.
- Has scored 155 goals and 395 points in 683 NHL games.

During "Hockey Day in Canada" on January 7, 2006, Darcy Tucker and his father were part of the opening face-off ceremony prior to a game between the Leafs and Oilers. When Darcy was a youngster, his father told him to watch the way Leaf captain Wendel Clark played the game. "That's a hockey player," Dale Tucker told his son.

games, and caught the attention of the Kamloops Blazers of the Western Hockey League. He spent four successful years in the British Columbia town and was a major force on the Blazer Memorial Cup teams. His last two junior seasons saw him score 52 and 64 goals, but he was only an eighth-round choice (151st overall) of the Montreal Canadiens in 1993.

Perhaps his lack of size (listed as 5'10", 178 pounds) scared away many NHL clubs from selecting him higher in the entry draft, but Tucker was determined to prove them wrong. He turned in a good year with the Habs farm team in Fredericton, New Brunswick, scoring 29 goals and totaling 93 points in 74 games, but the Canadiens dealt him to Tampa Bay in January 1998. A 21-goal season in Tampa seemed to put Tucker in the big leagues for good, but after scoring 14 at the start of the 1999–2000 season, he was dealt to the Maple Leafs. Tucker may have been perceived as too feisty a player for his own good, and he was not exactly a defensively responsible forward (minus 34 one year with the Lightning). But Toronto loved what they were getting and were quite willing to give up a good young player in Mike Johnson to land the hard-driving Tucker.

Since coming to Toronto, Tucker has developed a well-earned reputation for his willingness to do any-thing to win a game. He is unafraid to launch his body like a torpedo against players who are often much bigger. At times Tucker has crossed the line with what some consider borderline clean/dirty hits, depending on who's doing the analysis. He has given the Leafs a nasty edge but has also produced seasons of 16, 24 and 21 goals, showing he can be effective in more ways than one. The Leafs liked his competitive nature and quickly signed him to a long-term deal before the NHL's lockout season and always defended the gritty winger whenever he got himself into trouble. He has become a Toronto favorite (Leaf fans still will not forgive Ottawa's Daniel Alfredsson for his hit from behind on Tucker during the '02 playoffs) and represents the never-say-die attitude that has long been a trademark of the team.

The 2005–06 season saw Tucker enjoy his finest year, with 28 goals and 33 assists to go along with 100 penalty minutes. He should have scored more goals (he was stuck at 24 for a while), but he played much of the year with a rib injury. In typical Tucker fashion, he raised the ire of Buffalo coach Lindy Ruff with what the Sabres' mentor felt was a cheap shot at one of his players. Tucker did not respond too strongly (perhaps a sign that he is maturing), but his style did not change one bit.

YOUNG GUNS!

Exciting young talent on the verge of stardom in the new National Hockey League!

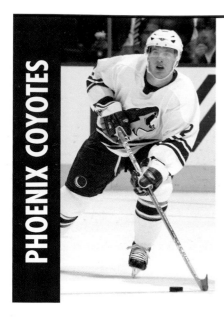

Keith BALLARD

DEFENSE, PHOENIX COYOTES, 5'11", 208 POUNDS.

- Drafted 11th overall by Buffalo in 2002.
- Traded to Colorado (2003) and then to Phoenix (2004).
- Recorded 26 points in 37 games for University of Minnesota in 2003—04.
- Scored eight goals and 31 points in 82 games for Phoenix in 2005—06.

BOSTON BRUINS

Brad BOYES

RIGHT WING, BOSTON BRUINS, 6'1", 195 POUNDS.

- Drafted 24th overall by Toronto in 2000.
- Traded to San Jose (2003) and then to Boston (2004).
- Scored 33 goals and 75 points for Providence (AHL) in 2004—05.
- Scored 26 goals and 69 points for Boston in 2005—06.

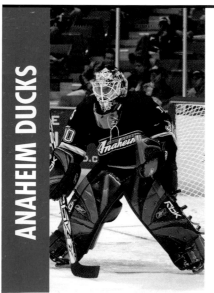

ANAHEIM DUCKS

Ilya BRYZGALOV

GOALTENDER, ANAHEIM DUCKS, 6'3", 180 POUNDS.

- Drafted 44th overall by Anaheim in 2000.
- Led AHL in games played (64) by a goalie in 2003—04 (winning 27).
- Played in 31 games for Anaheim in 2005—06 posting a 13-12-1 record.
- Recorded his first NHL shutout in '05—'06 and a .910 save percentage.

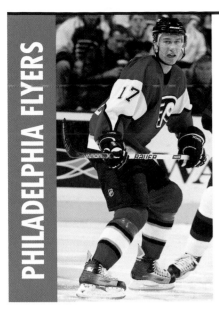

Jeff CARTER

CENTER, PHILADELPHIA FLYERS, 6'3", 175 POUNDS.

- Drafted 11th overall by Philadelphia in 2003.
- Recorded 74 points in 55 games for Sault Ste. Marie (OHL) in 2004–05.
- Recorded 23 points in 21 playoff games for Philadelphia (AHL) in 2005.
- Scored 23 goals and 42 points for Philadelphia in 2005–06.

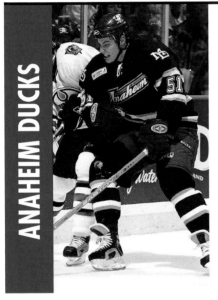

Ryan GETZLAF

CENTER, ANAHEIM DUCKS, 6'2", 210 POUNDS.

- Drafted 19th overall by Anaheim in 2003.
- Scored 86 goals for the Calgary Hitmen (WHL) in final three seasons.
- Scored 14 goals and 39 points in 57 games for Anaheim in 2005–06 season.
- Recorded seven points (three goals, four assists) in 16 playoff games in '06.

Chris HIGGINS

LEFT WING, MONTREAL CANADIENS, 5'11", 192 POUNDS.

- Drafted 14th overall by Montreal in 2002.
- Recorded 41 points in 28 games for Yale University in 2002–03.
- Scored over 20 goals twice for Hamilton (AHL, 2003–04 and 2004–05).
- Scored 23 goals and 38 points in 80 games for Montreal in 2005–06.

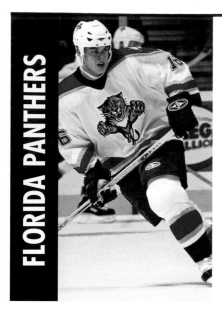

Nathan HORTON

RIGHT WING, FLORIDA PANTHERS, 6'2", 201 POUNDS.

- Drafted third overall by Florida in 2003.
- Recorded 68 points in 54 games for Oshawa (OHL) in 2002–03.
- Recorded 22 points in 55 games for Florida in 2003–04.
- Scored 28 goals and 47 points for Florida in 2005–06.

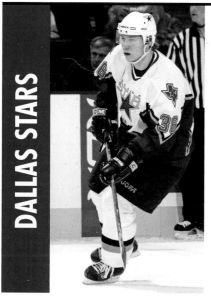

Jussi JOKINEN

LEFT WING, DALLAS STARS, 5'11", 183 POUNDS.

- Drafted 192nd overall by Dallas in 2001.
- Scored 23 goals and 47 points in 56 games in Finland during 2004–05.
- Scored 17 goals and 55 points for Dallas in 2005–06.
- Scored 10 shootout goals during 2005–06.

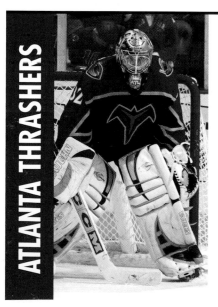

Kari LEHTONEN

GOALTENDER, ATLANTA THRASHERS, 6'3", 200 POUNDS.

- Drafted second overall by Atlanta in 2002.
- Won 58 contests for Chicago Wolves (AHL) in 96 games between 2003 and 2005.
- Posted a 20-15-0 record for Atlanta in 2005–06.
- Recorded a save percentage of .906 with two shutouts in 2005–06.

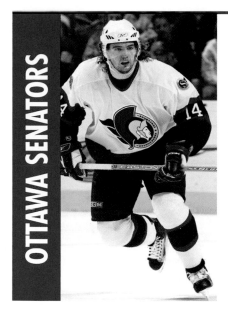

Andrej MESZAROS

DEFENSE, OTTAWA SENATORS, 6'1", 200 POUNDS.

- Drafted 23rd overall by Ottawa in 2004.
- Named to NHL All-Rookie team in 2005—06
- Scored 10 goals and 39 points in 82 games for Ottawa in 2005—06.
- Recorded a plus 34 rating in 2005—06.

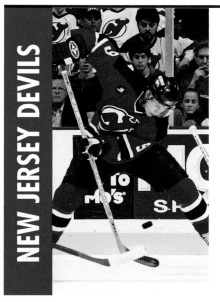

Zach PARISE

LEFT WING, NEW JERSEY DEVILS, 5'11", 185 POUNDS.

- Drafted 17th overall by New Jersey in 2003.
- Recorded 55 points in 37 games for North Dakota in 2003—04.
- Recorded 58 points in 73 games for Albany (AHL) in 2004—05.
- Scored 14 goals and 32 points in 81 games for New Jersey in 2005—06.

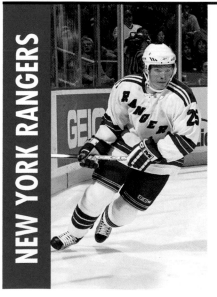

Peter PRUCHA

RIGHT WING, NEW YORK RANGERS, 5'10", 161 POUNDS.

- Drafted 240th overall by New York Rangers in 2002.
- Recorded 13 points in 16 playoff games for Pardubice in Czech Republic League.
- Scored 30 goals and 47 points for Rangers in 2005—06.
- Scored 16 powerplay goals for Rangers in 2005—06.

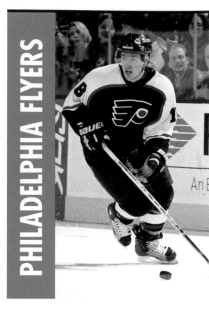

Mike RICHARDS

CENTER, PHILADELPHIA FLYERS, 5'11", 185 POUNDS.

- Drafted 24th overall by Philadelphia in 2003.
- Named to Memorial Cup tournament All-Star team in 2003.
- Recorded 15 points in 14 playoff games for Philadelphia (AHL) in 2005.
- Scored 11 goals and 34 points for Flyers in 2005–06.

Michael RYDER

RIGHT WING, MONTREAL CANADIENS, 6'1", 196 POUNDS.

- Drafted 216th overall by Montreal in 1998.
- Recorded 67 points in 69 games for Hamilton (AHL) in 2002–03.
- Scored 25 goals and 63 points for Montreal in 2003–04.
- Scored 30 goals and 55 points for Montreal in 2005–06.

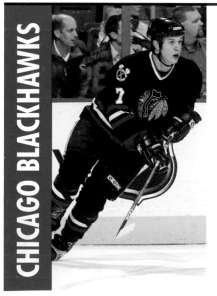

Brent SEABROOK

DEFENSE, CHICAGO BLACK HAWKS, 6'3", 215 POUNDS.

- Drafted 14th overall by Chicago in 2003.
- Recorded 54 points in 63 games for Lethbridge (WHL) in 2004–05.
- Recorded 32 points in 69 games for Chicago in 2005–06.
- Posted a plus 5 rating while playing 20:01 minutes per game in '05–'06.

Alex STEEN

LEFT WING, TORONTO MAPLE LEAFS, 5'11", 183 POUNDS.

- Drafted 24th overall by Toronto in 2002.
- Recorded 17 points in 50 games for MODO in Sweden during 2004—05.
- Scored 18 goals and 45 points in 75 games for Toronto in 2005—06.
- Scored nine powerplay goals and one short-handed goal in 2005—06.

Jarret STOLL

CENTER, EDMONTON OILERS, 6'1", 200 POUNDS.

- Drafted 36th overall by Edmonton in 2002.
- Recorded 106 points for Kootenay (WHL) in 2000—01.
- Scored 10 goals and 22 points for Edmonton in 2003—04.
- Scored 22 goals and 68 points in 82 games for Edmonton in 2005—06.

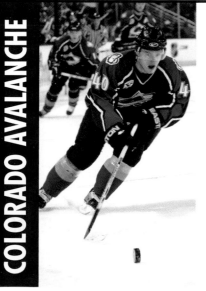

Marek SVATOS

RIGHT WING, COLORADO AVALANCHE, 5'9", 175 POUNDS.

- Drafted 227th overall by Colorado in 2001.
- Scored 38 goals and 77 points for Kootenay (WHL) in 2001—02.
- Scored 18 goals and 46 points in 77 games for Hershey (AHL) in 2004—05.
- Scored 32 goals and 50 points in 61 games for Colorado in 2005—06.

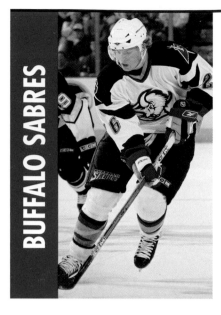

Thomas VANEK

LEFT WING, BUFFALO SABRES, 6'2", 210 POUNDS.

- Drafted fifth overall by Buffalo in 2003.
- Named MVP of NCAA championship tournament in 2003.
- Scored 42 goals and 68 points in 74 games for Rochester in 2004–05.
- Scored 25 goals and 48 points in 81 games for Buffalo in 2005–06.

CAROLINA HURRICANES

Cam WARD

GOALTENDER, CAROLINA HURRICANES, 6', 176 POUNDS.

- Drafted 25th overall by Carolina in 2002.
- Named WHL Player of the Year in 2004.
- Named winner of the Conn Smythe Trophy in 2006.
- Posted a 14-8-2 record for Carolina in 2005–06.

COLUMBUS BLUE JACKETS

Nikolai ZHERDEV

RIGHT WING, COLUMBUS BLUE JACKETS, 6'1", 186 POUNDS.

- Drafted fourth overall by Columbus in 2003.
- Scored 13 goals and 34 points for Blue Jackets in 2003–04.
- Recorded 40 points in 51 games for Moscow CSKA in 2004–05.
- Scored 27 goals and 54 points for Columbus in 2005–06.

PHOTO CREDITS

ACKNOWLEDGMENTS

The author would like to acknowledge and thank the contributors to the following sources that were consulted while writing this book:

Newspapers
Toronto Star, Toronto Sun, The Globe and Mail, National Post, Boston Globe, Detroit Free Press, and articles from the *Canadian Press* and the *Associated Press* that appeared in these newspapers or on various websites.

Websites
Slam Sports/Hockey: Canoe.ca; Sportsnet.ca; Legends of Hockey.net; NHL.com; NHLPA.com; RusHockey.com; Hockeybuzz.com; Detnews.com; Sympatico.ca; Globeandmail.com; Canada.com

Magazines
The Hockey News, 2005–06 season; *Hockey Digest; Prospects Hockey; Face-off Magazine; Icehockey World; Sports Illustrated; Maple Leafs Game Day* programs from the 2005–06 season.

Record Books
Official NHL Guide and Record Book (2005–06 season); *Total Hockey* (2nd edition); *Total NHL* (2003 edition); *World Cup of Hockey 2004 Media Guide; OHL Information and Player Register.*

Books
Hockey Scouting Report 2004 by Sherry Ross; *Hockey's Young Superstars* by Jeff Rud; *The Coolest Guys 2* by Gary Mason and Barbara Gunn.

Television
Hockey Night in Canada on CBC; The NHL on TSN; The NHL on NBC; Toronto Maple Leafs Hockey on TSN and Sportnet.

The author also wishes to thank Barbara Campbell, Dan Liebman, Lionel Koffler and Michael Worek at Firefly Books for their assistance and support in completing this book. Thanks also to designer Kimberley Young for her usual great work and to writer Steve Milton for his work in preparing and researching some profiles.

A special thank you to my wife Maria and my son David for their help and understanding.

PLAYER LIST